Rules and
Red Tape

Rules and Red Tape

A Prism for Public Administration Theory and Research

Barry Bozeman and Mary K. Feeney

Routledge
Taylor & Francis Group

LONDON AND NEW YORK

First published 2011 by M.E. Sharpe

Published 2015 by Routledge
2 Park Square, Milton Park, Abingdon, Oxon OX14 4RN
711 Third Avenue, New York, NY 10017, USA

Routledge is an imprint of the Taylor & Francis Group, an informa business

Library of Congress Cataloging-in-Publication Data

Bozeman, Barry.
  Rules and red tape : a prism for public administration theory and research / Barry Bozeman,
Mary K. Feeney.
     p. cm.
Includes bibliographical references and index.
ISBN 978-0-7656-2334-8 (cloth : alk. paper)—ISBN 978-0-7656-2335-5 (pbk. : alk. paper)
1. Bureaucracy. 2. Public administration. I. Feeney, Mary K. II. Title.

JF1501.B693 2011
351.01—dc22   2010044387

ISBN 13: 9780765623355 (pbk)
ISBN 13: 9780765623348 (hbk)

Contents

Rules and Red Tape

1

Situating Red Tape Research and Theory

Nearly every English speaker knows the term "red tape."[1] However, a shared term does not always equate to a shared meaning. When someone complains about red tape, it is difficult to know whether the person is bemoaning the amount of paperwork in an organization, tangled rules and regulations, capricious bureaucratic behavior, lethargic bureaucratic behavior, or the sad plight of having socially desirable, effective rules enforced to one's personal disadvantage. Popular usage of the term "red tape" requires no precision.

To illustrate the multiple popular meanings of "red tape," let us consider one government's attempt to obtain citizens' help in identifying problems in state government and possible solutions. In 2008, the state of Virginia set up a website to solicit and log citizens' concerns. The website, called "Virginia Ideas Website" (www.aitr.virginia.gov/ideas), was still functioning and popular as late as the first half of 2010. As one might expect, many of the entries complained about red tape. We provide one such entry below, posted in September 2008:

> **Reduce government red tape.** "There appears to be several hundred different agencies listed at the official Virginia government website. Many of them contain similar words in their agency titles. How much repetitive work is being performed by more than one agency? Why not consolidate agencies that do similar work, or eliminate some of them altogether? We could probably save thousands of dollars by downsizing the quantity of Virginia agencies."

This particular notion of red tape focuses on duplication and overlap, which is perhaps the single issue most commonly identified by government reformers as an administrative problem. Indeed, duplication and overlap was a central concern of the Hoover commissions on reform in the late 1940s (Arnold 1976); but are duplication and overlap really red tape?

Let us consider some other citizens' complaints about government behavior that might be considered red tape.

The *New York Times*[2] ran a story on the Mexican government's attempt (much like Virginia's) to solicit citizens' help in government reform, even offering a prize for the most egregious case of "useless red tape." The winning entry was a woman's explanation of the monthly bureaucratic odyssey required to obtain her son's life-sustaining medication. The published story generated a raft of emails posted on the newspaper's blog by *Times* readers.

Consider this posting from France:

> I am an American living in France, which by far tops the U.S. in terms of bureaucracy (hence the origin of the word). Get this: in order to effectuate any legal doings in France, one must always furnish certified . . . and officially translated birth and death certificates that are less than three months old—as if the information on these changes! A previous translation of the same birth certificate will not be accepted.

And this posting from Arizona:

> My driver's license had expired while I was living in New York City. When I returned to Tucson I went to the DMV to renew my license and told them what had happened. The clerk asked me to turn over my New York license and I told her I never had one. She said I would have to write to Albany for clearance because "somebody had to be driving." I pointed out (again) that I had been living in the city and used public transportation. She didn't buy it.

Are these instances of red tape? In the French case, the problem seems to be related to rules and procedures. The Arizona case seems less clear inasmuch as the rules, whatever they may be, are not enforced consistently. Is this red tape?

In a sweeping reform initiative called the National Performance Review, the Clinton administration sought to address a wide range of bureaucratic pathologies, but it is instructive that the compendium listing problems and reforms was titled *From Red Tape to Results: Creating a Government That Works Better and Costs Less*. Why would a government reform effort treating problems ranging from lack of employee empowerment to risk aversion to purchasing procedures choose to label them all "red tape"? One answer, of course, is the attractiveness of alliteration. However, the point remains—the term "red tape" often is a catchall.

According to Goodsell (1994, 63), red tape is a "classic 'condensation' symbol in that it incorporates a vast array of subjectively held feelings and expresses them succinctly." To put it another way, red tape has come to connote the worst of bureaucracy: gargantuan, cynically impersonal, bound up in meaningless paperwork, and beset by excessive, duplicative, and unnecessary procedures (Goodsell 1994; Rai 1983).

If red tape means nothing more than "bad bureaucracy," then the concept has value only for venting frustrations, not for scholarship, analysis, or serious managerial application. However, during the past several decades, scholars in public administration have sought to develop red tape as a legitimate and relatively unambiguous concept suitable for serious research. This book asks whether that effort has succeeded and what remains to be done.

Red Tape as a Focus of Scholarly Inquiry

While most people are comfortable with red tape as an epithet, many are surprised to learn that there is a scholarly field concerned with systematic learning about red tape. In fact, the past two decades have witnessed the emergence of a cottage industry of red tape research. In a relatively short time, red tape has gone from a topic ignored by researchers (though bemoaned routinely by public administration practitioners and the general public) to a research field occupied by at least thirty or so researchers, chiefly in the United States but also by a few from other parts of the world. As a result of these scholars' labors, we have seen books, several dissertations, and dozens of research articles, many of them published in the most influential scholarly journals in the field of public administration. Many of these scholars use a common definition of red tape as "rules, regulations and procedures that require compliance but do not meet the organization's functional objective for the rule" (Bozeman 2000).[3]

Since we are among those who have for years contributed to the red tape literature, we would like to think that something has been learned from the time and resources that so many scholars have invested. But to speak of research *activity* is not necessarily to speak of *knowledge*. What has been learned from this flurry of activity? Do we know more about red tape and related organizational phenomena than we knew in, say, 1980? Certainly researchers have developed propositions and causal claims, but how much veracity flows from the arguments and evidence provided by red tape researchers?

We have two central objectives for this book, both pertaining to the state of the art in red tape research. The first objective is to provide a critical summing up of red tape research and its findings. Our first core question is this: "As a result of the dozens of published studies about red tape, what do we now know about the phenomenon of red tape, its causes, and its organizational and social impacts?" The second objective is more ambitious—to use red tape research and theory to explain empirically based theory development in public administration. Our second core question therefore is this: "What does the experience with red tape research and theory reveal about knowledge development in public administration?" The second objective, using red tape research as a lens to understand scholarly public administration, is potentially relevant for the 99 percent of public administration scholars who invest their time in topics other than red tape.

We cannot hope to answer either of our core questions without a thorough-going review of red tape research and theory. Our book presents a detailed review, aiming to cover literally every published paper dealing with red tape. Thus, aside from possible insights into research and theory building, the book should prove of interest to those who wish to learn about the content, findings, and contentions of red tape research. Some of our readers may be scholars who focus on red tape, bureaucracy, and organizations, and these readers need little or no introduction to red tape research. But for those more interested in the critical and epistemological aspects of our book than the particular content of our case in point, we provide the brief introduction below.

Situating Red Tape Scholarship: Three Knowledge Domains

We think of red tape knowledge as operating in three domains, each overlapping at least to some degree with the others. We refer to these domains as "ordinary knowledge," "formal knowledge" (or scholarship), and "application knowledge" about red tape.

Ordinary Knowledge and Formal Knowledge of Red Tape

Popular usage of the term "red tape" is based on ordinary knowledge (Kennedy 1983; Lindblom and Cohen 1979). Ordinary knowledge of red tape, or for that matter any topic, comes from day-to-day experience and communication and is part of being an active member of society. People obtain ordinary knowledge not through formal study or investigation but in social encounters and exposure to mass media. Most well-educated individuals have a prodigious amount of ordinary knowledge and a relatively small amount of formal knowledge. For example, a university-trained engineer may have a significant amount of formal knowledge about the tensile strength of metals and might be able to apply that knowledge to the problem of structural flaws in bridge design. However, no matter how much such formal knowledge this engineer might have, she almost certainly has much more ordinary knowledge about a dizzying array of topics, such as the efficacy of over-the-counter cough medicines, the best and worst online travel websites, the peccadilloes of particular celebrities, and, perhaps, the rules, regulations, and red tape affecting civil engineers' government contracting relations.

Ordinary knowledge sometimes provides powerful, highly beneficial insights, but, just as often, it can be rife with ambiguity, and be misleading, counterproductive, or demonstrably wrong. People often make mistakes on topics such as the efficacy of over-the-counter medicines and they may have misperceptions about red tape in contracting. But whether ordinary knowledge is right or wrong, or in dispute, it plays a role in almost any decision context and any social issue. Most significantly for present purposes, ordinary knowledge comes into play in connection with formal knowledge, challenging it, complementing it, extending it, or competing with it. For example, the clash between ordinary knowledge and formal knowledge about biological evolution is as lively today as it was during the Scopes trial, when William Jennings Bryan pitted ordinary knowledge, folk wisdom, and deeply held religious beliefs against Clarence Darrow's expert witnesses' interpretations of formal knowledge.

In some areas of the natural and physical sciences, there is little or no competition between ordinary knowledge and formal knowledge, generally because of the lack of any ordinary knowledge. Presently, there seems to be no ordinary knowledge about chiral quarks, phage vectors, genome-wide insertional mutagenesis, or multiplicative ergodic theorems. This is not to make light of the *potential* for such ordinary knowledge. When the natural sciences begin to have obvious implications for near-term impact on human beings, ordinary knowledge develops quickly. Think of the case of climatology. Until recently, about the only ordinary knowledge pertaining to climatology was the *Farmers' Almanac*. But the mass media coverage and the political warfare surrounding climate change and its environmental impact have quickly changed climatology from the esoteric preoccupation of a few thousand scientists to a topic also including expansive ordinary knowledge.

The competition between ordinary knowledge and scholarly knowledge generally is greatest in the social sciences, not only because social science topics tend to be more easily understood than in the natural sciences, but also because nonspecialists more often have relevant experience. With respect to red tape, ordinary knowledge clearly is dominant in informing judgments and actions. Indeed, it could hardly be otherwise since very few people outside of a small community of university-based researchers are even aware of red tape scholarship.[4]

We have several reasons for emphasizing the role of ordinary knowledge about red tape. First, as we have already noted, it is important to understand the limited extent to which red tape research is recognized by most nonspecialists and the limited degree to which knowledge produced by red tape researchers has diffused beyond the confines of academic journals and books. Red tape research differs little from most academic enterprises in the degree to which it is separate from the "real world" of real problems, technologies, and solutions. One would, likewise, be hard-pressed to find much real-world penetration of research on, say, neo-institutional sociology, organizational networks, or postmodern interpretations of work and occupations, despite the existence of a sizable formal literature on these topics.

Second, we stress the prevalence of ordinary knowledge about red tape in recognition of the fact that it has directly influenced scholarly work. Until relatively recently there was no formal research on red tape. The work undertaken has been motivated to some extent by the very concerns prevalent in ordinary knowledge—vexation with malfunctioning bureaucracy. However, there is also a countertrend, also influencing the academic response to red tape—a concern about "bureaucracy bashing." The complex interplay between these concerns is explored later in this book. The point for the present is simple: red tape research has not been walled away. Even as a research construct, red tape has never been a hermetically sealed academic fancy.

A third point, important and not so obvious, is that ordinary knowledge about red tape provides not only motivation for developing formal knowledge but also research cues. Many research specialists see their task as improving on ordinary knowledge, and that attitude often seems well justified. When ordinary knowledge gives us mustard plasters and formal knowledge gives us germ theory, then we can with some confidence point to improved results. But in many of the social sciences, including red tape research, the relationship between ordinary knowledge and formal knowledge is less one of inferior and superior knowledge than different sorts of knowledge with different types of utility. This is a complex point that we shall explore throughout the book, but for the present let us simply say that ordinary knowledge about red tape tends to offer the benefits of context, emotive and expressive content, and narrative. By contrast, formal knowledge can provide the benefits of precision, generalization beyond context, and visibility of assumption, method, and inference.

Application Knowledge and Red Tape

With respect to any topic, including red tape, problem-solving activity uses knowledge and, at the same time, creates knowledge (Bozeman and Rogers

2002). The knowledge used in problem-solving activity may be trial and error (in situ), ordinary knowledge, or formal knowledge. The results of application and problem-solving activity generally create a new knowledge, often called craft knowledge (Delamont and Atkinson 2001), though we use the more general term here, "application knowledge." Application knowledge is the sort that practitioners tend to acquire and use. In the case of red tape, managers seeking to solve problems related to perceived red tape can proceed by inventing context-based approaches, or they can draw from ordinary knowledge, from formal knowledge, or all three at the same time.

Reynaud's (2005) study of rules and routines in the Paris Metro Electronic Equipment Maintenance Workshop offers a good example of how problem-solving activities (routines) help to interpret rules into appropriate usage. Routines-based analysis enables researchers to focus on the strategies that workers adopt in order to implement or follow rules and thus achieve organizational goals. Reynaud argues that rules are abstract and general because they are designed for different, specific cases, whereas routines are the means by which individuals interpret and implement rules. Reynaud concludes that the "first difference between rules and routines is that the former are *arrangements awaiting interpretation*, while the latter are *rules already interpreted*" (866). Thus the interpretation and implementation of rules is, essentially, application knowledge.

Let us consider a directly relevant instance of the development of application of red tape knowledge (Bozeman et al. 2008). In August 2007, the University System Office (USO) of the University System of Georgia (USG)[5] contracted with faculty of the University of Georgia's Department of Public Administration and Policy for a year-long study to assess "the quality of administrative procedures and the possible existence and severity of 'red tape' in the USO, primarily in the Office of Information and Instructional Technology." The research was explicitly premised on the previous work of this project's senior investigator (Bozeman 2000). As indicated in this project's scope of work, the study was explicitly designed to

> follow the methods set out in Bozeman's book, *Bureaucracy and Red Tape*, for assessing, managing and reducing red tape. The methods shall involve identifying rules that no longer attain the goals for which they were created and rules that, while perhaps still functional, entail an administrative and compliance burden that is excessive compared to their values in promoting the rules' and procedures' objectives.

The study focused on the Office of Information and Instructional Technology (OIIT). This choice was due to the willingness of the OIIT to participate and to serve as a test site for developing approaches and procedures for studying rules and regulations and assessing possible red tape. OIIT cooperated with the investigators by providing access to both employees and stakeholders. The research resulted in a report giving the results of the data analysis, identifying sources of red tape, and suggesting strategies for reducing red tape and improving services.

In some respects, the experience with the USG study was quite atypical. In the first place, it is very rare for clients to contact a researcher on any topic because they happen to have read a book or article produced by the researcher. Second, the demand for consulting work addressing red tape is much smaller than one might expect, given the pervasiveness of the problem. The reason? Soliciting research on red tape implies that it exists and that it might be a problem. With respect to red tape, denial and buck-passing are much more common strategies than head-on confrontation, especially when outsiders are involved. But except for these two important distinctions, the research in other respects perfectly exemplifies application knowledge. The researchers used many of the same measures and hypotheses found in the formal literature, but applied them intensely to the particular context and needs of the USG. One of the hallmarks of application knowledge is that it tends to be context-specific, focusing on the unique needs of particular organizations or institutions.

Knowledge Competition: Which to Use?

If ordinary knowledge sometimes competes with formal knowledge of red tape, application knowledge provides an even more formidable competition. In many cases application knowledge has the advantage of practitioners' deep experience with phenomena, close learning, and context-specific learning, and it is often more precise and less ambiguous than ordinary knowledge. Almost by definition, it is more utilitarian in its focus than is formal knowledge. Indeed, the question arises why we even need a formal knowledge of red tape when we have application knowledge.

The problem with that question is that it has exactly the same status as the question why we need a formal knowledge of public administration (in general) when we have application knowledge. This is a deep challenge for any practitioner-related field, one drawing data from practice. The most optimistic answer is that there is no reason why one type of knowledge should preempt the other. But the challenge goes farther and, thus, we might also say that while we recognize the value of application knowledge, formal knowledge can provide benefits not easily rendered by application knowledge. Formal knowledge is better codified, it is typically more precise, and it is more often aimed at generalization. Formal knowledge generally employs a wider set of analytical tools and methods, each carrying a different set of advantages and disadvantages, generally ones that are well known. At its best, formal knowledge can even prove useful for problems not identified or broadly experienced at the time the formal knowledge was created.

One of the key questions in the history of scholarly public administration is whether formal knowledge has its own epistemological warrant or whether it is valuable only as a means of informing and improving practice. We take the former position. If one takes the latter position, then public administration research has a paltry record and little reason for existing as a scholarly enterprise. If one takes the view that red tape research can and should flourish even if ignored by practitioners and even if it is or seems to be irrelevant to practice, then it is incumbent to make a claim for its value.

Certainly, red tape research or any public administration research can be justified on a curiosity basis. The fact that many areas of astronomy seem to have no practical bearing has not impeded research. A stronger rationale relates to a future time frame. To say that red tape research currently has limited applicability does not mean that it is forever destined to evade application. The history of social sciences is such that application of formal knowledge tends to proceed slowly, depending (in part) on the ability of researchers to produce valid, confidence-inspiring explanations and useful analytical tools. Application also depends on the ability and interest of researchers in communicating their results to nonspecialists. Finally, there is the demand side. Even if red tape researchers were to have powerful theories and tools, these could not be applied without clients for such knowledge. This latter requirement would seem unproblematic. However, as we mentioned earlier, practitioners seeking knowledge of red tape are tacitly acknowledging that red tape exists and that it is a problem—an acknowledgement not always politically expedient or in their own self-interest.

During the remainder of this book we will not often return to issues pertaining to either ordinary knowledge of red tape or to application knowledge. Both these topics are obviously important, especially the latter. Those interested in application knowledge about red tape can consult any of an array of highly practical and often useful sources, including materials from the National Performance Review (Gore 1993), rewards for employees who reduce red tape (U.S. GAO 2005), or awards for ideas to reduce red tape in the European Union (Europa 2009). While we acknowledge the great importance of the red tape application knowledge attendant on government reform and management improvement, that knowledge domain is not the emphasis of this book. We are concerned with the formal knowledge domain and examine others only to the extent that they have influenced formal knowledge or been influenced by it.

In this book, our focus is on this one small scholarly field—research and theory about red tape—and we consider popular views about red tape only to the extent that they influence the development of formal knowledge. This is not to say that research and popular views always diverge. But there is one very important difference between the two: many people use the term "red tape" as the term for almost anything they do not like about the functioning of bureaucracy, whereas red tape research tries to separate red tape from other bureaucratic pathologies. In popular usage, red tape is often viewed as equivalent to the number of rules and regulations in a bureaucratic entity or the number of rules ordinary citizens must grapple with in seeking services from a bureaucratic entity. However, for the most part contemporary research and theory about red tape focus not on the number of rules or even the burden they present, but rather on the extent to which rules, regulations, and procedures accomplish the goals they have been designed to serve.

A Learning Laboratory for Theory-Building

If our goal is to understand the theory-building enterprise in public administration, we must begin by acknowledging that no single research topic adequately represents the great variety of theory-driven public administration research. Each major research topic in public administration has nuances, evidentiary status, data concerns, and even research norms a bit different from every other topic. Nevertheless, there are some common elements in building public administration theory, and red tape scholarship provides a particularly instructive case in point. In the first place, if we are interested in empirical research, public administration does not present us with as many choices as we might assume. Public administration, even a contemporary public administration enamored of traditional social science methods, data, and statistics, remains epistemologically diverse, with as nearly as many scholars grounded in humanities or legalistic traditions as in quantitative, empirical research. Discourse, narratives, action theory, individual experience reports, nontheoretical case studies, best practice, management prescription, philosophical and ethical analysis, historiography—all these and more coexist in public administration with empirical, generalization-seeking social science research.[6]

A second advantage of focusing on red tape research as a theory assessment case is that it is of the right age, not too old to have calcified or to have scattered into many different directions, but not too young as to provide little product available for analysis. The first published empirical research in public administration with the term "red tape" in its title was produced in 1975 (Buchanan), but the first paper clearly focused on a red tape construct akin to contemporary usage was not produced until seventeen years later (Bozeman, Reed, and Scott 1992). Between 1975 and 1992, only a few papers were published that even touched on red tape (e.g., Baldwin 1990; Bretschneider 1990; Bozeman and Crow 1991; Kingsley and Reed 1991; Lan and Rainey 1992). However, more than fifty red tape papers have been published in the seventeen years between 1993 and 2010. Mid- and late-career public administration researchers who have paid any attention to red tape research have witnessed its entire development.

Advantage three: although empirical red tape research is arguably less than twenty years old, the topic has taken on the trappings of a core research topic. The volume of research serves as one indicator (see Figure 1.1). Another is the publication of reviews of the literature (e.g., Pandey and Scott 2002); literature reviews and syntheses require raw material. An indicator that red tape research has begun to mature is that it has attracted critics and objections. As one of those critics notes (and this is advantage number four), "it would be difficult to identify a concept that is more identified with the field of public administration than red tape" (Luton 2007, 530). Public administration owns red tape research in the sense that most of the scholarly work done on the topic is produced by public administration scholars and published in public administration journals. True, there are several other topics where public administration scholars predominate, but most of these are not characterized by aggregate data-based empirical research. The public administration research topics that are strongly empirical are ones shared with other fields. For example, topics as privatization and public budgeting have major contributors from economics and political science.

Aside from red tape research, public service motivation (PSM) (Coursey and Pandey 2007; Perry 1996; Perry and Hondeghem 2008) is perhaps the only public administration empirical research dominated by public administration researchers. While PSM is a good example of a public administration research domain, we could easily argue that PSM is a subset of the much broader and stronger intrinsic-extrinsic motivation research agenda in multiple fields (e.g., organizational behavior, industrial psychology, business). In fact, much public administration research is a subset of a larger field of research. For example, research investigating performance, performance-based pay, and incentives in the public sector has a parallel track in education, where researchers investigate performance and incentives of teachers (Aaronson, Barrow, and Sanders 2003; Ballou and Podgursky 1997; Figlioa and Kenny 2007; Hanushek and Rivkin 2004; Podgursky and Springer 2007; Springer and Winters 2009).

For public administration scholars, PSM is certainly within the domain of public administration. However, for those outside the field, PSM is quite similar to generic research on intrinsic motivation, with public service being one of the many ways in which individuals are motivated to work better or

Figure 1.1 **Public Administration Red Tape Journal Articles, by Year**

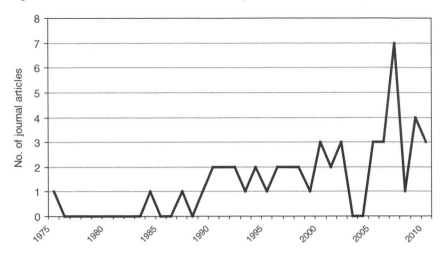

longer. Moreover, measures of PSM vary across culture and setting. For example, many non-American researchers talk about public service motivated behavior (Chanlat 2003; Pratchett and Wingfield 1996; Woodhouse 1997). Because research on intrinsic motivation continues in multiple fields and in multiple arenas, it does not offer the narrow case for measurement analysis that is available with red tape measures.

Note that we do not take public administration's domination of a field as a wholly positive attribute; in many respects it is a significant disadvantage. Topics taken up by only a few specialists armed with similar training do not always thrive. Cross-fertilization leads to knowledge innovation not only in public administration research, but also in other social sciences (Dryzek and Leonard 1988) and the physical sciences (Laudan 1977). However, if the relative insularity of red tape research and theory is in some respects a problem for its vitality as a research topic, the fact that the production and dissemination of red tape knowledge is closely held means that it is easier to track. Just as important, if one is interested in characterizing public administration research and theory development, then focusing on a topic not well integrated with other disciplinary strains provides some assurance that the forces driving theory development really are central to public administration. This is especially important in public administration, a field that has been characterized as a "borrowing field" (Waldo 1948).

A final justification for red tape research as a knowledge-building laboratory is its interesting interplay between research and theory. In examining red tape scholarship, we shall see that empirical research is sometimes informed by theory and theory is sometimes informed by empirical research. This seems like a modest accomplishment, but, as critics of every stripe acknowledge, it is one we cannot necessarily expect in public administration research. In the social sciences, much more so than in the natural and physical sciences, research and theory tend to develop along separate lines (Blalock 1966; Layder 1998). Some feel that this frequent partitioning explains much about the limited power of social sciences research.

Prelude to an Embedded Criticism of Red Tape Research and Theory

Most of the chapters in this book are devoted to developing concepts of red tape and to reviewing, integrating, and assessing research and theory about red tape. To a large extent this is done more or less on the fly, introducing various ideas about red tape, citing studies related to those ideas, and then providing commentary. However, the articulation and review chapters are in some respects a necessary prelude. These chapters provide a thorough grounding in research and theory of red tape and, we think, give some understanding of the ways in which knowledge accumulates in empirically based public administration. In the final two chapters we provide an assessment and criticism that are, at the same time, much more personal and critical than the reviews in the previous chapters. We refer to this as an "embedded" critical perspective because it is our reflection not as outsiders looking in but as persons who have conducted research in the field and who are reflecting on the limitations not only of others' work but of our own as well. Naturally, there are advantages and disadvantages to such an approach. Objectivity is not one of the advantages. However, we know the history and the ins and outs of knowledge production about red tape in a way that a removed reviewer would not. Moreover, in providing this embedded perspective, we seek not only to critique and ultimately improve red tape research, but also to identify research obstacles faced by most empirical researchers in public administration and perhaps to point to some new directions for diminishing these problems.

Chapter Overview

Finally, let us consider the remaining chapters in the book and the book's organization. Chapter 2 provides a "prehistory" of empirical research on red tape, examining related work in sociology, important early conceptual work on red tape, and the earliest developments toward a systematic theory of red tape and the beginnings of empirical research. Much of this chapter is a sociology of knowledge and reports some of the "inside baseball," including the relation of research projects not only to red tape research and theory but also to red tape researchers. Chapter 3 provides extensive summaries of the earliest systematic theory of red tape (Bozeman 1993, 2000) and more recent conceptual-theoretical developments. This sets the stage for Chapter 4, which not only focuses on empirical research on red tape, reporting propositions, data sources, and methods, but also considers connections between empirical research and previously reviewed theory as well as the self-contained theoretical implications of the empirical research. Chapter 5 focuses on relatively new concerns for red tape researchers—the relation of red tape to contracting and performance management. Chapter 6 sums up findings about red tape theory and research and suggests a research agenda. Chapter 7 sets a new, more personal, reflective tone while providing a history lesson in red tape research. Since much of the history relates to specific projects, especially the series of studies referred to as the National Administrative Studies Projects (NASP), the chapter is in part organized according to these projects and the lessons they provide. Chapter 7 also identifies some of the problems common to almost all public administration research and some possible solutions to those problems.

Notes

1. In French, the term "red tape" (literally, *bande rouge*) does not have the same meaning. This is not because the French have none of what we refer to as red tape. Tellingly, the French word for red tape is the English word *bureaucracy*. Our thanks to Professor Patrick Gilbert, University of Paris-Nanterre, for pointing this out.

2. Elisabeth Malkin, "For Redress of Grievances, Mexicans Turn to Bureaucracy Context," *New York Times*, January 8, 2009, www.nytimes.com/2009/01/09/world/americas/09mexico.html?_r=1. The woman who had to endure a monthly bureaucratic odyssey to get medication for her son won a government-sponsored contest to identify Mexico's most useless red tape. See also the comments on this article at http://community.nytimes.com/comments/www.nytimes.com/2009/01/09/world/americas/09mexico.html.

3. While one might expect that researchers working on the same topic would tend to use the same definitions, concepts, and measures, organizational researchers rarely converge on usage.

4. However, the familiarity of the educated general public with red tape research may change soon. One of the chief mechanisms by which formal knowledge is conveyed to nonresearchers is through textbooks. Now that red tape research is beginning to be discussed in influential textbooks (e.g., Rainey 2009) and presumably read by thousands of persons taking university courses in public administration, it will perhaps provide an alternative to experiential knowledge and other types of ordinary knowledge.

5. The USG is the umbrella administrative unit for all state colleges and universities in Georgia and is responsible for, among other things, providing system-wide rules and services for such shared needs as purchasing, software development, and personnel standardization.

6. Not convinced about the relative paucity or influence of empirical research in public administration? Try this exercise. Log on to Google Scholar and in the search box type "Public Administration." You will, of course, get thousands of returns. While the items are not strictly ranked in terms of citations, all of the most cited papers will be in the first ten or so pages. If you rank the items by citation, you will find that no empirical research article appears among the first forty on the list. Nor is this due to the dominance of books, though books are well represented on the high citation list. If you look only at journal articles, you will find only a handful of empirical research papers in the 100 most cited journal articles. Of course, this might also be the result of the fact that empirical research is relatively new to public administration scholars and that the most commonly cited, seminal works—for example, Herbert Simon's *Administrative Behavior* (1957)—are from an era when empirical research was not often published.

Why Red Tape Is
Not So Black and White

In this chapter and the next, we review a decade's worth of theorizing about rules and red tape. Most of the theoretical work on rules and red tape during that period has been developed from just a few sources (Bozeman 1993, 2000; Bozeman and DeHart-Davis 1999; March, Schulz, and Zhou 2000; Schulz 2003). One of the purposes of this chapter is to present a new conceptualization of red tape, a concept we refer to as "multidimensional red tape," a concept that addresses some of the limitations of previous ones. But to understand the genesis of red tape theory, it is useful to consider the history of red tape as a researchable concept, including the relationship of rules theories to red tape.

As we shall see in this chapter and later ones, contemporary research tends to treat red tape as a distinct bureaucratic pathology. One definition often used in contemporary red tape research and theory is this one:

> *Organizational red tape:* Rules, regulations, and procedures that remain in force and entail a compliance burden for the organization but make no contribution to achieving the rules' functional objectives. (Bozeman 1993)

While there are significant limitations to this concept, ones we review below, the concept has the important advantage of viewing red tape in much the same way as most ordinary citizens do: something that is undesirable and to be avoided when possible. Another advantage, at least in some respects, is that it grounds red tape in rules and procedures. Not *everything* that goes wrong in bureaucracies should be called "red tape." But as we shall see below, the route to a rules-based conception of red tape and to the research based on it has not been smooth. Along the way, red tape concepts have required some disentanglement. In the first place, it is very easy to confuse red tape with "formalization," a close conceptual relative. Second, many early public administration theorists discussed "good red tape," arguing that much of what some people think of as red tape is actually a useful if sometimes vexing procedural protection. This distinction still proves troubling in some ways. Finally, the operational steps between accepting a rules-based, negatively connoted concept of red tape and actually applying it in research have not been easy. A review of red tape "prehistory" helps us understand some of these difficulties and points of confusion.

After we provide some background on the origins and development of red tape concepts, we give careful scrutiny to theories of rules. We feel that those who study red tape still have much to learn from the study of rules, especially if one assumes, as we do, that red tape is really a rule or set of rules that have for one reason or another proved ineffective and burdensome.

Conceptual Origins

What most of us think of as red tape has probably existed as long as governments have existed. The term "red tape" has existed since the sixteenth-century reign of Henry VIII, when Cardinal Wolsey's administration produced scrolls bearing government edicts and tied them with red tape. The recipients began using the term "red tape" to refer to complex and unwieldy government rules and pronouncements. Scholarly work on red tape is of more recent vintage. Indeed, more than 90 percent of all published work about red tape has been published since 1990.

This chapter provides a prehistory of red tape research and theory. We have a dual purpose in this enterprise. In the first place, early red tape research and theory are in part a reaction to what existed in prehistory, including explicit statements of perceived limitations of related work. In the second place, the prehistory is important to understanding the embedded criticism provided later in this book, wherein we provide a firsthand account of developments in red tape research and theory, including an informal sociology of knowledge.

We assume that systematic research and theorizing about red tape began in the 1980s, and our concern here is with the question "what scholarly work presaged red tape research?" There are two important pre-1980 streams: (1) closely related work in sociology, focusing chiefly on organization structures and formalization, and (2) in public administration, the work of Herbert Kaufman, explicitly addressing red tape, but in a somewhat whimsical way and with limited attention to developing a researchable red tape concept. We consider each of these below and then examine the reasons why public administration researchers developed a body of red tape research differing significantly from both the Kaufman and the formalization traditions.

Organization Structure and Formalization

Organizational sociology provides an important element of the prehistory of red tape theory and research. Not only does this field examine organizational dimensions and behaviors similar to red tape, it also provides an important underpinning that affects subsequent red tape research. Organizational sociology has had the advantage (from the standpoint of theory development) of being little interested in reform and much interested in explanation. Partly as a result of this detachment, organizational sociologists have a view of organizations that helps us to understand the differences between unpopular but effective elements of bureaucracy and those aspects of bureaucracy that are simply ineffective in the sense that they do not accomplish social or organizational goals. This insight, while not specifically dealing with red tape, is fundamental to red tape theory—as we see in subsequent chapters of this book.

To understand the relation of formalization theory to red tape, we must begin with a brief overview of sociological concepts of structure. Richard Hall (1991, 48) provides a useful, unpretentious definition of organization structure: "It is the way in which the parts are arranged." Hall presents several other scholars' definitions of structure, including this not so simple one: "a complex medium of control which is continually produced and recreated in interaction and yet shapes that interaction: structures are constituted and constitutive" (Ranson, Hinings, and Greenwood 1980, 3).

Hall's definition is useful in capturing the basic notion, but the Ranson and colleagues' definition adds some value for all its complexity. It makes the point that structure is patterned human interaction (a common sociologically oriented perspective on structure) and, at the same time, the result of that interaction. The same word is used to refer to the process and the product produced by the process.

According to Hall (1991), organization structure serves three fundamental functions. In the first place, it shapes organizational outputs and provides the framework for the activity intended to achieve organizational goals. Second, it regulates variations in individual behavior within the organization; that is, it sets limits and controls certain behaviors, leaving others uncontrolled and at the discretion of members of the organization. Finally, it provides a setting for the exercise of authority within the organization, signaling who is in charge, responsibilities, appropriate lines of communication, and superordinate-subordinate relationships.

If those are the functions of structure, and if bureaucracy is the structuring of organizations, then it is not so difficult to understand why bureaucracy is so often unpopular. Perrow (1972) views bureaucratization as a trade-off between efficiency and inflexibility. Too little bureaucracy and efficiency is lost as the organization spins out of control. Too much bureaucracy and organizations become inflexible and unwieldy, stifling the very activities that they were set up to enhance.

To this efficiency-inflexibility trade-off we can add others. Perhaps the most important of these is the trade-off between organizational coordination and individual freedom. Coordination is essential to any organization. If organizational members do not coordinate their activity, little can be achieved. While some organizational tasks rely more on interdependence than others do, few major tasks are wholly independent. Indeed, if all major organizational tasks were independent, there probably would be no need for the organization. At the same time, coordination also implies control. While some control is required, the inevitable question is how much control is necessary to ensure coordination, standardization, and efficient use of resources.

The reason bureaucracy can never be popular with persons working in the bureaucratic organization (much less those dealing with it from the outside) is that bureaucracy *inevitably* pits the interests of the organization against those of the individual. In the best of circumstances, organizational members working in a bureaucracy are called upon to limit their discretion, constrain their use of resources, and submit to hierarchical controls in order that the organization might have the coordination and control necessary to achieve a collective purpose. To the extent that the individual organizational member's interests converge with those of the collective, the sacrifice is worth making. But in the worst of circumstances, the organizational member is called upon to submit to controls that do not promote task achievement, that do not support the goals of the collective, and that serve no legitimate social or organizational function (Kreiner, Hollensbe, and Sheep 2006). This is bureaucracy at its worst.

Considering the bureaucracy's need to control behavior and constrain individual discretion, we see the potential for all bureaucratic organizations to create red tape. Bureaucracy constrains, and when those constraints serve no legitimate purpose, organizations, their members, and those they serve become ensnared in red tape.

Formalization as Physiology, Red Tape as Pathology

A significant part of an organization's "physiology" is the set of officially sanctioned behaviors embodied in the codified rules to which the organization

22

is subject. Organization theorists have been quite inventive in their development of concepts and measures of formalization, but the definition provided below is simple and relevant:

> *Formalization:* "the extent to which rules, procedures, instructions and communications are written." (Pugh, Hickson, and Hinings 1969, 75)

Other concepts of formalization focus on the number or extent of rules (Briscoe 2007). However, neither the number of an organization's rules nor the extent to which procedures are formally codified tells us whether the rules are effective. Neither a high nor a low level of formalization is inherently "bad." In some instances, high levels of formalization enhance needed controls, accountability, or safeguards. In other instances, formalization is pathological and stifles effectiveness.

Why Formalization Is Important

As we shall see in the next chapter, red tape theory is concerned with rules, regulations, and procedures. Most contemporary researchers define red tape in terms of one or more aspects of ineffective rules. Bozeman (1993) provides perhaps the most stringent definition—rules, regulations, and procedures that have a compliance burden but do not achieve the functional objective of the rule. But others have defined or measured red tape in terms of other aspects of rules, including especially their roles in causing delays of organizational functioning. Later in this book we shall inventory concepts and measures of red tape (see also Pandey and Scott 2002). The basic point is that both formalization and red tape concepts focus on problems pertaining to rules or to the interaction of rules and structure.

Given its importance and close relationship to red tape research and theory, we consider formalization theory in some detail. Scott provides a good account of the importance of formalization, beginning with the idea that formalization actually *defines* organization. Scott's definition of formalization is broader than some others in that it examines all organization structure, not just rules. According to Scott (1987, 33), "a structure is formalized to the extent that the rules governing behavior are precisely and explicitly formulated and to the extent that roles and role relations are prescribed independently of the personal attributes of individuals occupying positions in the structure." Without prescribed roles and behaviors, established through sets of formal rules, formal organizations cannot exist (Simon 1957). If a group's behavior is entirely based on unpredictable, illegitimate, and informal behaviors, the group is not by any conventional definition an organization. The formalization issue, then, is not "whether" but "how much" (Rivkin and Siggelkow 2003).

According to Scott (1987), the organization's formal structure not only mediates performance but also is the manager's instrument of performance. The manager has little or no control over the informal, personalized, and ad hoc behaviors of employees; it is the formalized structures, as represented by rules, procedures, organizational charts and formal plans, that give direction to sanctioned behavior. Thus, the degree of formalization relates closely to the potential for managerial control of organization members' behaviors (Clegg 1981). One of the enduring questions in organization and management is which aspects of behavior to require formally and to codify and which aspects to keep informal and leave to the discretion of employees. The answer to that question often tells us much about the effectiveness of particular organizations. The answer also relates to issues of red tape inasmuch as red tape often emanates from the desire to provide formal control of organizational activities that operate more effectively when uncontrolled or controlled informally by work norms (Bozeman 2000).

While organizational members do not always find formal relations as satisfying as ones based on informal, personalized relations, the tasks, duties, and behaviors formally prescribed in organizations' structures nonetheless offers many advantages. In the first place, they help separate the person from the behavior. This is an advantage in that role performance does not depend on any particular individual. Thus, job mobility, promotion, and even the death of organizational members present fewer barriers to organizational stability and functioning (Gouldner 1950; Lieberson and O'Connor 1972; Pffefer and Salancik 1977). The formalization of roles also has the advantage, in some cases, of easing work relationships among people who do not like one another or who do not know one another.

Red Tape Versus Formalization

In general, the red tape research notes a distinction between formalization and red tape. Specifically, researchers note that formalization is neutral, while red tape is negative or bad (Bozeman and DeHart-Davis 1999; Bozeman and Kingsley 1998; Bozeman and Scott 1996; Pandey and Bretschneider 1997; Pandey and Scott 2002). Bozeman and Loveless (1987) go further in describing this distinction by noting that red tape and strong internal controls do not necessarily go hand in hand. In fact, organizations that are highly formalized can have low levels of red tape, and organizations with weak internal controls can have high levels of red tape. Welch and Pandey (2007) offer a methodological test of this assertion that red tape and formalization are different concepts. In their analysis of the interaction between intranet usage and red tape in state human service agencies, they test formalization (extent of record-keeping in organizations) and red tape as separate independent variables and as an exogenous organizational variable. They conclude that intranet reliance reduces red tape, but red tape has no effect on intranet reliance or information quality and that formalization is negatively associated with information quality but positively associated with intranet reliance and red tape. Welch and Pandey note that although formalization is characteristically positively associated with general red tape, it is not a significant determinant of procurement red tape. In sum, although formalization and red tape are related, they are distinct concepts.

Formalization has consequences well beyond the issue of red tape. Nevertheless, an understanding of red tape presupposes knowledge of the nature and significance of formalization. Knowing how systems of rules evolve or become more formal is relevant to knowing how rules "devolve," or become less effective. Regarding red tape theory, one especially important means by which rules evolve is in response to the organization's search for increased power or legitimacy or to clients' political or constituent demands (Rosenfeld 1984; Stevenson 1986; Warwick 1975). One sign that political demands have been addressed is the adoption of new formal rules and structures (Seidman 1970). In some instances, political pressures for government to create or reallocate value lead to increased formalization, in others to new programs and new agencies (Kaufman 1986).

Herbert Kaufman and the Concept of Beneficial Red Tape

It is noteworthy that Herbert Kaufman, one of the foremost students of public agency creation and expansion, authored a work that was for many years the only book-length treatment of red tape and, indeed, one of the few works of any sort dealing with red tape—*Red Tape: Its Origins, Uses, and Abuses* (1977). Kaufman's book is still read more than thirty years after its publication, and many of its insights are as fresh today as they were then. However, Kaufman provides neither a theory of red tape nor a systematic treatment of the topic. Indeed, despite using the term "red tape" on nearly every page of this 100-page book, Kaufman never actually provides a definition. This is not really surprising given Kaufman's intent to write a whimsical, widely accessible book rather than to provide a systematic, thoroughgoing treatment of the topic. He does begin the book by noting that when "people rail against red tape, they mean that they are subjected to too many constraints, that many of the constraints seem pointless, and that agencies seem to take forever to act" (4–5). Thus, he includes several elements common to most discussions of red tape—vexation, constraint, and delay.

One legacy of Kaufman's work, one still perplexing red tape researchers, is the notion of "beneficial red tape." Kaufman's concept of negative red tape is set side by side with beneficial red tape. For those who study red tape as, first and foremost, an organizational pathology, the idea of beneficial red tape is not easy to digest.[1] The notion of beneficial red tape stems in part from the quite sensible point that what one person views as red tape, another might not. One line of reasoning might be described as an administrative "tragedy of the commons":

> Every restraint and requirement originates in somebody's demand for it. Of course, each person does not will them all; on the contrary, even the most broadly based interest groups are concerned with only a relatively small band of the full spectrum of government activities. . . . But there are so many of us, and such a diversity of interests among us, that modest individual demands result in great stacks of official paper and bewildering procedural mazes. (Kaufman 1977, 29)

Thus, part of the reason for red tape is the sheer number of specialized demands for government action. This idea runs through much of Kaufman's work on bureaucratic politics and clienteles (e.g., Kaufman 1986). Process protection also gives rise to red tape. Kaufman notes that had we "more trust in . . . our public officers, we would feel less impelled to limit discretion by means of minutely detailed directions and prescriptions" (1977, 58–59). Kaufman points out that much red tape could be avoided if we were willing to reduce the checks and safeguards now imposed on government employees. But he does not advocate doing away with the extensive rule-based safeguards, noting that were we to do away with red tape, "we would be appalled by the resurgence of the evils and follies it currently prevents" (59). Thus, for Kaufman, the negative aspects of red tape are trumped by other public administration values such as transparency, accountability, fairness, protection of rights, and due process.

Kaufman is certainly not the only student of bureaucracy who suggests an important rationale for seemingly excessive rules and procedures. According to Landau (1969), duplication and overlap in some cases provide important benefits. In an interesting argument, Landau observes that "the deliberate removal of redundancies grinds an organization down to subsistence level, so restricting its repertoire of responses as to render it incapable of effective performance" (1991, 12). In other words, duplication and attendant inefficiencies can sometimes provide long-run benefits.

Several writers (e.g., Benveniste 1983, 1987; Goodsell 1985; Thompson 1975) argue that red tape sometimes provides benefits in the form of procedural safeguards that ensure accountability, predictability, and fairness in

26

administrative and policy decisions. Kirlin (1996) makes the important point that government provides an institutional framework for a wide array of human activity and that focusing narrowly on managerial efficiency undervalues government's role in the design of institutions and policies.

As an accountability mechanism, red tape comports with—and even flows from—larger democratic and constitutional values that emphasize tolerance, diversity, and participation in the political process. Thus, according to this view, the pervasiveness of bureaucratic red tape mirrors our system of governance, a system designed to be redundant and hence, inefficient, in both structure and execution.

Consistent with Kaufman's (1977) assertion that red tape is integral to our political culture, Meyer suggests that red tape is a necessary feature of our federal system: "The quantum shift in the scope of federal activities when superimposed upon a decentralized system of state and local government created a host of intergovernmental ties where none had existed previously, and it gave rise to formal procedures governing these relationships" (1979a, 230). Meyer also suggests that privatization, a value ingrained within our political culture, serves as another source of red tape. Like the red tape that flows from intergovernmental relationships, this form of red tape stems from the documentation and other administrative requirements that are attached to federal funds as a means to ensure compliance with federal guidelines. But in the larger context, red tape may be viewed as a product of our political culture and the expectations that flow out of citizen demands and our constitutional system of governance. The need for adequate levels of accountability allegedly gives rise to red tape.

Several studies examining the impact of red tape point to possible benefits. Foster (1990) found that the likelihood of rule compliance is strongly mediated by factors such as client empathy and peer group pressures. In numerous instances, such factors led to significant rule-bending, ranging from passive noncompliance to open sabotage. While red tape is often assailed as a source of nonresponsiveness in public organizations, one study found that nonresponsiveness is related more to limited resources and to the degree of discretion that workers exercise (Mladenka 1981). Similarly, Goodsell (1981) and Maynard-Moody and Musheno (2000) found a favorable predisposition toward rule-bending for clients perceived as the most needy or most capable of benefiting from the rule-bending. In Goodsell's study, both physical proximity and interpersonal contact were more critical determinants of services than the extent of rules themselves. Snizek and Bullard (1983) and York and Henley (1986) report that standardization of work procedures actually enhances job satisfaction because of increasing clarification of role expectations. Baldwin (1990) was unable to detect any effects of red tape upon motivation levels among managers. But others (Blau and Scott 1962; Ivancevich and Donnelly 1975) have found that bureaucratization reduces job satisfaction. To sum up, some scholars view red tape not as pathology but as a mixed blessing—both harmful and beneficial at the same time. Usually the harm comes from its inefficiencies, costs, and the frustration it creates. The benefits arise from its protections and guarantees of accountability. But the two-sided view of red tape presents confusion, perhaps an unnecessary confusion. We take note of studies in the "beneficial red tape" tradition, but in this book the term "red tape" is not associated with benefit nor is the term neutral. Red tape is a bureaucratic pathology.

Red Tape as Pathology

While Bozeman's (2000) definition of organizational red tape is perhaps the one that has had the most scrutiny and development during the past several years, the idea that red tape is an organizational pathology is certainly not new. The origins of pathological red tape in theories of bureaucracy are difficult to trace, but one early part of the lineage is Merton's (1940) classic study of bureaucratic personality. Merton argues that organizational demands for rule adherence lead to goal displacement among individuals working within bureaucratic organizations. Rules become ends in themselves, and adherence to formalized procedures interferes with the adaptation of these rules to special circumstances. Accordingly, the rules that were designed to increase efficiency, in general, produce inefficiency in special or exceptional circumstances. Merton further suggests that sustained exposure to entrenched rules creates a tendency toward rigidity among individuals within bureaucracy. This may occur because bureaucratic organizations tend to reward rule-oriented workers more than those who display less of a rule orientation (Edwards 1984).

Since Merton's pathbreaking study, a number of other scholars have followed in the same tradition of identifying red tape as a bureaucratic pathology (e.g., Argyris 1957; Hummel 1982; Thompson 1961) and focusing on the role of bureaucrats and their psychological world in producing red tape (Bozeman and Rainey 1998; Pandey 1995).

The empirical research on red tape (reviewed in a subsequent chapter) has, for the most part, reflected the popular view of red tape as an organizational pathology. Buchanan (1975) describes red tape in terms of excessive structural constraints. Baldwin (1990) distinguishes between formal and informal red tape. Formal red tape pertains to burdensome personnel procedures, whereas informal red tape concerns constraints created by such external sources as the media, public opinion, and political parties. Perhaps the closest to popular usage is Rosenfeld's (1984) definition of red tape as the sum of government guidelines, procedures, and forms that are perceived as excessive, unwieldy, or pointless in relationship to official decisions and policy.

Research studies in the red-tape-as-pathology tradition (e.g., Baldwin 1990; Bozeman, Reed, and Scott 1992; Bretschneider 1990; Feeney and Bozeman 2009; Kingsley and Reed 1991; Pandey and Kingsley 2000) suggest that government is often the cause of red tape, whether the effect is manifested in public or private spheres. That is, red tape flows from external governmental influences and particularly governmental regulations (Baldwin 1990), resulting in conditions of "bureaucratic inflexibility" (Rai 1983).

The pathology tradition seems to resonate with everyday experience and is close to popular usage. The beneficial red tape tradition makes the important point that some of the rules we find frustrating, wasteful, or inefficient are nonetheless beneficial because they ensure accountability, preserve rights of procedure, or provide protections from abuses of power.

Resolving the Confusion of Pathology Versus Benefit

The point made by Kaufman (1977) and others is that many of the rules, regulations, and procedures viewed as red tape provide benefits in terms of control, accountability, and even public safety and security. An alternative means of making the same point is simply to distinguish between rules, regulations, and procedures that are beneficial and those not conferring benefits—"red tape." This is not as easy as it sounds but is nevertheless a good strategy for sorting through bureaucratic problems.

Taking the stance that red tape is inherently a bureaucratic pathology may actually advance the normative concerns of beneficial red tape adherents. If we face head-on the need to sort good rules from bad, beneficial elements of rules from destructive ones, procedural guarantees and accountability may receive more direct attention and deliberate support. To those, such as Kaufman, who view red tape as an inevitable concomitant of government action, the crucial question is "how much red tape should you tolerate to get satisfying amounts of what you want?" (Kaufman 1977, 60). But the red-tape-as-pathology approach takes a different view. Namely, if rules provide accountability, they are not red tape. The rules might be constraining, unpopular, and costly, but if they achieve an important and legitimate goal, such as enhanced accountability, they are not red tape. Red tape rules, regulations, and procedures confer no benefits and, thus, the question is not "how much do we need?" but "how do we eliminate them?"[2] If red tape were the key to preserving accountability and procedural protections, then the world leaders in citizen safeguards would be the impoverished, administratively underdeveloped nations of the world that, by all accounts, greatly outpace the United States and other industrialized nations in creating red tape.

From Beneficial Red Tape to Contemporary Red Tape Theory

Much of the early work on red tape was directly motivated by perceived limitations of, respectively, formalization research and the view presented by Kaufman (1977) and others (e.g., Waldo 1948) using the term "red tape" as, essentially, synonymous with the number of rules or with administrative burden. According to the beneficial red tape view, red tape was often just another term for accountability. According to formalization research, which did not deal directly with red tape, the key issue was the extent to which rules are written and behaviors officially prescribed. Neither of these views fully clarifies red tape as an organizational pathology—the most common meaning of red tape. This is not to say, of course, that red tape is more important socially or managerially than either accountability or formalization, only that it is a different phenomenon with meaning that goes beyond what is encompassed by either formalization or accountability. The quest for this residual meaning—the destructive and pathological aspects of rules, regulations, and procedures—provided much of the motive for a public administration red tape research and theory agenda.

While most red tape research and theory since at least the 1990s may be viewed as a repudiation of the notion of beneficial red tape, the focus on pathological aspects of rules has to some extent proved a problem. The effects of rules are more complicated than simply being red tape or not being red tape. Rules have highly varying degrees of effectiveness and diverse outcomes, affecting people diversely. As we see throughout this book (please pardon the pun), red tape is not so black and white.

Theory of Rules and Red Tape

The development of red tape theory has been intertwined with the development of theories of rules.[3] In part, this is because early fieldwork on rules (e.g., Bozeman 1993; Kieser and Kubicek 1992; Zhou 1993) provided the grist for developing a "rules-based" orientation to red tape theory. While a focus on rules certainly seems a defensible approach to red tape theorizing, it is not the only approach that might have been taken. All theories are in a sense path-dependent. When decisions are made, either tacitly or self-consciously, to focus on a domain of phenomena and an attendant set of concepts, those decisions tend at least temporarily to foreclose other explanatory approaches.

What are some of the red tape concepts that might have developed in a parallel universe? The possibilities are not endless. Since the earliest meaning of the term, red tape has referred to documents and written promulgations, something very close to rules, sometimes identical to rules, regulations, and procedures. Nevertheless, there are other possibilities. For example, red tape research tends not to have focused on *policies* per se but rather on administrative procedures and rules and the implementation of broader policies. In part, this is owing to the fact that scholars have focused chiefly on *bureaucratic* red tape. If we examine public policies closely, it is not difficult to identify elements in the policies themselves that would meet some definitions of red tape in terms of the delays, inefficiencies, and vexation created.[4]

Similarly, red tape research in public administration has not focused on rule-making, laws, or procedural rules. Rather, it has focused on organizational rules and their effects on managers and, to a lesser extent, stakeholders. Red tape has been operationalized as rules that impede efficiency and effectiveness, rather than the ways in which laws and policies create burdens and obstacles for citizens or individual organizational members. Similarly, there has been little public administration research focused on the ways in which red tape is related to accountability, equity, representation, legitimacy, fairness, and other public values.

Another "path not taken" in red tape theory is structure-as-red-tape. If we think of formalization theory in organizational sociology as perhaps the closest relative of red tape theory, then we see that it would not have taken too much theory-building effort to use formalization as a starting point for red tape theory. Indeed, formalization has been quite influential on red tape research and, particularly, development of measures. Buchanan's (1975) early empirical work, titled as red tape research, used formalization measures. It has not been difficult to adapt formalization research to the task of developing new measures of red tape. Many of the actual measures used by researchers are closer to classic notions of formalization than to red tape as defined in theory (e.g., Bozeman 2000; Kaufman 1977).

The study of organizational rules has a long history in organization theory (Crozier 1964; Levitt and March 1988; March and Simon 1958), but during the period in which red tape theory began to develop, organizational rules had for some time been neglected. During the 1950s and 1960s, sociologists' studies of rules focused chiefly on their effects on the psychological states of individual bureaucrats or on their impacts on power relations. Merton (1940) focused on goal displacement and emphasized the importance of rules in facilitating harmony and predictability among employees with different types or degrees of authority. Crozier (1964) focused on rules as a protection against an employee's superior and, especially, the possibility of arbitrary action, as well as on the ways in which rule creation results in vicious cycles where rules continually grow but never sufficiently eliminate uncertainty.

Since the 1960s, researchers have taken a more quantitative approach to understanding rules in organizations. Starting with the Aston School large-scale study of organizations (Pugh et al. 1969), researchers aimed at understanding the ways in which organizational size and differentiation are related to bureaucratization and formalization. Researchers also began to investigate the ways in which rules are affected by the organizational environment (DiMaggio and Powell 1983; Meyer and Brown 1977; Tolbert and Zucker 1983). Most important, the growth of empirical research on rules has resulted in a focus on understanding the dynamic creation, revision, and death of rules.

Recent studies of bureaucratic rules have focused on the politics and law of rule-making, examining processes more than impacts. Some studies focus on rules of one particular sort or pertaining to a particular policy domain, such as environmental policy (e.g., Magat, Krupnick, and Harrington 1986; McGarrity 1991; Reynaud 2005). Others examine the relationship of rules and rules processes to governance structures (e.g., Frant 1993) or interest groups (e.g., Furlong 1997). Kerwin (1994) provides one of the best and most comprehensive overviews of rule-making processes, including useful information about the formulation, management, and oversight of rules. Similarly, Beck (2006) offers an empirical assessment of a set of rules in order to test hypotheses about the development and evolution of rules. Taking a very different approach, Manning (2008) shows through case studies that the interpretation of rules is guided by social context, which can lead to quite different outcomes for the implementation of the same rule.

Although most studies of rule-making give limited attention to the impacts of rules, there is a growing literature focusing on the ways in which rules are formed and how they change—or the dynamic nature of rules (March, Schulz, and Zhou 2000; Miner 1991; Zhou 1993). A rule is born, revised to meet the organization's needs, and eventually suspended or censored (see Figure 2.1). This research aiming to understand the dynamism of rules relies on rules' histories and studies of the determinants of rule birth and the evolution of rules. In a study of rule formation and change at Stanford University from 1891 to 1987, Zhou (1993) finds that rules are generally formed in response to external crisis and shocks and change as the result of internal learning and adaptation. In a more recent study, Schulz and Beck (2000) find that 25 percent of organizational rules are revised each year and 5 percent are suspended. The creation, adaptation, and suspension of rules demonstrate how an organization evolves, learns, and adapts. Although birth, revision, and suspension are the typical life history of a rule, there are exceptions—rules that are not revised or are never suspended.

Schulz (2003) developed a simulation model to explain the ways in which rule changes are affected by organizational tolerance for obsolescence. Schulz notes that organizational rules can become permanently institutionalized when

Figure 2.1 **Rule History**

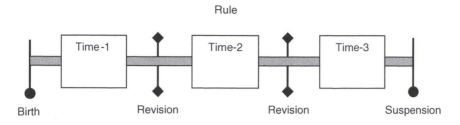

Rule

Birth   Revision   Revision   Suspension

Source: Adapted from Schulz and Beck (2000) and Schulz (2003, 1080).

their obsolescence is tolerated. Essentially, individuals in the organization ignore or tolerate a useless or inappropriate rule because revising the rule would cost more than simply ignoring the rule. Although Schulz does not call these obsolete, permanent rules "red tape," we view Schulz's simulation model as an important theoretical contribution to red tape research. For example, Schulz notes that rules often face competing pressures within an organization, especially in organizations that seek to balance reliability, legitimacy, and efficiency—a balancing act especially common to public organizations. In such "competing pressure organizations," whether public or private, one can expect an increased tendency for obsolescence and thus an increased likelihood that there will be red tape.

Thinking Systematically About Rules

Rules are the central organizing component of an organization and are present in bureaucracies, technologies, hierarchies, practices, policies, procedures, job descriptions, procurement and purchasing contracts, accounting and budgeting procedures and guidelines, personnel policies, strategic plans, and delineations of jurisdictions (Kieser and Kubicek 1992; Levitt and March 1988; Miner 1987; Schulz 2003; Zhou 1993). Researchers note that rules are created, revised, reduced, expanded, and suspended, and thus dynamic (March, Schulz, and Zhou 2000; Schulz and Beck 2000), but also they can be institutionalized, permanent, and unchanging (Dobbin and Dowd 2000; Meyer et al. 1985; Schulz 2003; Sutton and Dobbin 1996; Sutton et al. 1994).

Developing rules-based red tape theory has entailed conceptual analysis of rules (Bozeman 2000). We review briefly some of the central concepts of rules, as used in red tape theory. We began by breaking down rules into elemental components. While sociologists and organizational theorists note that rules can be written or unwritten (encoded or not encoded), we are primarily interested in formal rules, those that are written. Formal rules have the advantage of not only being written and thus easily measured, but are typically related to stronger knowledge about the rule. Research indicates that as rules age they are associated with increased knowledge and thus increased adherence and stability (Schulz and Beck 2002).

Since our concern is with formal, organizationally sanctioned rules, an enforcement provision is vital because it distinguishes between formal rules and informal, norm-based guidelines. This is *not* to suggest that informal rules are less important. Many studies (e.g., Roethlisberger and Dickson 1939) have documented the strength of informal norms and group-based dicta. We simply recognize that written rules and unwritten norms and behavior are qualitatively different and generally have distinct outcomes for individuals and organizations. Empirical research has shown that written (encoded) rules have a stabilizing effect for organizations, while rules and behaviors that have accumulated over time but are not encoded tend to destabilize rules (March, Schulz, and Zhou 2000; Schulz 1998a; Schulz and Beck 2000). While unwritten rules are less stable than written rules, research has found that informal norms, or routines, are critical for filling in gaps between formal rules and ensuring that rules are applied in a purposeful manner (Reynaud 2005). In an assessment of new rules for a productivity bonus in the Electronic Equipment Maintenance Workshop of the Paris Metro, Reynaud finds that routines are important for "sense making" and to adjust, modify, and expand new rules to effective implementation. In sum, informal rules (rules not encoded, routines, or norms) are important means for interpreting new rules and navigating around obsolete rules, but they are of less importance to an understanding of rules as red tape.

All formal rules, the only kind of rule of interest here, have three common dimensions (Bozeman 2000): (1) behavioral requirements, (2) implementation mechanisms, and (3) enforcement provisions. Rules tell organizational members what must be done, by whom, and under what circumstances, thus ensuring continuity of actions and practice. Each formal, organizationally sanctioned rule specifies some behavior that is either required or prohibited (prohibition is just another requirement—the requirement to refrain). Rules guide behavior (Cyert and March 1963; Levitt and March 1988), resulting in stability within organizations. Whether rules are defined from the view of evolutionary economics (Nelson and Winter 1982), transaction-costs economics (Williamson 1981, 1985), resource-based and knowledge-based perspectives (Foss 1996; Grant 1996; Teece and Pisano 1994), or legal analysis (Dobbin and Dowd 2000; Dobbin and Sutton 1988), they are created and evolve in order to drive the behavior of individuals and organizations.

Rules may be straightforward, such as "No smoking," or they may be inordinately complex, such as requirements for actions during a nuclear plant accident. In addition to setting behavior requirements, rules indicate when and how and who should implement a behavior. Implementation components of rules tell, for example, that the no-smoking provision applies to all employees at all times when they are *in* the office building, but that behavior is not regulated when they are on official business but outside the building. Similarly, the rules for nuclear plant accidents will set boundary conditions defining an accident and specify not only the actions to be taken but also the parties responsible for acting.

For purposes of a rule-based theory of red tape, a most important assumption is that a rule (regulation, procedure) is a *social* concept and has no existence without social meaning. This is because rules are all about behavioral requirements. Since a behavioral requirement of a rule is a defining characteristic, and since behavioral requirements are inherently social, it follows that rules themselves are best viewed as social artifacts. In their review of rule-based models of organizational learning, Schulz and Beck (2002) note that rules, rule histories, and the connections between rules enable researchers to understand organizational social systems. Because rules are path-dependent and interconnected (Zhou 1993), analyzing rules and rule changes enables researchers to understand how an organization learns and facilitates, limits, coordinates, and enables activities. Because rules are revised to deal with a changing environment, rule texts and rule histories are a record of organizational knowledge (Schulz and Beck 2002).

Any rule can be viewed as having behavioral requirements, implementation mechanisms, and enforcement provisions, but also an objective for the rule. Since rules are not universal, it is also important to understand which persons are subject to the rule (i.e., workers in Acme organization, citizens of Ferndale, or all citizens of the United States). Another boundary issue is the domain of rules and policies to which any particular rule is attached, the "rule ecology."

Rule Objectives

If red tape is viewed in terms of achieving (or failing to achieve) formally sanctioned objectives, then any assessment must begin with some knowledge of the rule's objective. However, this obvious starting point often immediately sets a problem for understanding rules and red tape. Many rules are poorly defined and their objectives are not directly stated. Sometimes this poses few problems because the rule's objectives are easily inferred. Thus, if a company adopts a no-smoking rule, employees do not need to be told the objective. In other cases, objectives are not as clear and not easily inferred.

Most important, many rules break down at their very inception due to a lack of clarity about objectives.

Let us take the example of a no-smoking rule. This rule, on its surface, seems quite easily understood. We just stated that if a company adopts a no-smoking rule, employees do not need to be told the objective. However, it is important to note that just because a rule has a clearly communicated objective, that objective is not necessarily sensible or socially desirable. From the standpoint of organizational analysis and red tape theory, knowledge of a rule's objective is important because it indicates the behavior that the rule seeks to induce or prohibit. In our no-smoking example, the objective can be an important factor in how rules are designed, implemented, and enforced.

Let us consider two contrasting instances of a seemingly simple rule. In March 2003, the City of New York passed a ban on smoking in all public establishments. This rule, or ban, was promoted on the basis of workers' rights (i.e., the right of wait staff, bartenders, and others to work in a clean, smoke-free environment). The no-smoking legislation enabled the City Department of Health and Mental Hygiene to follow up on complaints of violations and allocate fines of $200 to $400 for the first violation, $500 to $1,000 for the second, and $1,000 to $2,000 for the third. Three violations in one year can result in the revocation of the owner's license.

In comparison, in 2005, the state senate and governor of Georgia approved a statewide smoking ban. This ban aimed to protect the health of minors (children under age eighteen). Thus, adult-only venues in Georgia (e.g., over-eighteen bars, restaurants, and entertainment venues), outdoor sports venues, retail tobacco shops, and outdoor places of employment remain eligible for smoking. Fines in Georgia range from $100 to $500. The objectives of these two rules, which both ban smoking in public establishments, not only re-sulted in very different forms of legislation and penalty structures, but, more important, define the limits of behavior. Smokers in Georgia might be more likely to break the rule, given the lower fine level. Restaurants in Georgia, if they have a large number of smoking patrons, may move to ban entry to minors. Additionally, rule compliance might be higher in New York, where all public establishments are smoke-free, as compared to Georgia, where there are numerous exceptions to the rule. In sum, the objective of a rule may result in lower compliance or increased confusion about rule implementation and enforcement.

Even when there is no connection between rules' objectives and actual outcomes, rules nonetheless require some minimal level of shared or sym-metrical values. For those interested in ensuring compliance with rules, a key factor is the strength of the value served by the rule. Compliance may be based on fear of sanctions or other people's perceptions, a desire to get ahead or receive positive evaluations. But in many cases, a person's compliance is based on an interest identical to the functional object of the rule. Thus, even workers who smoke may readily agree not to smoke indoors because they are sympathetic to the objective of the rule—better air quality in the workplace. Similarly, owners of polluting industrial firms may actually support strong pollution controls, so long as they believe that their competitors are subject to the same rules and same levels of enforcement.

All rules entail a compliance resource requirement, even if that requirement is not specified. The compliance resource requirement is the answer to the question "What level of resources would be needed to comply with the requirements set by the rule?" This is *not* to say, of course, that the compliance resource requirement is a good approximation of the resources that will actually be expended in connection with a rule. From a practical standpoint, making good estimates of the compliance resource requirement is a vital part of making good rules and avoiding red tape. But in many instances, determining compliance resource requirements is a tricky proposition. Thus, when the Environmental Protection Agency (EPA) requires all the companies within a given geographic attainment area to meet a given standard for nitrogen oxide emissions, it is almost impossible to get a good estimate of the compliance resource requirement of such a regulation.

Rule Ecology

Rules do not exist in a vacuum. They are affected not only by external social events, but also by changes in the physical world (Beck 2006; Schulz 2003). Rules are path-dependent and are also affected by other rules (interdependent). In general, the rule ecology is that part of the social and physical environment that impinges upon compliance and upon the rule's effects. Let us consider the example of rules about emission standards for catalytic converters. The rule ecology is dynamic and might change in a great many ways. Some possibilities include (1) new information emerging about the costs of bringing automobile catalytic converters up to standard; (2) further development of solar or electrical vehicles; (3) rising (or declining) use of mass transit; (4) motorists organizing, protesting, and writing elected representatives about the annoyance of complying with auto inspection rules; (5) lack of service stations and garages willing to undertake inspections; (6) improved air quality because of environmental reforms in other policy arenas; and (7) new scientific evidence about the effectiveness of catalytic converters. These illustrations give some indication of the complexity of rule ecologies. The effectiveness of rules depends upon several factors (both internal and external to the organization) outside the sometimes simple behavior modification sphere of the rule.

Technology, political action, available resources, knowledge, social change, and even world events can affect the outcomes of rules.

Recent research also notes that because organizational rules are dynamic, they are subject to the amount of oversight and monitoring provided by the organization itself. Schulz (2003) notes that if an organization fails to oversee and monitor rules, it is at a higher risk of tolerating obsolescent rules, which over time will result in the inability to revise those rules to the new environment. According to Schulz, "Obsolescence is likely to be more tolerated when organizations lack the energy to monitor their rules" (2003, 1092).

Compliance Burden

In public administration research, the concept of formalization focuses on the number of formal rules, while organizational theorists measure the amount of rules as "rule mass," or the number of pages of paper dedicated to outlining general and specific rules. But for an understanding of red tape, the amount of rules is much less important than the compliance burden associated with the rules. The full impact of rules cannot be adequately determined without knowing something about the resources and energy required to comply with the rules (Foster 1990; Foster and Jones 1978). A new set of federal guidelines on sponsored research accounting might well have a quite different impact on, say, a small consulting firm with a single accountant than on a major university employing thirty accountants and financial managers. Thus, it is useful to distinguish between the amount of rules and the resources required to comply with them. *Compliance burden* is defined as the total resources *actually* expended in complying with a rule (Bozeman 2000).

Compliance burden is, roughly speaking, a direct "cost" of a rule. Compliance burden is *not* the full cost of a rule. To calculate the full cost of an implemented rule, we would need to know the sum of compliance burden, implementation burden, the cost of rule formulation, and the opportunity costs imposed by the rule. Nor is compliance burden the amount of resources *required* to meet the rule, but the amount that the complying organization actually *expends*. For example, imagine an organization that develops a handbook outlining a set of rules to manage the flow of traffic in the parking garage. The management sends the handbook to all employees. It costs the organization a certain amount of money and effort to write, publish, and distribute the garage driving manual. However, the employees already have a set of typical driving norms. Therefore, if no one follows the new rules outlined in the handbook and if the organization fails to enforce the new rules—that is, if there is no compliance and no enforcement—there is no cost to compliance burden.

People or organizations seeking to comply with rules may expend either more or less resources than are actually needed to meet the rule. In complying with a rule, why would anyone spend more resources than actually required? In some instances, more resources might be spent because the complying individual or organization favors the rule's objectives, a sort of voluntary contribution. In other cases, extra resources might be expended to achieve some personal objective. For example, a recently chastised firm might spend more resources on environmental cleanup than required simply because it wishes to take out advertisements trumpeting the firm's good works. The favorable publicity may boost sales.

In some cases, overcompliance (or undercompliance) is a matter of poor prediction. One of the themes developed throughout this book is that rules are predictions of human behavior and often go awry because of human indeterminacy. In creating and implementing a rule, people are saying, in effect, "if a rule requires behavior x, under conditions j (or holding conditions constant), the result will be outcome y." All rules entail behavior assumptions and predictions. Sometimes the rules are very simple and the predictions simple. But the more complicated the behaviors required and the more complex the assumptions, the more likely that the implicit predictions will fail. Assessing compliance burden is only one of many crucial issues relating to the fact that rules predict behavior. The effectiveness of rules and the red tape generated from rules both relate to the predictive character of rules.

Implementation Burden

Rules entail not only a compliance burden but, in most instances, an *implementation burden*. There are some rules that are truly self-implementing, but most entail at least some level of energy and resources, even if it is nothing more than posting a sign. In many instances, the implementation burden and compliance burden are borne by different organizations. Thus, when a state environmental agency regulates, the agency may bear an implementation burden while the regulated business may bear the compliance burden.

We can define the implementation burden as the total resources actually expended in implementing a rule (Bozeman 2000; see Schulz 1998 for somewhat different usage). The implementation burden may have even more of an impact on bureaucratic behavior than the compliance burden. In an experimental study of bureaucratic discretion and control flowing from rules, Scott (1997) found that subjects who were making decisions about simulated welfare cases were much more affected by the *intensity* of the rules (his term for compliance burden) than the *number* of formal rules. The rule implementers were willing to substitute their discretion for organizational rules when it was relatively easy (from a rule compliance standpoint) to do so and were much less likely to use discretion when the compliance burden increased.

39

Rule Density, Rule Mass, and Rule Incidence

From the perspective of the managers of organizations, the critical issue often is not the compliance burden associated with any particular set of rules and regulations, but the compliance burden required for all the rules, regulations and procedures to which the organization is subject. While regulators tend to think only about the rules they impose, managers think about the sets of rules and regulations to which they are subject and the resources available to comply with them. Whether the rule is from the Occupational Safety and Health Administration (OSHA) or EPA may make little difference to complying managers or regulated organizations; indeed, managers might not even know the origin of some rules.

Rule density, which relates to this issue of aggregate rules and the resources required to comply with them, is defined as the "total resources devoted by the organization to complying with all its rules, as a percentage of total resources available to the organization" (Bozeman 2000). Rule mass refers to the size of a set of rules, expressed as the number of pages describing the general and specific rules (Beck 2006).

Using the concepts of rule density, rule mass, and compliance burden helps in thinking about the implications of bureaucratization for management theory. Figure 2.2 depicts the relationships among total organizational resources and total compliance burden with differing rule densities calculated from a line dividing the X axis (total resources) and Y axis (total compliance burden). If we take total resources as a reflection of the volume and "energy" of organizational activities, we can consider the implications of combinations of total resources ("energy level") and total compliance burden ("bureaucratization level"). The chief lesson of the model depicted in Figure 2.2 is that each organization has a finite set of resources that can, in principle, be used in a number of different ways. These resources are the organization's energy. Just as the human body consumes resources and uses calories (burns energy), organizations use their resources and burn energy. If a high percentage of the organization's energy is devoted to complying with rules, less is available for achieving other tasks. We can speculate about the implications of the organization types corresponding to the various levels of energy and compliance (the legend under Figure 2.2). Thus, a high energy/low compliance organization likely has few external controls. This is not inherently good or bad. The extent of control should depend on the nature of the organization's missions and its interdependence with other organizations. Similarly, we can speculate that a low energy/high compliance organization is the classic overworked, overcontrolled bureaucracy. It has relatively few resources but many formal demands put upon it. The

Figure 2.2 **Rules Density Typology**

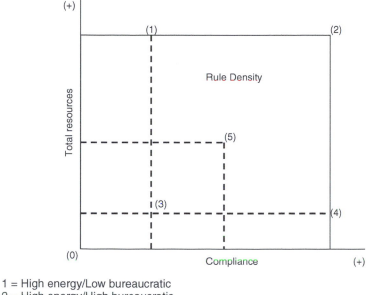

1 = High energy/Low bureaucratic
2 = High energy/High bureaucratic
3 = Low energy/Low bureaucratic
4 = Low energy/High bureaucratic
5 = Medium energy/Medium bureaucratic

general point is that considering the organization's energy level compared to its compliance requirements can give some insight into its ability to take on new tasks and its potential for change.

Regardless of the potential importance of the propositions about under- and overcontrol, rule density, or rule incidence, these issues are *not* issues of red tape. Red tape occurs not because of the number of rules, but when rules consume resources and fail to achieve objectives.

Since the concepts presented in this chapter are in some cases new ones, some relationship to simple questions might be useful. Table 2.1 organizes several of the most important concepts according to the questions they address with respect to rules and their effects: What? How Much? Who? To What Effect? Armed with a set of concepts that allows us to discuss rules, red tape, and their components and consequences, we turn in the next chapter to the primary concern of this book—the *causes* of red tape.

41

Table 2.1

Rules and Their Consequences: Organizing the Concepts

What?	How much?	Who?	To what effect?
Rules	Compliance burden	Rule incidence	Rule efficacy
a. Behavior	Implementation	Rule ecology	Rule density
requirements	burden		
b. Implementation	Red tape		
mechanisms			
c. Enforcement			
provisions			
Functional object of rule			

Bureaucratic Pathology

If compliance burden is, roughly speaking, the direct cost of a rule, *rule efficacy* is the direct benefit of a rule. As is the case with compliance cost, there may be impacts that are not direct. Often, rules provide benefits to some purpose other than the functional object of the rule. For example, fuel economy rules tend to have not only energy savings benefits but also reduce harmful emissions and, by encouraging the purchase of smaller cars, can in some cases reduce deaths in automobile accidents. We can define rule efficacy as "the extent to which a given rule addresses effectively the functional object for which it was designed" (Bozeman 2000).

This definition of the benefit of rules does not enable much precision. As discussed earlier in this chapter, many rules have an extremely murky functional object. Certainly, there is no requirement that the functional object be clear-cut or universally agreed upon. Indeed, some scholars argue that ambiguous and vague rules enable implementers to better adjust the rule into practice. Reynaud (2005) notes that routines and norms help to transform vague rules into useful practice. However, while it is possible that organizational members can exploit vague rules to improve implementation, it is also possible that value rules will result in additional rule creation and increased rule sets (Beck 2006). Indeed, it is often the case that the functional object is open to diverse interpretations. The classic example of an ambiguous rule in the public sector is the injunction to "rule in public interest." More than a few regulatory statutes include broad language instructing regulators to act in the public interest. Walter Lippman (1955, 4) defined the public interest as what we would choose if we "saw clearly, thought rationally, and acted disinterestedly and benevolently"—a stringent set of requirements. In most cases, however, the functional object of the rule is more concrete than that.

Usually, measuring rule efficacy presents problems—explaining the paucity of empirical research in this area. Generally, the simpler the rule, its ecology, and its functional object, the easier it is to measure rule efficacy. To return to our recurring example, if we develop a no-smoking rule, put up a sign implementing the rule, and then measure incidence of smoking (or, alternatively, air quality) before and after the rule implementation, we can probably get a satisfactory index of rule efficacy. It is possible that a convention of nonsmoking Mormons will come through the airport and confound the results a bit, but the before-after measure would probably be useful nonetheless. Most cases, however, are not so simple; consider measuring the efficacy of rules that limit and restrict smoking (e.g., Georgia) rather than those banning smoking altogether (e.g., New York). Consider another case introduced above—state-mandated inspections of automobile catalytic converters. The functional object of the rule is enhanced air quality. But so many factors can affect air quality that any attempt to evaluate results by tracking ambient air quality is unlikely to shed much light on the effectiveness of the inspections. Nor do we know much from the number of inspections or even the number of inspections failed (or even more confounding, the presence of cars from out of state). Such factors as variance in the stringency of the inspection and garage owners' profit-motivated false positives come into play. Even if we were able to come up with an entirely satisfactory measure of rule efficacy, the determination of the compliance burden of state-mandated inspections is inordinately complicated. For example, how do we value the literally thousands of hours citizens devote to inspections, hours that would have otherwise been devoted to leisure and work?

The red tape concept introduced below does not take a rigid cost-benefit perspective on rules. It is in some circumstances useful to think of red tape as rules with net negative cost-benefit ratios. But given the enormous measurement problems and the ubiquity of rules that are truly odious and provide no benefit, the concept of red tape presented here is extremely conservative—rules with *no* benefit.

Red Tape Defined: "No Redeeming Social Value"

Two red tape concepts have dominated post-1990s red tape research theory; each has some range of utility. One definition, *organizational red tape*, assumes that effects are unitary. The other, *stakeholder red tape*, assumes that a rule may be red tape for one set of stakeholders, but functional for another. The theory developed here is based on two definitions of red tape, one an authority-based definition and centering on the organization implementing the rule, the other stakeholder-based.

Organizational red tape: Rules that remain in force and entail a compliance burden for the organization but make no contribution to achieving the rules' functional objective.

This is the red tape concept we presented earlier in the chapter. It has the advantage, an important one, of not viewing the amount of rules as identical to or indicative of red tape, thus dispensing with the confusing notion of "good" red tape. A central assumption in the concept of organizational red tape, one that should be made explicit, is that it is contingent on the relationship of the rule to the functional object. The functional object is defined in terms of an authoritative, official statement of purpose. That official statement can come from the organization or from an authoritative controller of the organization (e.g., a parent organization, a superordinate government bureau, or a legislative or judicial body). But each formal rule has a formal statement of purpose.

A potential drawback of the authority-based definition of red tape is that it fails to note that rules can have very different meanings and impacts for different stakeholders. Thus, what may seem useless red tape to an organizational client or customer may seem an important work-processing rule to a manager. For example, rules designed to protect workers and prevent discrimination in the hiring process might seem burdensome and taxing to a job applicant.

In some cases, there are analytical and practical advantages to viewing red tape as subject-dependent. Thus, a second definition of red tape is presented below, a subject-dependent concept, focusing on stakeholders.

Stakeholder red tape: Rules that remain in force and entail a compliance burden for the organization but make no contribution to objectives valued by a focal stakeholder.

It is easy to see that stakeholder red tape provides theoretical advantages over organizational red tape. From a general policy standpoint, as opposed to the perspective of a single organization, stakeholder red tape is more important. However, despite the social importance of this red tape concept, it is not at all easy to develop a satisfactory research construct. For this reason, among others, very little red tape research has focused on stakeholder red tape.

From the standpoint of research, the organizational red tape concept is more practical. It is less complex, it is based on a formal statement of the purpose of the rule, and it is more amenable to measurement. Stakeholder red tape is particularly useful when analyzing coalitions of interests in organizations or when the focus is not on the organization as unit of analysis. But stakeholder red tape leads quickly to complexity, often so much complexity that explanation of rules' impacts becomes almost impossible. Given the central premise that human indeterminacy and unpredictability are among the most important issues in assessing the effects of rules, we can see the virtual impossibility of predicting outcomes for diverse sets of stakeholders. But if stakeholder red tape is not the easy concept, it has some value as an ideal construct. The more stakeholders, the greater the problems in sorting out stakeholder red tape. In a government organization, we might expect at least the following stakeholder types:

- Parent agency
- Political superiors (e.g., Congress)
- Central management agencies (e.g., Office of Management and Budget)
- Interorganizational partners (both public and private sector)
- Clients and clientele groups
- Intraorganizational coalitions

A rule that is red tape for one group within a category may not be red tape even for another group in that same category. Thus, the category "intraorganizational coalitions" might include such diverse sets as the psychologists in the personnel department, the cohort of younger middle managers, and employees interested in innovation and change. Each of these coalitions may have unique sets of values and different functional objects to be served (or not served) by the organization's rules and procedures. What this means, from the standpoint of researching red tape, is that comprehensive and valid measurement of a stakeholder concept of red tape is inevitably a prodigious task, one undertaken by few red tape researchers.

New Concept: Multidimensional Red Tape

In developing any social sciences concept, researchers often face a dilemma. On the one hand, it is important that the concept capture as much phenomenological reality as possible. On the other hand, if the concept is to be much use for developing empirically based theory, then it should enable constructs and measures. As we see in the discussion above, these two criteria often clash. Stakeholder red tape has face validity and embodies the useful idea, one expressed well by Waldo (1948), that individuals vary not only in their perceptions about red tape but also in the concrete effects rules have upon them. By contrast, the organizational red tape concept, while more amenable to research, fails to recognize the multiple perspectives and effects of red tape.

These two concepts of red tape share one limitation: they provide stringent concepts of red tape. If we define red tape as making *no contribution whatsoever* to organizational (or stakeholder) goals and purposes, a miniscule propor-

45

tion of rules actually qualifies as red tape (DeHart-Davis 2009). Having such a stringent notion of red tape limits the utility of research red tape, especially with respect to its practical value for managers and policy-makers.

In historical context, the development of a stringent concept of red tape seems understandable. Early work on red tape sought to bring some clarity to the muddle that had been created by the idea of beneficial or "white" tape, a concept confounding high cost and high value rules. There was also a need to distinguish between theories and measures of formalization and rules effects, especially deleterious effects. Organizational and stakeholder red tape definitions, stringent as they are, helped to carve a niche for red tape research distinguished from formalization research.

While organizational and stakeholder red tape concepts retain utility for researchers, theory requires a red tape concept more closely aligned with experience. Thus, we introduce another rules-based red tape concept: multidimensional red tape.

> *Multidimensional red tape:* Rules that remain in force and entail a compliance burden for the organization or its stakeholders, but that are ineffective with respect to at least some of the organization's or the stakeholders' objectives for the rules.

Multidimensional red tape represents a significant departure from organizational and stakeholder red tape, but a step in the direction of organizational and managerial reality. Its utility for research remains to be seen, but it is at least possible that the added complexity entailed in this red tape conceptualization will advance research.

The multidimensional red tape concept provides several advantages. In the first place, its requirements are not so stringent. Rules need not be utterly useless to qualify as red tape—the definition is based on a lack of effectiveness rather than a total lack of (positive) effect. Related, the concept recognizes that a rule may be effective in some domains or rule objectives while qualifying as red tape in others. Unlike organizational red tape, there is no presumption of either a single objective (legitimate functional object) for a rule nor is there a single perspective on the effectiveness of rules. The multidimensional red tape concept, by allowing some aspects of rules to qualify as red tape, while others do not, greatly expands the practical utility of the concept. Another advantage of multidimensional red tape is that it retains the useful notion of red tape as pathology. The definition is not relaxed to such a degree that it encourages a retreat to the "beneficial red tape" oxymoron or that it gets bogged down confusing challenging and sometimes burdensome goals such as accountability or procedural protection with red tape. Red tape remains an organizational and managerial problem, no organizational fantasy here, but the concept depicts red tape as interrelated and interdependent components of rules, some components perhaps quite effective and others not effective. In other words, it seems to us that reality is served.

Despite the advantages of multidimensional red tape, limitations remain. The previous conceptions of red tape as having no redeeming value at least seemed to provide guideposts helping to identify red tape. In any organizational or managerial concept, there is the question of qualifying rules. What qualifies as leadership, job satisfaction, intrinsic motivation, and so forth? In organizational red tape the answer seems easy—a rule is red tape if it accomplishes nothing. However, the specificity of the organizational red tape concept has proved more apparent than real. Few rules accomplish nothing whatsoever; moreover, it is a daunting task to document that this is indeed the case. Empirical research on red tape has in most cases taken the tack of using perceptions about whether rules accomplish nothing, but, aside from the problem that perceptions do not seem to capture all we might wish about red tape, there is the problem that people in the same organization have different perceptions about the same rule. Nonetheless, noting that organizational red tape presents its own problems in no way shrinks the operational problems of multidimensional red tape.

In moving from concept to construct, an obvious and important problem with multidimensional red tape is that its focus on rule effectiveness does not and cannot provide a precise demarcation about when rules have become sufficiently ineffective as to qualify as red tape. If we assume, quite reasonably, that there is great variance in the effectiveness of rules, even great variance in the extent to which they are ineffective, then when is the line crossed from a not-so-good rule into red tape status? We suggest this problem is not so great as it appears and, especially, that it is not much different than the problems one finds with a great many concepts. Let us consider some major social concepts that have been used for many years. With respect to the concept of alienation, how do we know that people are sufficiently distanced from others that they should now be described as "alienated"? With respect to leadership, when exactly does a person show requisite behaviors to be described as a "leader"? Or what about "job satisfaction"? At what level and on which job satisfaction items do we conclude finally that a person is "satisfied"? There appears to be no reason why rules-based red tape constructs need any sharper demarcation points than do other organizational research constructs.

It seems to us that greater operational difficulties are posed by the idea of multiple stakeholders considering different goals for rules. However, this complication seeks to address a limitation of previous red tape definitions. Why should red tape focus entirely on the legitimate goals of organizations?

Putting aside for the moment the question of whether the goals themselves may be problematic, we can certainly suggest that in the hurley-burley world of actual policy-making, official policy-makers, much less stakeholders, rarely agree exactly what is to be accomplished by provisions of rules, regulations, and procedures. It is well known in policy-making that those supporting particular policies (and, by extension, particular rules flowing from them) often have in mind competing objectives for the exact same policy provisions. Why should this not be the case, or why should the case be viewed as irrelevant, with respect to organizational rules and stakeholders? Still, the operational difficulties may not be so easy to surmount. After we determine (or posit) stakeholders, we would likely need to elicit responses about their diverse objectives for rules and the relative value for those objectives. One stakeholder may put great value on efficiency and very little on privacy protection, whereas another stakeholder may have exactly the opposite values. Similarly, a rule may prove quite effective for one of those values but may be so ineffective for another as to constitute red tape. There are well-established methods for eliciting diverse and conflicting values, especially contingent value methodology, thus far used chiefly in environmental policy (Cummings, Brookshire, and Shulze 1986).

Figure 2.3 provides a depiction of the multidimensional red tape concept, showing that red tape can be viewed as a threshold variable.

Conclusion

Organization theory uses terms in so many different ways that it sometimes seems that up is down and left is just a variation of right. But in this book when we use the term "red tape," the meaning will not be far removed from the ways in which people normally talk about it. Red tape is bad. It is not an aid to accountability or legitimacy or a means of ensuring participation. Rules that appropriately hold organizations accountable may not be popular with the people constrained by them, but they are not red tape. Nor is red tape the same as having a great many or overly detailed rules. The amount of rules is formalization, and the level of formalization and the rule mass may tell us little or nothing about the amount of red tape. Many rules do not imply effective rules. Few rules do not imply effective rules.

An important subtext is that the number of formal rules needed in one type of organization may be quite different than is needed in another type. Some organizations require few rules and need to maintain a high level of autonomy to further their mission. Sometimes large organizations may need an extensive number of rules, especially if the organization has many branches, but research also finds that the number of employees in an organization is not

Figure 2.3 **Three Red Tape Concepts**

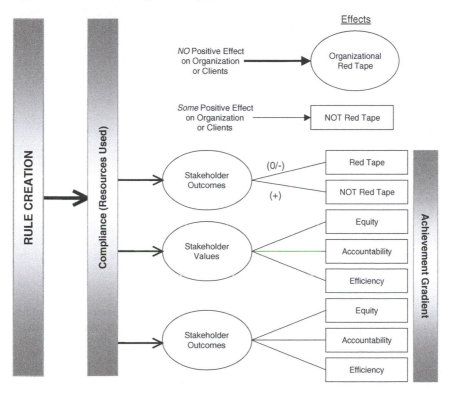

related to the rule mass (Beck 2006). Organizations that prize creativity and innovation may need few rules. Some organizations may be self-regulating if their members follow strong professional norms that are compatible with the organization's mission. Other organizations need extensive rules. This is likely the case, for example, with organizations charged with providing specifically mandated services on an equitable and standard basis, as well as organizations that must manage a large number of different branches (Beck 2006). Thus, in assessing whether organizations' rules are red tape or not, the judgment cannot be made apart from knowledge of the objectives the rules seek to serve. Rules that are observed but that do not further the objective qualify as red tape. The fact that we do not like particular rules does not qualify them as red tape. The fact that we dislike the objective that the rule serves does not qualify the rule as red tape. Red tape is pathology, involving the waste of resources. The waste of resources in complying with red tape pertains not to bureaucratic requirements and controls but to the formulation and implementation of rules that, for one reason or another, do not work. All the above-mentioned concepts of red tape have this in common. However, the utility of the respective concepts will likely depend on the extent to which one needs a straightforward conception of red tape in connection with a single organization or whether one requires a more nuanced concept focused on the organization and its stakeholders and taking into account the fact that rules reflect multiple dimensions for which people have multiple and sometimes conflicting goals.

Notes

1. One contemporary approach to red tape research that *seems* akin to Kaufman's is DeHart-Davis's (2009) work on "green tape." However, on closer examination, her work is more in line with contemporary approaches (i.e., pathological red tape); the distinction is that rather than focusing on causes of red tape she seeks to analyze the components of effective rules and regulations.

2. While this view of red tape has proved useful in promoting research and reducing ambiguity, if we focus on stakeholder or multiple perspectives on rules, then the question of what is and is not judged red tape becomes more complicated. We return to this point in later chapters.

3. A note on usage: the term "rules" is used throughout the remainder of this book as shorthand for "formal rules, regulations, and procedures."

4. It is worth noting that some red tape publications *have* focused on specific policies and on the red tape to which the policies give rise. For example, Bozeman and DeHart-Davis (1999) examined red tape inhering in Title V air quality permitting policies. Other rule-based studies have assessed the creation and development of rules (e.g., Reynaud's [2005] study of the Paris Metro Workshop) and the dynamic development of rules (e.g., Beck's [2006] study of rules at a German bank).

3

Elements of Red Tape Theory

The study of red tape presents many puzzles, including this one: why has empirical research on red tape developed to a much greater degree than has conceptual and theoretical work on red tape? In some fields, this puzzle would have an easy answer: that scholars gravitate to measurement and the testing of quantitative hypotheses in part because theory usually requires more extensive work and in part because theory does not easily fit into the standard unit of academic research, the twenty-page journal article. But in public administration, this answer fails to satisfy. Public administration remains distinct from other social sciences. Public administration has not fully embraced quantitative-empirical[1] research. Even today, conceptual work in public administration is at least as common as quantitative empirical work, and the empirical research that is published tends to be less cited than books, conceptual work, and practice-oriented publications.

We note the scarcity of theoretical work on red tape in part to explain why much of this chapter focuses on two closely related theoretical works (Bozeman 1993, 2000), works providing the only comprehensive theory of red tape. To be sure, there are theories of rules (reviewed in the previous chapter) and there is theory produced from empirical research on red tape (reviewed extensively in the next chapter). But conceptual theory-building separate from empirical work on red tape has been less common and generally piecemeal.

This chapter has several objectives. First, we provide a concise review of the red tape theory, drawing chiefly but not exclusively from Bozeman's (1993, 2000) efforts to develop comprehensive theory. Second, we consider the extent to which empirical researchers have tested the models and propositions set forth in conceptual theory. Finally, we begin to discuss the relation between theoretical and conceptual work on red tape, with its attendant concepts and propositions, and empirical research on red tape.

Bozeman's Theory: Rule-Inception and Rule-Evolved Red Tape

Figure 3.1 is a conceptual model depicting Bozeman's theory of red tape (adapted from Bozeman 2000). We begin here not only because it remains the only broad, fully articulated theory of red tape, but also because it has affected subsequent empirical research.

As we see from Figure 3.1, a fundamental assumption of the theory is that red tape can occur at the same time as rules are created or rules can evolve into red tape over any period of time, depending upon transformations related to the implementation or enforcement of rules. Red tape "built-in" at the beginning of rules is referred to as "rule-inception" red tape, and red tape occurring as rules are implemented and they evolve is referred to as "rule-evolved" red tape. Related to rules theory reviewed in the previous chapter, the theory assumes that all rules can be thought of as having a behavior requirement, an implementation plan, and enforcement mechanisms and, most important, that any of these has the potential to contribute to red tape.

Another particularly important aspect of the model theory depicted in Figure 3.1 is that it shows the two very different ways of assessing red tape, in terms of, respectively, impacts on organizations and their members and impacts on organizational stakeholders (which usually include a broad set of actors such as clients, customers, supervising agents, and resource providers, among others).

The theory specifies a number of "red tape threats," divided according to whether they are threats during the creation of the rule or subsequently in its implementation. There is no implication that these are the only causes of red tape, but the theory seeks to be as comprehensive as possible in identifying the particular means by which legitimate rules become red tape. In the next section, we review the factors leading to rule-inception red tape.

Rule-Inception Red Tape

Often rules, regulations, and procedures have "built-in" red tape, red tape that is part of the rule's creation. In some instances, persons who are not acting in the best interest of the organization or its stakeholders create rules. Self-serving rules are not easy to establish in the full light of day, but are much easier to develop in relative obscurity. Often rules are cloaked in symbols or apparently pure motives hiding self-serving origins. No one actually says, "Here is a rule

Figure 3.1 **Bozeman's Model of Red Tape and Its Determinants**

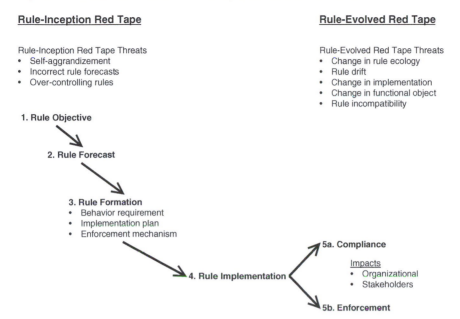

Rule-Inception Red Tape

Rule-Inception Red Tape Threats
• Self-aggrandizement
• Incorrect rule forecasts
• Over-controlling rules

Rule-Evolved Red Tape

Rule-Evolved Red Tape Threats
• Change in rule ecology
• Rule drift
• Change in implementation
• Change in functional object
• Rule incompatibility

1. Rule Objective

2. Rule Forecast

3. Rule Formation
• Behavior requirement
• Implementation plan
• Enforcement mechanism

4. Rule Implementation

5a. Compliance

Impacts
• Organizational
• Stakeholders

5b. Enforcement

we shall observe because it will enhance my power," but, nonetheless, many rules serve only a self-aggrandizing function.

While we should never underestimate veniality as a cause of bad rules, it seems likely that most rules, even ones that are bad, ineffective rules at the very outset, originate not from narrow self-interest but from failed attempts to serve the collective interest. In all likelihood, the amount of red tape and inefficiency occurring as a result of self-serving rules in public organizations is much less than is the amount of red tape created to forestall self-serving behaviors. The late Elliot Richardson, attorney general and secretary of defense during the Nixon administration and secretary of commerce during the Ford administration, noted that "critics need to be reminded that much of what they dislike most about government—the complicated regulations, the red tape, the costly layers of supervisors—is the direct consequence of distrust in government" (Richardson 1996, 27). This echoes Kaufman's (1977, 59) conclusion that the combination of distrust and democracy causes "the profusion of constraints and unwieldiness of the procedures, which afflict us." Pandey and Welch (2005) note that public managers have little incentive to create rules to advance personal interest and promote side-payments (Downs 1967) because they are less likely than private employees to benefit from the economic returns that these types of rule might bring their organization.

Instances of rule-inception red tape are many, but the causes relatively few. Here is a categorization of causes (Bozeman 2000):

1. *Incorrect rule forecasts:* rule-makers' assumptions about the relation of means to ends turn out to be wrong.
2. *Illegitimate functions:* rules are self-serving and do not promote a legitimate, sanctioned organizational purpose.
3. *Negative-sum compromise:* rules are a compromise, serving more than one objective, though none well.
4. *Overcontrol:* rules established for managerial control and accountability impose so much control that the business of the organization and its clients is impeded.

Incorrect Rule Forecasts

Many dysfunctional rules have their origins in misunderstanding of the relation between means and ends. In several instances, the reason for the inefficacy of rules is simple—persons designing the rules have insufficient understanding of the problem at hand, the relationship of the rule to the perceived problem, or other people's likely application or response to the rule. The fact that this occurs so often should not surprise, since forecasting human behavior is inordinately complex.

Every rule contains, implicitly or explicitly, a forecast about human behavior: "If we implement Rule X, Behavior Y will occur." At the time of origin, there is only a forecast, not a proof, because there is no valid, in-context evidence for a forecast. The fact that the rule worked a certain way in another organization may be useful supporting evidence, but not a valid test of the forecast. The implementation of the rule provides the only valid test of the veracity of the forecast. Considering the hazards and inherent uncertainties of forecasting (Girosi and King 2008; Helmer and Rescher 1959), it should come as no surprise that rule forecasts are often proved wrong.

Some rules entail easily understood patterns of causation and, thus, apparently less risky rule forecasts. Let us say, for example, that an organization located in a dense urban area wishes to help reduce traffic congestion. Among possible options: changing work hours to nonstandard ones. The causal reasoning would be simple enough:

1. Workers cause traffic congestion arriving and leaving at the same time.
2. Our organization's workers will be required to arrive and leave at a different time than other workers.
3. Therefore, traffic congestion will be reduced.

Acting on this reasoning, the organization develops a rule requiring half its employees to arrive at 10:30 A.M. and depart at 6:30 P.M. Now let us use some of the concepts developed thus far to analyze the rule. The *functional object* of the rule is reduction of traffic congestion. The *rule forecast* is that changing arrival and departure hours will decrease congestion. The *compliance burden* might include, among other possibilities, the inconveniences borne by the employees and the problems of coordinating work activities among employees arriving and leaving at different times. The rule is judged *red tape* if it does not accomplish the functional object. If it accomplishes the functional object, it may or may not be a "good rule," but it is not red tape. How might it be a "bad rule" but not red tape? One possibility is that the coordination costs entailed by employees arriving at different times would prove enormous. Thus, the functional object is served—reducing traffic congestion—but at too high a price.

Even in this relatively simple example, the rule forecast might prove wrong. Perhaps the change in work hours would mean that fewer employees would use public transportation because scheduling focuses only on rush hours. Or the mixing up of employees' work hours might cause the breakup of car pools. The point is that all rule forecasts, even seemingly simple ones, involve uncertainty and thus susceptibility to incorrect rule forecasts (Reason 1990). In many instances, the causal assumptions underlying a rule forecast are extremely complicated (Kerwin and Furlong 1992; West 2005), especially when there are numerous spillover effects and unanticipated consequences pertaining to the rule's functional object. Doubtless, much red tape results from incorrect rule forecasts and, related, the failure to adjust the rules in the face of contravening evidence.

Incremental learning, perhaps public administration's most significant contribution to management theory (e.g., Lindblom 1959; March and Simon 1958; Simon 1957), often is ignored in rule-making and implementation. Decades ago, March and Simon (1958, 141) provided a metaphor to compare "optimal" decision-making to "satisficing," the difference between "searching a haystack to find the *sharpest* needle in it and searching the haystack to find a needle sharp enough to sew with it." But for the most part, March and Simon were focusing on decisions and actions taking place within single organizations. Implementing a set of rules at one level of government (e.g., federal) to be diffused throughout the scores of agencies at another level (e.g., state) and having an impact on millions of citizens is more akin to searching for the sharpest needle at the bottom of the ocean.

It is not particularly difficult to envision the factors likely to lead to incorrect rules forecasts. The most important issues have to do with the complexity and interdependence of the forecasts and the extent to which redundancy and "backup" are built-in (Ting 2003). If the desired outcomes can be achieved even when some predictions turn out incorrect or when some systems fail, then the likelihood of red tape occurring from incorrect rules forecasts is reduced. Interestingly, the study of redundancy in high-reliability systems might have something to teach us about promulgating effective bureaucratic rules. LaPorte and colleagues' (LaPorte and Consolini 1991; LaPorte and Thomas 1990) studies of high-reliability organizations, such as air traffic controllers and nuclear power plants, provide lessons about predicting organizational outcomes in "tightly coupled" organizations and missions with little margin for error. LaPorte and Consolini (1991, 28) observe that high-reliability organizations must be "alert to surprises or lapses that could result in errors small or large that could cascade into major system failures from which there may be no recovery." This is not so different from large-scale implementation of regulatory rules—the ability to expect *and accommodate* surprises is equally critical for ensuring that rational plans for systems of bureaucratic rules do not go awry once implemented in the messy real world (Leveson et al. 2009).

Illegitimate Functions

Rules should serve a legitimate, organizationally sanctioned, or, in the case of public agencies, politically sanctioned functional object. In the public sector, the organization is not the sole provider or arbiter of legitimacy. Superior executive agencies, legislative bodies, judicial authorities, and, ultimately, the electorate determine legitimacy. In the private sector, the case is not as different as it might seem because private firms are subject to public laws. Indeed, the legitimacy of corporations owes much to the state and its licensing and chartering procedures. Business organizations with high degrees of "publicness," a term referring to the degree of external control by political authorities (Bozeman 1987; Bozeman and Moulton, in press), must look not only to themselves and to stockholders as sources of legitimacy but to law and public policy. Nevertheless, it is accurate to say that, in general, legitimacy is internal and organizational with private firms but external and extra-organizational with government firms.

Regardless of the *source* of legitimacy, a rule serving an individual's or group's self-interest, but no legitimate function for the organization, qualifies as red tape. The reason is simple: a compliance burden is produced, but no legitimate functional objective is served—the very definition of red tape used here. Thus, if an employee in the accounting division sets a rule requiring additional reporting on travel reimbursement forms for the unsanctioned purpose of expanding his or her knowledge base and organizational power, the result is, by definition, red tape.

Negative-Sum Compromise

Decisions about rules often reflect compromise. In some instances, a rule may be established that serves so many diverse objectives that a considerable compliance burden is sustained but *none* of the objectives is achieved. Rule-makers seek to do too much and end up doing little or nothing. Often rules built on overly elaborate compromise serve too many masters.

It is easy enough to think of examples of large-scale public policies to illustrate negative-sum compromise. More than a few of the laws passed each year by the U.S. Congress seek to serve too many interests. But let us consider an example within the realm of the regulatory bureaucracy. In many instances, energy policy, environmental policy, and economic development policy are hard to disentangle. Some state government agencies have simultaneous responsibilities in the three policy arenas. Let us assume that a state government energy agency is interested in stimulating the industrialized (prefabricated) housing market in order to promote energy efficiency. The agency quickly finds that there are significant and often unpredictable spill-overs in the areas of pollution and economic development policy. While most industrialized housing currently available represents great energy efficiency improvements over the existing housing stock, much of these energy savings are because the houses are well sealed. Another way of saying "well sealed" is "poor ventilation" (Bayer 1990). The result is that prefabricated buildings are especially prone to so-called sick building syndrome (Kriess 1993). The public manager's task, in such an instance, is to set standards for industrialized housing that will, at the same time, take advantage of energy savings, provide for adequate ventilation, and do both at a cost that will permit the industry to develop and be competitive with stick-built homes. Thus, at least three conflicting cardinal values must be juggled—energy efficiency, ventilation, and construction and materials cost (Roulet et al. 2006). Not surprisingly, regulations serving multiple, conflicting values often result in the realization of none. In such cases, rules expand with no objective served, and thus red tape emerges from combined good intentions.

Overcontrol

The most common source of rule-inception red tape, overcontrol, may be the most difficult source of red tape to weed out. Unlike some sources, over-control is neither inadvertent nor incidental. Overcontrol goes to the heart of management and governance. It arises from the depths of political culture via limited government norms and public distrust of authority, but also from the shallows of particular managers' insecurities. Given the differences in cause and effect between political overcontrol and managerial overcontrol, they deserve separate treatment.

Managerial Overcontrol

Generally, managerial control objectives result in internal rules, and managerial overcontrol results in internally derived red tape. Few question the need for management control. Managers' responsibilities for obtaining organizationally sanctioned objectives necessitate developing tasks and rules ensuring that subordinates will take coordinated actions to achieve the objectives. Even in organizations with limited hierarchy and strong participation norms, some degree of managerial control remains vital. The issue, again, is one of balance. Too much managerial control is no less stultifying than too little.

With too little control, the organization cannot achieve coordination so effort is expended to little purpose. With too much managerial control, initiative is crushed, too much time is devoted to control and reporting, and tasks serving organizational objectives get deflected. Exerting *appropriate* levels of control and formalization is crucial to organizational effectiveness. Unfortunately, it is never easy to determine just how much control to exert or which activities should be formalized and which should remain discretionary.

One of the less explored topics in management research is guidelines for formalization. Clearly, rules cannot cover every contingency; thus, the "informal organization" is inevitably important. The informal organization, under some circumstances, can even "preserve the organization from the self-destruction that would result from literal obedience to the formal policies, rules, regulations and procedures" (Dubin 1951, 68). But one of the most common responses to uncertainty and ambiguity is seeking control through formalization. As we know from extensive discussion in previous chapters, formalization is not the same thing as red tape; but they are often related. It is typically (but not always) the case that organizations that are extremely rule-bound have a high likelihood of generating red tape.

The organizational psychology of overcontrol holds much interest for organization theorists and managers. There is no shortage of ideas as to why it is that managers sometimes strive mightily to control the uncontrollable and to overcontrol when effectiveness requires delegation of power. Perhaps, as Thompson (1961) maintains, managerial overcontrol results from the inherent ambiguity of managerial work in bureaucracies, especially in public bureaucracies. Perhaps Downs (1967) is correct that all bureaucrats maximize self-interest and usually perceive control as in their self-interest. But whatever the reason, and however unfortunate the consequences, to manage is to control—Landau and Stout (1979) notwithstanding—and usually to overcontrol.

Political Overcontrol

Managerial overcontrol plagues almost all organizations; political overcontrol affects almost all government organizations and more than a few private organizations. Many of the "unnecessary rules and regulations" industry officials complain about are political overcontrol, but in many instances, industrial officials' complaints really are more about the disjunction of private interests and public ones.

Political control of business enterprise certainly is appropriate, and even the most enthusiastic adherents of the market will, if pressed, acknowledge that at least some government-imposed regulation is needed. If nothing else, they wish to be protected against predatory business practices of competitors. Without externally imposed rules and regulations, unsafe working conditions would abound, industrial pollution would remain unchecked, insider trading would wreak havoc, dangerous products would be foisted on unwitting consumers, industrial espionage would rise to new heights, and the necessary ingredients of market efficiency could not be achieved.

When not taken to the extreme, complaints made by business and public agencies about undue political controls often have much validity. It is always difficult to sort out self-interested carping from valid complaints about red tape, but it is not so difficult, on a case-by-case basis, to identify red tape aimed at political overcontrol. Let us consider two examples, one of which is, in retrospect, easily identified as political overcontrol, and another that was, at the time, widely alleged as overcontrol but now is generally accepted.

First, let us consider the case of the surgeon general's warning about the health risks of tobacco products. When initially introduced, a great many people, not just the tobacco industry, decried these rules as intrusive government interference and government-imposed red tape. While few informed citizens disputed the health hazards of tobacco, research at that time was still somewhat inconclusive. One reason is that much of the research was done by the tobacco industry and was proprietary. As public domain research began to catch up, the idea that regulating tobacco was unnecessary or red tape was dismissed by nearly everyone, even many in the tobacco industry (Bayer and Stuber 2006).

Sometimes allegations of unreasonable rules and red tape have a clear ring of truth. One publication (Moloney 1996) featured the story of the owner of an Evanston, Illinois, doughnut shop who was nearly put out of business after an inspection by the Occupational Safety and Health Administration (OSHA). The inspection of her thirty-person bakery resulted in fines for such infractions as failing to warn employees of the hazards of household dish-washing liquid.

Obviously, bureaucratic overcontrol happens, it is a problem, and it is

59

an easy target of humor. But considering the literally millions of directives implemented each day, is it possible to avoid an occasional lapse or excess? Does the isolated anecdote, no matter how biting, really tell us much about the functioning of bureaucracy? An excellent case in point is OSHA. Unquestionably, OSHA sometimes implements rules that seem nitpicking, and, unquestionably, many people in business do not like OSHA and its rules, whether nitpicking or not. But consider since OSHA was formed in 1970 that the overall workplace death rate has been cut in half (OSHA 1995). While no one knows exactly what percentage of that reduction is attributable to OSHA, common sense suggests that at least some significant percentage is likely due to regulation. Given that more than 6,000 U.S. citizens die annually from workplace injuries and that workplace injuries cost the U.S. economy more than $110 billion per year, the issues of workplace regulation should not be trivialized, even if there is some demonstrable overcontrol.

High Compliance and High Opportunity Cost Rules

High cost rules do not qualify as red tape, not so long as they continue to achieve a legitimate functional objective. Nevertheless, rules that are extremely costly in relationship to their achievements can be at least as harmful as red tape.

To this point, we have not directly considered the *opportunity cost* of rules. In connection with rules, we can use the term "opportunity costs" in its traditional usage: "the cost of using resources in terms of the value of the best alternative good these resources could have produced" (Apgar and Brown 1987, 393). The implication for organizational rules is that it is important to consider not only the compliance burden (cost) and benefits associated with a rule, but also the benefit that might have been obtained had the cost spent in compliance been spent on some other activity.

The issue of the opportunity costs of rules is really one of management policy and strategy. To say that a rule is not red tape is not to say that it is a good rule. In many instances, a rule that serves an important function may do so at too high an opportunity cost. As such, it might be a poor rule, but not red tape. Some bad rules are red tape and some bad rules are bad for other reasons and are not red tape. It is sometimes difficult to distinguish between a poor rule and a good rule accompanied by high compliance and opportunity costs. This difficulty sets practical managerial challenges, but for the red tape theorist or researcher, confusing red tape with rules that are largely ineffective or that are minimally effective but a bad social investment can undermine knowledge of both red tape *and* organizational performance. One of the initial motivations for improved conceptualization of red tape was to separate the phenomenon from the many other types of bureaucratic malfeasance or inefficiency. Without careful attention to the exact nature of rules' limitations, it is difficult to continue to develop useful theories and propositions about red tape.

Rule-Evolved Red Tape

Once-effective rules often lose effectiveness over time, sometimes to such an extent as to devolve into red tape. Rules do not always maintain their effectiveness. The "devolution" of functional rules to red tape can be caused by characteristics of the organization making the rule or by the individuals enacting the rule. Often it requires many people acting in concert to turn a good rule into red tape. From empirical research, we know relatively little about why and how good rules turn into bad ones. Since very little red tape research has been longitudinal, the evolution of rules receives insufficient attention. But we can consider conceptual theories and hypotheses about why good rules go bad.

To a large extent, the change of effective rules into red tape mimics natural processes. Just as natural systems, ranging from the human body to the universe itself, tend to run down, so do rules. It may seem odd that something as intangible as a rule can actually wear out from use. Organisms' cells wear down due to the strict natural limits imposed by aging and quite literal wear and tear. Naturally, there is no similar process with rules. However, rules can wear down because the more people who use or execute them, the greater the likelihood that the rules will be implemented incorrectly or in unstable ways or that the rules will be misinterpreted or changed in random or undesirable ways. On the other hand, it is conceivable that widespread use of a rule will result in its more effective implementation. It is possible that if numerous actors regularly enact a rule, it will become a routine resulting in the reduction of red tape and other, less effective rules. The key in this case is organizational learning about rules and adjustments in implementation (Pentland and Feldman 2005).

The Evolution of Rules

Rule change is a different social process from rule creation, responsive to different social and political factors. There is remarkably little empirical evidence about the processes of rule change. In the previous chapter, we mentioned Zhou's (1993) work, one of the few formal studies of rules change. Examining more than 100 years of organizational rules developed and implemented at Stanford University, Zhou found differences between rules' founding rates and change rates. Founding rates were largely due to historical period effects, but did not relate to organizational complexity, changes in organizational learning, or government policy change. Rule founding seemed chiefly related to organizational crises of various sorts, consistent with organization theorists' views that rules serve as means of coping with uncertainty (e.g., Cyert and March 1963). By contrast, rates of rule change were relatively stable across historical periods and seemed more a function of organizational learning processes, particularly problem detection and correction.

Before discussing ways in which organizational rules become red tape, we consider two features of organizations that make them vulnerable to rule-evolved red tape. "Organizational phantoms" relates to the fact most people work under organizational rules created by persons no longer with the organization. "Organizational entropy" is the tendency for organizational and management systems to run down or disintegrate.

Rules to Red Tape: Reasons for Rule-Evolved Red Tape

There are several processes by which rule-evolved red tape occurs:

- *"Organizational phantoms" and rule drift*—rules were developed long ago, for purposes now obscure, by people who may no longer be with the organization. In such cases, if the rule continues to be implemented, the rule may change (drift). Without a secure knowledge of its objectives, red tape my result.
- In *implementation change*, there is change not in the content or basis of the rule, but in the way it is executed.
- There may be a *change in the functional object* of the rule, rendering the rule unneeded or less effective.
- The rule and its implementation may stay the same, but some external change can undermine the rule's efficacy; that is, there is a *change in the rule's ecology*.
- *Rule strain* occurs as the sheer number of rules increases, with a corresponding increase in compliance burden, until the marginal benefit from rules becomes less and less and, then, negative.
- *Rule incompatibility* occurs as new rules are promulgated that may be effective but, at the same time, undermine the effectiveness of old ones.

Organizational Phantoms and Rule Drift

One fascinating aspect of bureaucracies is the linkage of the organization's "living" with the organization's "dead." If we include among the "dead" not only the literally dead, but former organizational members who have retired or taken other jobs, we can speculate that *most* of the internal rules under which organizations operate were created by people no longer working there. In the absence of frequent revisiting of organizations' rules, regulations, and procedures, these phantoms hold much power (Schulz 2003).

Organizational phantoms are a major culprit in rule drift. Rule drift occurs when the meaning and spirit of a rule get lost in organizational antiquity as contemporaries inadvertently change the rule or its meaning. Sometimes individuals enforce a rule or comply with it without having any idea why the rule was formulated or what function it serves. Perhaps the need for the rule no longer exists. Rules may be observed ritualistically even if there is no understanding of the manifest purpose of the rule. Indeed, mysterious rules may even be venerated ("that's just the way we have always done things here . . .") for the stamp of organizational peculiarity or legend they confer (Islam and Zyphur 2009).

Rule drift is not always a matter of the length of time that has passed since the rule's origins. Other factors that may be related to rule drift include personnel turnover (in the case of internal rules), changes in client composition (for external rules), and the reorganization of organizations and programs. Rule drift is particularly likely in organizations where rules are enacted only infrequently. Rules enacted by the same people within the same context over brief, regular periods are likely to preserve content. The familiarity of frequently enacted rules reduces the likelihood of unwitting change. Special-occasion rules are generally more likely to be misapplied in any of several ways, including change in content. This explains, in part, why emergency procedures, rules that are by definition vital, are so often poorly enacted. Rule drift is often caused by lack of familiarity with the rules' content, which, in turn, is explained by a lack of opportunity for enactment. Thus, the disastrous effects of nuclear "events," space station docking accidents, and toxic waste spills often are compounded because rules infrequently executed are poorly executed. In natural disasters such as Hurricane Katrina, infrequently exercised and poorly understood rules exacerbate already bad situations (Kunreuther and Pauly 2006).

Besides the infrequency of rule enactment, the number of people interacting also affects rule drift. If the same 100 people enact a rule 100 times each day, there is limited likelihood for drift. But if the rule is enacted 100 times each day by 100 *different* people, there is much greater likelihood for rule drift. Indeed we can think of rule drift in terms of a simple equation,

pRule Drift f([nE] [nA]),

where the probability of Rule Drift is a function of

nE = the number of occasions of rule enactment over time, and
nA = the number of people administering the rule.

This point can be expressed in another way as well. Table 3.1 is a four-celled table that presents a rule enactment typology relating the number of rule enactment occasions to the number of persons enacting the rules. Rules may be enacted with more or less frequency. If a large number of persons are enacting the rules, then rule enactment is "distributed"; if few people are enacting the rules, rule enactment is "concentrated." Each of the four types has particular meaning for predicting rule drift. In the infrequent/concentrated case, few people enact rules rarely—for example, in a nuclear plant accident. However, there are many other instances of relatively unimportant rules being implemented infrequently by few. Indeed, some rules are enacted infrequently *because* they are relatively trivial.

Least troublesome is the frequent/concentrated case—relatively few people enacting rules frequently. There is little reason to expect rule drift in such cases. This is not to suggest that administration is necessarily efficient in such cases. Those enacting the rule may become bored with their jobs and thus give less attention to the implementation of the rule. But even in such cases there should be a good understanding of the content of the rule and little reason to predict a shift in the rule's behavioral requirements. A simple example in this category is the case of air traffic controllers. The rules are usually clear-cut and well understood and, by all reports, usually well executed. The persons executing the rules understand them so the content is not altered through drift. Any problems are caused not by rule drift, but by fatigue, poor communication and implementation of the rule, or some other such source.

The highest threat for rule strain is the infrequent/distributed case—rules enacted infrequently, but by many people. The classic case is large-scale civil emergencies, such as natural disasters. The infrequent distributed case is particularly relevant as a causal factor in rule drift and, in general, a particularly acute problem in the evolution of functional rules into red tape. By contrast, the case of frequent/distributed poses somewhat less hazard for either rule drift or red tape inasmuch as those implementing the rules have more routine practice in their allocation.

Implementation Change

Sometimes rule content changes in undesirable ways and creates red tape; in other cases, there is no change in rule content but a change in the rule's implementation. For one reason or another, individuals begin to implement the rule in a different manner than before. Naturally, not all changes in rule implementation are red tape; some are sensible and functional adjustments to changed circumstances or unique features of special cases. But when the change undermines the achievement of the

Table 3.1

Rule Enactment Typology

Number of rule enactments/Concentration of people enacting	
(H,L)	(H,H)
Frequent/Concentrated	Frequent/Distributed
Auditors	*Welfare eligibility determinations*
(L,L)	(L,H)
Infrequent/Concentrated	Infrequent/Distributed
Parole review	*Election administration*

rule's functional object, then changes in implementation can transform a working rule into red tape.

In cases of rule drift, the content changes, whereas in cases of change in implementation the content stays the same. But from a practical standpoint it is often very difficult to sort out the difference between the two. Probably the most common changes in implementation have to do with the amount of discretion with which the rule is applied. Most rules *assume* that some discretion will be used in their application. For most rules, it is neither possible nor desirable to specify all the possible conditions to which the rule should apply. Nor is it possible in most cases to specify exceptions. Discretion often saves us from ourselves and gives us a way out of obviously ridiculous circumstances that the rule-makers did not foresee.

One similarity between rule drift and implementation change as sources of red tape is that they are sensitive to many of the same causes and interpretation. Thus, the rule enactment typology introduced above for rule drift is relevant for change in implementation. Similarly, both problems are often a function of rule complexity.

Implementation change is not only one of the most common sources of red tape, but also a particularly nettlesome one. Often, there is no easy remedy. Effective management requires initiative and discretion. Effective management also requires attention to the rules and stability in their administration. There is a rich literature (e.g., Gruber 1987; Leazes 1997; Wamsley and Wolf 1996) in public administration and political science on the inherent conflicts among the values of administrative efficiency, discretion, stability and fairness in application of rules, and ability to deal sensibly with exceptions and special needs. The boundaries among these values are rarely clear and it is often difficult even to develop rules of thumb. Thus, implementation change is worrisome because it is required for good management, yet it is also a source of red tape. When managers exercise discretion or bend rules, it is rarely clear whether the consequence will be red tape or a needed adjustment of the rules.

Change in the Functional Objective

Sometimes the functional objective of the rule changes in ways that render the rule obsolete or otherwise useless. There may no longer be a need to achieve the objective of the rule, but the rule remains in place nonetheless, with compliance burden intact.

Let us consider a simple example. The city of Oakdale requires each of its agencies to issue each year a strategic plan with a twenty-year planning horizon. The functional object of the rule is to provide the city council with information about the agencies so that it can make wise decisions about allocating resources to each agency. Because of a budget crisis, Oakdale's Office of Public Statues and Monuments has just been dismantled by the city council: all operations terminate at the end of the fiscal year. Requiring the Office of Public Statues and Monuments to provide a strategic plan would be red tape because the functional object has changed—there is no need for a long-range plan for an agency with a short-range future.

In this simple example, the likely culprit is habituation. That is, there are powerful routines in bureaucracy and politics that seem to take on a life of their own. Bureaucratic organizations work according to routine and seasonal requirements. It is now the end of the fiscal year, so it is time to spend money; it is now the end of the planning cycle, so it is time to develop the next year's strategic plan. Often old habits take time to catch up with new circumstances.

In many instances, problems with change in the functional object occur as a result of organization phantoms. That is, the rule's objective was set up by people no longer with the organization; the objective has been lost along the way, but the rule remains. The functional object is obscured; the rule compliance behavior, much more visible, remains.

Change in the Rule's Ecology

Even if the rule's functional object does not change, circumstances might occur that mitigate the rule's usefulness. For example, a rule requiring carbon copies of memoranda makes little sense if almost all communication is electronic. In this case, the rule's ecology includes the organization's adopted communications technology. This is a simple example of ecological change transforming a rule into red tape, but the situation is often similar for broader, more significant rules embedded within a much more complex ecology.

An example of changes in rule ecology occurred in a bizarre locale: outer space (Cowen 1994). Space commerce began slowly in the 1960s with communications satellites and grew steadily until it encompassed a number of fields, including space manufacture of metal alloys, pharmaceuticals, and electronic materials: in short, any product made more easily or cheaply under weightless conditions in orbit. The problem is that the makers of tariff and customs policy never gave much thought to products emerging from outer space. As Tony Calio, then deputy administrator of the National Oceanic and Atmospheric Administration (NOAA), observed, "Customs laws were fine when they first started, but no one anticipated producing products in space. And space, like the high seas, is considered beyond the national borders" (Cowen 1994, A4). The result, then, was that the need for rules no longer matched with the rules ecology. This mismatch was remedied later when rules were changed so that products made by U.S. companies in space were not taxed as imports.

In all likelihood, certain classes of rules are more prone to harmful effects of change in ecology. The culprit is not, of course, the change, but the continuing existence of the unmodified, suddenly useless rule. Change does not necessarily create red tape; usually red tape is created by a failure to *adapt* to change. If those affected are close at hand and communication is frequent, it is likely that the flaws in the rule will be swiftly communicated.

Rule Strain

Organizations with a high rule density often create strain and inefficient use of resources. "Good" rules, but too abundant, can have a net negative effect. Five good rules may be within the organization's capabilities; ten good rules may, simply because of limited compliance capability, cause the organization or individual to interpret and apply rules less effectively. To put it another way, red tape may be caused by organizations having compliance and implementation burdens that cannot be met with existing resources. This deficit in resources leads to shortcuts or lip service paid to rules with the result that rules, even ones that have strong content and are directed appropriately toward a legitimate functional object, might be transformed into red tape.

While rule strain can occur in any of a variety of ways, a particularly perverse possibility is that it might occur as a result of efficiency-based strategies, such as downsizing and "right-sizing." When already lean personnel rosters are further cut, with no concomitant reduction in workload, the capacity to meet compliance requirements may be taken beyond the critical point. If the organization controls the preponderance of its rules—that is, if the rules are internal in their origin—then it may have the flexibility and the good sense to cut back compliance burden. But when the preponderance of rules are external in their origin, as in most government agencies, there is particularly high potential for rule strain and red tape. Rule strain is not always associated with personnel decrements. Often it is simply a matter of more and more compliance and implementation burden with no increment in resources.

Rule Incompatibility

Often rules build one on top of the other. If rules are inconsistent or at cross-purposes, their net effect may be damaging (even if particular rules remain effective with respect to their functional object). *Rule incompatibility* means that rationality added to rationality may sum to irrationality. This is not a matter of the volume or density of rules (as in rule strain), but the incompatibility of rules.

Let us consider a simple example of rule incompatibility. It is reasonable for an organization to establish a rule requiring employees to log each telephone number on long-distance calls. Despite the time and trouble required, if personal use of long-distance is becoming a major expense, the logging rule may be justified. Similarly, it is reasonable to establish a rule requiring all long-distance telephone callers to use an assigned dialing code keyed to an individual calling account. What makes no sense is to have both rules in force at the same time.

In some cases, rule incompatibility is not so easy to judge—especially for rules at a high policy level. There are many "incompatibilities" in public policy that may seem inefficient, illogical, or just plain stupid, but that are simply conforming to a set of political rules that may be internally rational.

Empirical Research Testing the Models and Propositions

In this section, we consider the extent to which empirical researchers have tested the models and propositions set forth in Bozeman's theory of red tape. In general, there has been little research directly testing this or any other conceptual theory of red tape. For example, there is no public administration research testing for rule-evolved red tape. We have found no empirical research investigating change in red rule ecology, rule drift, change in rule implementation, change in the functional object of a rule, or rule incompatibility and how they may or may not be related to the evolution of rules into red tape. Red tape studies rarely examine the history of rules or changes in rules. In short, there are many avenues still unexplored.

Extant Conceptual and Theoretical Analyses of Red Tape

Although the empirical red tape research does not address many components of Bozeman's theory, there is an extensive literature on red tape and its impacts on organizations and their members. There are also a few empirical studies investigating red tape's effects on organizational stakeholders (Feeney and Bozeman 2009; Walker and Brewer 2008; Welch and Pandey 2007). Pandey and Moynihan (2006, 3) argue that the vast majority of empirical red tape public administration studies are not well-tied to Bozeman's theory of red tape, because his theory is "broad in scope and is not anchored to specific referents" (3). Pandey and Kingsley (2000, 782) modified Bozeman's definition of red tape by clarifying that red tape is "impressions on the part of managers that formalization (in the form of burdensome rules and regulations) is detrimental to the organization." Pandey and Scott (2002, 565) argue that this modified definition has two key benefits:

> It avoids the necessity of a detailed case study of every rule for determining organizational/social significance of the rule's functional object (see Bozeman and DeHart-Davis 1999 to get a sense of the complexities involved in doing a rule-based operationalization) and, rather than leaving determination of organizational/social significance as an open matter, it provides a clear guideline. Simply put, red tape exists when managers view formalization as burdensome and detrimental to organizational purposes. It is, therefore, not necessary to go beyond managerial perceptions in creating operational definitions based on the theoretical construct Pandey and Kingsley espouse.

Thus, for the sake of convenience, the empirical research has moved away from individual rule assessments to account for red tape and instead moved in the direction of measuring managers' perceptions of red tape (this point is discussed more thoroughly in Chapter 4).

Although there have been only a few tests of various aspects of Bozeman's comprehensive theory of red tape, empirical red tape researchers have developed and tested middle-range theoretical and conceptual models of red tape. There have been steps toward operationalizing and testing parts of Bozeman's typology of red tape, including ordinary red tape, external control red tape, pass-through red tape, and interorganization red tape. Below we discuss these three developments.

Theoretical and Conceptual Models

Among the red tape theory advances since Bozeman's (2000) comprehensive theory is Pandey and Welch's (2005) multistage model of managerial perceptions of red tape (see Figure 3.2). Drawing from the empirical red tape literature, Pandey and Welch's model aims to investigate differences in red tape perceptions across public and private organizations. In contrast to many of the hypotheses presented by Bozeman (2000), this theoretical approach rejects the notion that public managers create red tape but rather proposes that public managers are subject to and must learn to manage red tape created by others. The model asserts that public managers' perceptions of red tape are conditioned by organizational environment and context and subjective workplace attitudes (e.g., alienation).

Using structural equations, Pandey and Welch (2005) test the proposed model and the endogenous relationships and find support for three of their four proposed hypotheses. They conclude that administrative delay and work alienation are positively related to managerial perceptions of red tape. They also find that perceptions of personnel red tape increase work alienation. They find no support for the proposed positive connection between administrative delay and work alienation (see dotted line in Figure 3.2).

A second effort to develop a theoretical and conceptual model of red tape is Moon and Bretschneider's model for red tape and information technology (IT) innovativeness (see Figure 3.3). Moon and Bretschneider (2002, 275) propose a structured theory with an endogenous relationship between perceived IT innovativeness and organizational red tape, defined as "a set of procedural characteristics of an organization that reflects structural, cultural, and environmental factors." The authors conclude that red tape can have a facilitating influence on IT innovation because high levels of red tape can lead an organization to innovate around the problem and that IT innovativeness in turn can reduce the level of perceived red tape.

In their examination of public organizations' rule-based constraints and the implementation of intranet technologies in state human service agencies, Welch and Pandey (2007) test a theoretical model that integrates the public administration red tape literature with the sociotechnical perspective on organizations. Figure 3.4 illustrates the model where high red tape indicates lower organizational effectiveness. Welch and Pandey's model proposes that there are exogenous relationships between three constructs—centralization, formalization, and communication—affecting an organization's technology implementation and innovativeness. Drawing from Bozeman's theory of red tape, they also note that external stakeholders (e.g., courts, politicians, other agencies, the public, and private not-for-profit and for-profit organizations) increase red tape in organizations.

Welch and Pandey propose two hypotheses about the relationships between red tape and intranet technology implementation:

H1:   Higher levels of red tape will negatively affect the level of intranet technology implementation (in terms of reliance and information quality) in public organizations.

H2:   Higher levels of intranet implementation (in terms of reliance and information quality) will reduce the level of red tape in public organizations (2007, 386).

Figure 3.2   **An Explanatory Model of Managerial Perceptions of Red Tape**

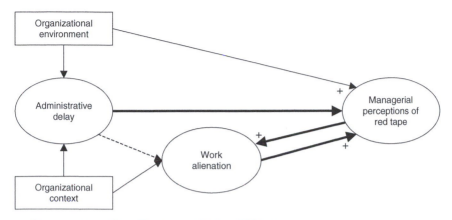

Source: Adapted from Pandey and Welch (2005, 4).

Figure 3.3   **Exploratory Model of Interdependence of Perceived Red Tape, IT Innovativeness, and Organizational Factors**

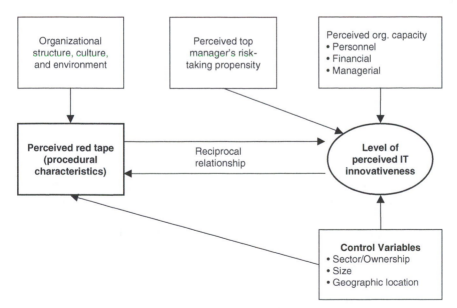

Source: Adapted from Moon and Bretschneider (2002, 276).

Figure 3.4   **Theoretical Model for Intranet and Organizational Effectiveness**

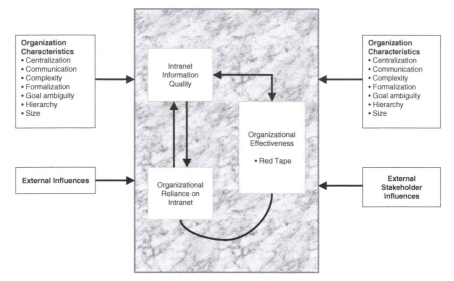

Source: Adapted from Welch and Pandey (2007, 382).

Their empirical model provides no support for the first hypothesis, perhaps because "the attraction of the technology overrides the negative influences that red tape might have on implementation" (393). They find strong support for the second hypothesis, concluding that high intranet reliance lowers red tape. Thus, conceptual models investigating the relationships between red tape and managerial red tape, innovativeness, and intranet technology show that red tape perceptions are conditioned by environment and context and that red tape has complex, endogeneous relationships with the ways in which managers work and perceive their work environments.

While the preceding examples do not add up to an extensive effort to develop theoretical and conceptual models for understanding red tape, they do point to a growing interest in understanding the ways in which red tape is related to other concepts. The conceptual models in the literature find that red tape is endogenously related to IT innovativeness (Moon and Bretschneider 2002) and administrative delay and work alienation (Pandey and Welch 2005).

Red Tape and Other Theories

A second, common theoretical approach to understanding red tape is pairing red tape measures with other important organizational and public administration theories. For example, red tape researchers have investigated the relationships between red tape and public service motivation (Moynihan and Pandey 2007b; Pandey, Kingsley, and Scott 2001; Pandey and Rainey 2006; Scott and Pandey 2005); red tape and formalization (Feeney and DeHart-Davis 2009; Welch and Pandey 2007); and red tape and theories of organizational effectiveness and performance (Pandey, Coursey, and Moynihan 2007; Pandey and Garnett 2006; Rainey, Pandey, and Bozeman 1995; Welch and Pandey 2007). This approach, while not grounded in a theory of red tape, does advance the understanding of red tape as an important construct that influences our understanding of other important theories.

Empirical research has found that red tape is negatively related to public service motivation (PSM) (Moynihan and Pandey 2007b). For example, Scott and Pandey (2005) find that public managers with higher levels of PSM report lower levels of perceived red tape, while those who report a high attraction to public policy-making report the highest levels of perceived red tape. Thus empirical research on red tape and PSM has served to enhance researchers' understanding of both constructs. While Bozeman's theory of red tape does not specifically address the ways in which individual motivations may affect red tape perceptions, this research could be used to further develop Bozeman's theory.

In empirical investigations of red tape and its effects on organizational performance, the research is somewhat mixed. On the one hand, researchers have found that red tape has a direct negative association with perceived effectiveness and performance (Pandey, Coursey, and Moynihan 2007). On the other hand, other researchers (Brewer, Hicklin, and Walker 2006; Brewer and Selden 2000) have found no statistically significant relationship between red tape and agency performance. Walker and Brewer (2009a) find that red tape actually has both positive and negative effects on government performance, with internal red tape lowering performance and external red tape increasing some dimensions of quality and quantity. The ways in which red tape is related to organizational and managerial performance remain under investigation; however, Walker and Brewer's work does point to an important theoretical development in both areas, as performance researchers seek to understand the role of red tape in hindering or aiding performance and red tape researchers seek to understand the outcomes of red tape, for both organizational members and external stakeholders.

Operationalizing a Red Tape Typology

There have been a few steps toward operationalizing and testing Bozeman's typology of red tape. The general/organizational red tape scale is a good example of a measure of ordinary red tape. This measure presents a scale from 0 (no red tape at all) to 10 (a great deal) and asks respondents to assess the level of red tape in their organizations. This measure appears in a number of research studies and has proven itself to be relatively stable in that a number of researchers have produced consistent findings with this measure. For example, researchers have found that there are significant differences in the level of red tape reported in public and private organizations (Bozeman, Reed, and Scott, 1992; Bretschneider 1990; Feeney and Bozeman 2009; Lan and Rainey 1992; Pandey and Kingsley 2000; Rainey 1983; Rainey, Pandey, and Bozeman 1995).

The research on external control red tape, while not always described as such, seeks to understand the ways in which the external environment and control affect red tape or perceptions of red tape in organizations. Walker and Brewer (2009a) and Brewer and Walker (2010b) find that public managers perceive that external factors increase red tape in their organizations. For public managers in their study, red tape is the result of external, uncontrollable factors. In a separate analysis, Walker and Brewer (2008) conclude that when chief officers feel more able to influence the external environment, the level of perceived red tape in public organizations increases. In their analysis of red tape perceptions among a variety of public sector employees, Walker and Brewer (2008) use the following five measures to estimate the external context and how it affects perceptions of red tape internal and external to organizations: (1) service need, (2) diversity of service need, (3) change in service need, (4) ability to influence, and (5) external political context. Table 3.2 describes these measures of the external environment, the first three being archival measures and the remainder drawn from survey respondents' perceptions. The findings from their model are complex, but overall Walker and Brewer conclude that because the external environment differently affects corporate officers, chief officers, and service managers, red tape perceptions are contingent on organizational position.

More recently, Bozeman, Brewer, and Walker (2008) sought to directly address Bozeman's (2000, 126–131) theory of external control model of red tape. The authors argue that they "test an entire theory of red tape rather than a part of a theory or an hypothesis derived from theory," as done by earlier empirical red tape research. The authors seek to determine the probability that an organization will have red tape, based on its propensity to create red tape or have rules that are subverted, inappropriately altered, or poorly implemented and thus become red tape. Using "diagnostic indicators," Bozeman and colleagues note that the external control model asserts that external control is the determinant of the probability that rules, external in origin, will become red tape. Similarly, rules that are subject to the control and interpretation of multiple, diverse stakeholders will have a high probability of becoming red tape.

Table 3.2

Five Measures of the Organization's External Context

Measure	Description	Type
1. Service need	Percentage of lone parent households as a measures of level of service need because income data are not readily available at the local authority level	Archival measure of the environment that focuses on service need
2. Diversity of service need	A Hehrfindahl index of ethnicity that gives a proxy for "fractionalization" within the local authority area.	
3. Change in service need	Percentage change in population 1991 to 2001.	
4. Ability to influence	The service was/is able to exert a lot of influence over the social and economic context, external political context, and internal political context during the last year.	Perceptual measures that focus on the malleability of external environmental influences
5. External political environment	The external political context in which the organization operates: changing rapidly, uncertain, or very complex during the last financial year.	

Source: Brewer and Walker (2005).

Figure 3.5 illustrates Bozeman's external control model of red tape, where an organization's red tape is positively associated with the number of organizational entities and units developing rules. Externally imposed rules are assumed to have less ownership by organizational members and thus be more likely to be misapplied or corrupted.

Based on their hypothesis that levels of external control red tape are increased because of entropy and nonownership of rules but moderated by communication feedback, Brewer and colleagues (2008) measure external control red tape using five measures to operationalize the dependent variable, red tape: two global measures and three subsystem measures. Entropy was measured using an index titled "internal political climate" and three variables derived from secondary data: social class diversity, population density, and nonemployment rate. Nonownership was measured using the proportion of voters who are in the Labour Party. Client feedback was measured using two measures: (1) responses to the survey item "Most managers place the needs of users first and foremost when planning and delivering services" and (2) a direct measure of Best Value Performance Indicators consumer satisfaction.

Figure 3.5 **External Control Model of Red Tape**

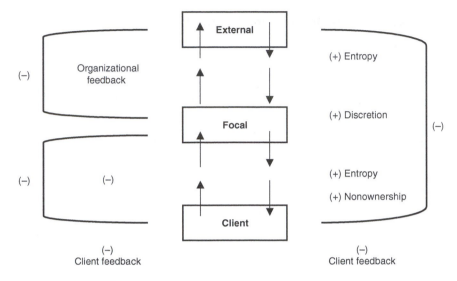

Source: Adapted from Bozeman (1993, 292).

Brewer and colleagues' (2008) test of Bozeman's model of external control red tape finds that the relationship between external control and red tape is compounded by entropy, which in turn affects the communication of rules, discretion over rules, and nonownership of rules. They conclude that external control leads to higher levels of red tape and that this relationship is moderated by informal communication among user-focused managers, but that consumer feedback does little to moderate the relationship. They conclude that organizational red tape is best managed by interorganizational communication and increased trust inside of organizations and not by external reforms and rules. Thus, we see a growing effort to return to connecting the empirical red tape research to theory.

Empirical research investigating the relationships between red tape and individual public managers' decision-making examines the ways in which external control red tape affects individual decision-making. Kingsley and Reed (1991) conclude that a higher number of external meetings and interactions with external actors does not increase decision-making and red tape. In fact, they find the opposite: a higher number of internal meetings increases managers' perceptions of red tape in the decision-making process. Similarly, Turaga and Bozeman (2005) find that there is no relationship between the number of external participants involved in organizational decision-making and red tape. Both sets of researchers conclude that it is possible that external control affects organizational-level red tape, but not red tape at the individual, decision level.

While there is work testing the external control component of Bozeman's typology of red tape, there is no test of pass-through red tape and only one published study of interorganization red tape. In 2007, Feeney and Bozeman (2009) administered a survey to 159 managers at the Georgia Department of Transportation (GDOT) and 176 of the consultants contracting with the agency; responses were received from 95 public managers and 96 private consultants. The researchers asked about red tape in the respondents' respective organizations and the red tape associated with the respondents' interactions between the organizations via contractual relations.[2] The researchers then tested the relationships among sector, time communicating, time allocated to paperwork, and contract experience and red tape. Feeney and Bozeman found that, similar to previous studies, public sector managers perceive significantly higher levels of red tape in their organizations as compared to private sector managers. The authors found no significant differences between the public managers' and private consultants' perceptions of red tape in their contracting relationships. The researchers note that it is possible that because the consultants have a long history of working with GDOT, they have developed coping mechanisms for dealing with government red tape and thus have diminished perceptions of red tape in their relationships. This research provides a test of Bozeman's theory of interorganizational red tape and also sheds light on stakeholder red tape—showing that compared to the state agency respondents, members of stakeholder organizations have quite similar perceptions of red tape in contracting.

Relation of Theoretical and Conceptual Research

We focused in this chapter on red tape theory and on research that in part flows from theory. However, as we shall see in the next chapter and most of the book, the tie between red tape theory and research is usually tenuous. Much red tape research is largely self-contained. That does not imply that it ignores previous theory or research, only that it uses them to a minor degree and, instead, focuses on developing new hypotheses, often ones that are more closely in line with the data available to the researcher. This is a different sort of theory-building, relying less on posited propositions and more on inductive, but can nonetheless be quite valuable. One disadvantage of such inductive, opportunistic research is that it makes the task of review and synthesis more difficult. When studies rely more on "data push" than "theory pull," they tend to be more scattered. This is not to say, however, that they tend to be inferior as explanations of red tape. In many cases, the more inductive research is quite inventive and, by looking at new data and new hypotheses, can develop new theory or redirect old theory. It is probably fair to say that most empirical research in public administration is in the deductive or opportunistic mode. One point of interest in this book is to compare and contrast the research that begins with puzzles posed in theory with research that begins with problems apparent from data and available measures. The textbook answer would be that the theory-based research would ultimately prove more valuable, but we are not so sure. The value of theory-based research depends on the availability of quality theory, and in red tape the supply is not vast.

Notes

1. We use the term "quantitative-empirical" to distinguish from case studies, one of the more popular types of public administration research. Case studies are obviously empirical but not in most instances quantitative. Hereafter, when we say "empirical research," we mean quantitative empirical. When we refer to case studies, we will specifically identify case studies rather than including case studies and the case study method under the more general label "empirical research."

2. Respondents were asked, "If red tape is defined as 'burdensome administrative rules and procedures that have negative impacts on the organization's effectiveness,' how would you assess the level of red tape in the contracting relationships between GDOT and private firms?" Response categories ranged from 0 (almost no red tape) to 10 (great deal of red tape).

Empirical Research on Red Tape

A close and continuing concern with the logic and procedure of analysis remains a prime necessity for any discipline if it is to locate its center and clarify its principal points of reference.

—Landau 1972, 178 (quoted in McCurdy and Cleary, 1984, 53)

Seeking to advance red tape theory, public administration scholars are engaged in honing definitions, developing concepts, gathering data, testing hypotheses, and assessing the reliability and validity of those efforts, with the goal of developing generalizable information about red tape in organizations. In this chapter we review the empirical research that has been conducted to test red tape theory, focusing on the concepts, measures, and data collection efforts used in an assortment of journal articles testing hypotheses about the relationships between red tape and organizational outcomes.

One of the greatest challenges in academic theory development is moving from theory to empirical research and back to theory development. Ideally, theory development and empirical testing of theory occur simultaneously and support each other. In the case of red tape research in public administration, and perhaps in much of social science research, this process often proves less iterative and more compartmentalized than one would hope. In the field of public administration, a relatively young social science and one that is tightly connected to practice and professionalism, balancing theory and empirical research is particularly challenging. Not only are methodological and empirical approaches in the field relatively new and underdeveloped, but also this underdevelopment is, arguably, a result of the applied nature of the field. Organizational reformers and public officials generally have limited patience for the intricacies and microcontroversies of methods and statistics and, instead, wish to have ready, clearly applicable solutions. In public administration, the demand for reform and innovation, and scholars' understandable desire to seem relevant, often prove the enemy of careful knowledge development. However, despite these challenges, public administration scholars and red tape researchers in particular have conducted a significant amount of empirical work in a short period of time, offering an important basis from which to assess progress.

This chapter reviews the red tape empirical literature and assesses the extent to which it tests and advances theory. There are two general streams of red tape research. The first is the study of red tape as related to corruption and bribery in the political economy and economics literatures. The second stream of red tape research, and the one most important to this book, is in public administration. As noted by Walker and Brewer (2008), the ontology of red tape is critical to understanding red tape research because the method by which red tape is conceived and discussed plays an important role in how it is measured, assessed, and addressed. Although some scholars (Guriev 1999; Mauro 1995) do not explicitly define red tape, but use the term interchangeably with cumbersome bureaucratic regulation and corruption, this chapter focuses on research that provides explicit measures of red tape and seeks to advance red tape theory. Thus, we are concerned with empirical research engaged in theory development, defining red tape as a negative phenomenon, rather than red tape as corruption, such as collusion or bribe extortion (Guriev 1999, 2004), so-called positive or beneficial red tape (Guriev 1999, 2004), or "green tape" (DeHart-Davis 2009), or determinants of effective rules.

Even focusing on that body of red tape research conforming to a pathological concept of red tape, we see that the public administration field has during the past twenty years produced an abundance of research on red tape. This research has focused on developing a more detailed understanding of red tape, detailing the definition and components of red tape and developing consistent, reliable, and valid red tape measures. In general, the public administration literature has examined samples of managers and organizations in developed Western nations, especially the United States and the United Kingdom, failing to offer national comparisons of red tape.[1] Additionally, the red tape research, like much of the empirical research in public administration, has tended to rely on "homegrown" datasets, funded by small personal research funds and graduate student labor or relationships that researchers have with particular agencies and organizations (Wright, Manigault, and Black 2004).

In this chapter we discuss the ontology of red tape in public administration.

We discuss the definitions, data sources, arguments and assumptions, methods, models, and samples that commonly appear in the public administration red tape literature. Because empirical public administration red tape research tends to rely on assessments of red tape using cross-sectional, primary data collected from surveys, there is an extensive literature based on perceptions and self-reported data. We discuss this literature by way of its measures. We begin by reviewing the operationalization and measurement of red tape, noting the definition of red tape and the data collection approaches in the public administration literature (e.g., primary survey data, secondary survey data, document analysis, and organizational documents). Second, we present a detailed appraisal of self-assessed red tape, offering a detailed analysis of the following measures: General Red Tape Scale (GRT), Personnel/Human Resource Red Tape, and Managerial Subsystem Red Tape (e.g., procurement, information system, communication, and budgetary red tape). We note the common use of these measures, some of the hypotheses tested and findings confirmed through these tests, and their weaknesses. Third, we discuss measures of red tape as delays, noting the hypotheses and findings in this research. Fourth, we review the general findings of the red tape empirical research. We conclude with a critical assessment of the empirical red tape research and the ways in which it has worked toward developing evidence for a theory of red tape and the extent to which the accumulated evidence seems to advance explanatory theory.

Operationalizing and Measuring Red Tape

Defining and Operationalizing Red Tape

In 1984, Rosenfeld defined red tape as "guidelines, procedures, forms, and government interventions that are perceived as excessive, unwieldy, or pointless in relationship to decision making or implementation of decisions" (603). While a useful definition for red tape, this failed to distinguish between good rules and bad rules, or rules that might cause delays but serve an important purpose. In 1993, Bozeman's theory defined organizational red tape as "rules, regulations, and procedures that remain in force and entail a compliance burden for the organization but have no efficacy for the rules' functional object" (283). Much of the modern empirical red tape research has built upon Bozeman's (2000) more straightforward definition of red tape as "burdensome administrative rules and procedures that have negative effects on the organization's performance." For example, DeHart-Davis (2007) offered the following definition of red tape, "burdensome administrative policies and procedures that have negative effects on the city's performance," while others (DeHart-Davis and Pandey 2005; Yang and Pandey 2009) define red tape as "burdensome rules or procedures that have an adverse effect on organizational performance." Pandey, Coursey, and Moynihan (2007) narrow Bozeman's definition, situating it within the formalization literature by noting that "red tape exists when managers view formalization as burdensome and detrimental to organizational purposes," confirming Bozeman's assertion that red tape imposes a "compliance burden for the organization but makes no contribution to achieving the rule's functional object" (2000, 82). Despite the widespread use of Bozeman's definition, especially in public administration, the research literature includes other definitions and constructs for red tape; for example, Kaufman and Wei (1999) define red tape as regulatory burden such as tax, licenses, and delay.

In their discussion of quantitative research measurement in public administration, Wright, Manigault, and Black (2004) note that researchers who offer detailed descriptions of their research, including their guiding definitions and assumptions, not only guide the consumer of the research, but also enable theory development by ensuring that other researchers can track, replicate, and follow the assumptions and limitations of the research. Wright argues that in order to properly assess empirical research and its contributions to theory, researchers must provide two types of information: (1) "general background information such as the source of their measure and the method of data collection used" and (2) "information describing and supporting how each study variable was operationalized" (751). While there are examples of poor data reporting throughout the public administration field, the red tape empirical research generally displays thorough data reporting and measurement. Public administration researchers using red tape measures almost always cite previous use of those measures and often the theory driving those measures.

Data Sources

Most of the red tape research in public administration comes from primary survey data. For example, Pandey and Bretschneider (1997) analyzed data from the National Association of State Information Systems mail survey to the directors of each program agency. Bretschneider (1990) compared red tape in public and private organizations and its effect on time to complete tasks using data from the National Study of Information Resources Management in State Government, which included responses from 1,005 data processing managers (622 public, 383 private). Bozeman and Bretschneider (1994) compared red tape perceptions in public and private research centers using data from phase 2 of the National Comparative Research and Development Project, which mailed questionnaires to research directors from a sample pool of 1,341 research centers (733 responses). This reliance on primary survey data for empirical red tape research is not surprising since public administration research relies heavily on self-administered surveys (Houston and Delevan 1990). For example, Wright, Manigault, and Black (2004) found that from a sample of 143 articles, half relied on self-administered surveys, and two-thirds of the 3,211 measures used in those articles were drawn from self-administered surveys. While it is disheartening to think of public administration as a field so devoid of public investment and research funding that one of its strongest theoretical and empirical contributions has come from such small-scale research projects, at the same time it is remarkable how many dissertations, books, peer-reviewed journal articles, conference papers, and careers have grown out of these small-scale research projects.

To date, few red tape studies utilize secondary data to test red tape hypotheses. One exception is Parsons (1991), who looks at data of targeted public transfers to estimate the impact of the complexity of screening procedures in the U.S. welfare system on individuals' willingness to apply for benefits. This measurement of public transfers data related to willingness to apply for services is an indirect measurement of red tape and the costs associated with navigating that red tape to access services.

In addition to the abundance of surveys collecting primary data on red tape, researchers have relied on red tape data collected from organizational documents. For example, Zhou (1993) collected data from the minutes of the Stanford University's Academy Council and Faculty Senate and other university publications, and DeHart-Davis studied documents and conducted interviews to gather data for her dissertation, "Environmental Permit Costs: The Roles of Red Tape, Communications, Experience and Subcontracting," at Georgia Tech in 2000 and for subsequent publications (DeHart-Davis and Bozeman 2001).

Public administration researchers have made a concerted effort to operationalize red tape measures. As individual researchers have administered studies and operationalized red tape through different means and methods, the field has grown a considerable literature that can be used to assess the progress of operationalizing red tape. The literature relying on self-reported survey data tends to fall into two categories. The first set of research asks respondents about the level of rules, restrictions, and constraints in their work environment. We label this first type of operationalization "self-assessed red tape." The second asks respondents to note the amount of time, delay, and paperwork associated with completing tasks. We label this second approach "red tape as delay." Below we discuss some of the ways in which researchers have operationalized these two categories of red tape and the strengths and weaknesses associated with these approaches.

Self-Assessed Red Tape

General Red Tape Scale

The research relying on self-reported assessments of red tape relies heavily upon the GRT Scale (also known in various research studies as the General Administrative Red Tape Scale, Global Scale, Global Measure of Red Tape, and Organizational Red Tape Scale). The GRT Scale was first developed by Rainey, Pandey, and Bozeman (1995) along with a measure of Rule Enforcement Red Tape (see Table 4.1). While there is no additional research advancing the measure of Rule Enforcement Red Tape, the GRT Scale has appeared in a number of subsequent survey instruments, including the National Administrative Studies Project (NASP) II, a survey of managers in Departments of Health and Human Services; NASP III, a survey of public and nonprofit managers in Georgia and Illinois; a study of red tape among Georgia Department of Transportation managers and their contractors (Feeney and Bozeman 2009); the English Local Government Dataset study of Best Value (see assorted works of Walker and Brewer); and a survey of managers in four cities in Kansas (assorted works of DeHart-Davis). Due to its widespread use, the GRT Scale has emerged as a staple measure for red tape in the public administration literature, appearing in more than twenty peer-reviewed journal articles (e.g., Brewer and Walker 2010a, 2010b; Bozeman and Kingsley 1998; DeHart-Davis 2007; Feeney and Bozeman 2009; Moon and Bretschneider 2002; Moynihan and Pandey 2007a; Pandey and Kingsley 2000; Pandey and Rainey 2006; Scott and Pandey 2005; Walker and Brewer 2008, 2009a, 2009b; Welch and Pandey 2007; Yang and Pandey 2009). As a result of the widespread use of the GRT Scale, researchers have concluded that public sector employees consistently report significantly more red tape in their organizations as compared to private (Feeney and Bozeman 2009; Rainey, Pandey, and Bozeman 1995) and nonprofit sector respondents (Feeney and Rainey 2010).

The GRT Scale offers one of the best examples of consistent, cross-research application of an empirical measure in public administration research. The measure has appeared in an assortment of research instruments applied in a variety of research settings. The scale has appeared in surveys administered to public, private, and nonprofit managers, departments of health and human services, city managers, and public managers and their consultants.

The GRT Scale has been used extensively for hypothesis testing as both a dependent variable and independent variable. Consider some of the following uses of the GRT Scale:

Table 4.1

Measures of Red Tape

GRT Scale: If red tape is defined as burdensome administrative rules and procedures that have negative effects on the organization's effectiveness, how would you assess the level of red tape in your organization? For this measure, the respondents are asked to rate the item on a 10-point scale, with 10 indicating the highest level of red tape and 0 indicating no red tape.

Rule Enforcement Red Tape: The index was constructed by summing the following items, with a 1 to 4 scale with 1 indicating strong agreement:

1. The employees here are constantly being watched to check for rule violations.
2. People here feel as though they are constantly being watched to see they obey all the rules.

Source: Rainey, Pandey, and Bozeman (1995).

- Pandey and Kingsley (2000) use a work alienation scale, organizational size, respondent education level, and time in current position to predict organizational red tape in public and private organizations, measuring red tape in terms of the GRT Scale.
- Scott and Pandey (2005) predict variance in the GRT Scale as related to public service motivation, controlling for organizational size, hierarchy, and centralization.
- Feeney and Bozeman (2009) also use the GRT Scale as a dependent variable, testing hypotheses about differences across sector and the relationship between communication, intersector collaboration, and work experience and red tape perceptions.
- DeHart-Davis and Pandey (2005) use the GRT Scale as an independent variable to test their hypothesis that higher levels on the scale will be associated with higher levels of alienation among public managers.
- Moynihan and Pandey (2007) test a hypothesis that red tape, measured by the GRT Scale, will be related to lower levels of public service motivation.
- Bozeman and Kingsley (1998) predict that managers in organizations with higher degrees of red tape, as measured by the GRT Scale, will tend to perceive less risk-taking than managers in organizations with lower levels on the scale.

The GRT Scale has been used to test a number of hypotheses, and at times the same hypotheses across multiple studies (e.g., public and private managers report different levels of perceived red tape in their organizations). The results have been relatively stable, providing a considerable degree of convergent validity. Moreover, because red tape researchers consistently tie this measure to Bozeman's theory of red tape (even when not providing direct tests of that theory), consumers of red tape empirical research are given the requisite information to assess the face validly and instrumental utility of the GRT Scale (Welch 2004).

Personnel Red Tape

In addition to the GRT Scale, one of the most common and persistent measures in the public administration red tape literature is Personnel Red Tape (PRT). The PRT Scale, or some variation of this scale, has appeared in multiple survey instruments. Rainey, Pandey, and Bozeman (1995) operationalized the first measure of personnel red tape using data from phase 1 of the NASP I,[2] asking respondents to indicate their level of agreement (using a 4-point scale ranging from strong disagreement to strong agreement) with the following five items:

1. Even if a manager is a poor performer, formal rules make it hard to remove him or her from the organization.
2. The rules governing promotion make it hard for a good manager to move up faster than a poor one.
3. Due to rules, pay raises for managers are based more on longevity than on performance.
4. The formal pay structures and rules make it hard to reward a good manager with higher pay here.
5. The personnel rules and procedures that govern my organization make it easy for supervisors to reward subordinates for good performance [reversed].

In their analysis, the authors summed the responses to these five items to create the PRT Scale. They concluded that there were significant differences between public and private managers' perceptions of personnel rule constraints.

A decade later, using data from the NASP II survey, Pandey and Moynihan (2006) reduced the PRT Scale measure by one item, summing responses to the following four questionnaire items and labeling the scale Human Resource Red Tape:

1. Even if a manager is a poor performer, formal rules make it hard to remove him or her from the organization.
2. The rules governing promotion make it hard for a good manager to move up faster than a poor one.

3. The formal pay structures and rules make it hard to reward a good manager with higher pay here.
4. The personnel rules and procedures that govern my organization make it easier for superiors to reward subordinates for good performance [reversed].

Pandey and Moynihan found that Human Resource Red Tape is negatively related to organizational mission effectiveness, but that developmental culture and political support from elected officials mitigate the negative effects of human resources red tape on mission effectiveness. They concluded that when organizations have a low developmental culture, an increase in human resources red tape is related to sharp declines in mission effectiveness, while the decline in mission effectiveness is less dramatic at organizations with medium developmental culture and slight at organizations with high levels of developmental culture. They concluded that the relationship between red tape and performance is moderated by political support and culture.

As noted in Table 4.2, a number of red tape researchers have developed and used measures for PRT in different instruments and settings and for different analyses. Brewer and Walker (2010a, 2010b) and Walker and Brewer (2009a, 2009b) used similar questionnaire items to develop measures of personnel red tape, which they labeled personnel and administrative subsystem measures, noting that they operationalized these measures as a subcomponent of red tape. Meanwhile, Pandey, Coursey, and Moynihan (2007) described human resources red tape as red tape associated with procurement, budgeting, information systems, and communication.

The individual survey items used in the PRT Scale, or variations of these individual items (through indexes, summation, and factors analysis)—as both dependent and independent variables—offer strong, consistent evidence that personnel rules and regulations vary significantly across the public and private sector (Bozeman and Kingsley 1998; Pandey and Kingsley 2000; Rainey, Pandey, and Bozeman 1995) and the public and private nonprofit sector (Feeney and Rainey 2010), and that public managers have some ability to make these rules more or less burdensome (Walker and Brewer 2009b). These PRT measures, gathered through multiple instruments (see appendixes for a full description of the following studies: Syracuse Metropolitan Organizational Theory Project, NASP I, NASP II, English Local Government Dataset) and from multiple samples (public, private, and nonprofit managers, city, county, state, and federal government), have proved reliable and valid measures of rules and regulations related to rewards and removal in the public sector. Moreover, the widespread use of these items, whether a 5-point or 7-point Likert scale, has enabled researchers to understand not only sector distinctions

Table 4.2

Personnel Red Tape Questionnaire Items

Questionnaire Items
1. Even if a manager is a poor performer, formal rules make it hard to remove him or her from the organization.
2. The rules governing promotion make it hard for a good manager to move up faster than a poor one.
3. The formal pay structures and rules make it hard to reward a good **manager** with higher pay here.
4. The personnel rules and procedures that govern my organization make it easy for superiors to reward subordinates for good performance (reversed).
5. Due to rules, pay raises for managers are based more on longevity than on performance.
6. Producing a low quality of work decreases my chances for promotion.
7. Because of the rules here, promotions are based mainly on performance
8. The formal pay structures and rules make it hard to reward a good **employee** with higher pay here.

Measure name	Question-naire item	Scale type	Data source	Citation
Personnel Red Tape	1, 3	Likert 1–7	English Study of Best Value	Walker and Brewer 2009a, 2009b
Promote/Rules	7	Likert 1–4	NASP I	Bozeman and Kingsley 1998
Pay/Rule	5	Likert 1–5	NASP I	Bozeman and Kingsley 1998
Promote/Quality	6	Likert 1–4	NASP I	Bozeman and Kingsley 1998
Personnel Red Tape	1, 3	Likert 1–7	English Study of Best Value	Brewer and Walker 2010a, 2010b
Personnel Red Tape	1, 3	Likert 1–7	English Study of Best Value	Walker and Brewer 2008
Personnel Red Tape	1, 3	Likert 1–7	English Study of Best Value	Brewer and Walker 2006
Personnel Red Tape	1, 3	Likert 1–7	English Study of Best Value	Brewer, Hicklin, and Walker 2006
Personnel Red Tape	1, 2, 3	Likert 1–5	NASP II	Chen and Williams 2007
Human Resource Red Tape	1, 2, 3, 4	Likert 1–5	NASP II	DeHart-Davis and Pandey 2005
Personnel Flexibility	1, 7, 8	Likert 1–4	NASP III	Feeney and Rainey 2010
Personnel Red Tape	1, 2, 3, 4	Likert 1–5	NASP II	Pandey and Garnett 2006
Personnel Red Tape	1, 2, 3, 4, 5	Likert 1–4	NASP I	Pandey and Kingsley 2000
Human Resource Red Tape	1, 2, 3, 4	Likert 1–5	NASP II	Pandey and Moynihan 2006
Personnel Red Tape	1, 2, 3, 4, 5	Likert 1–4	NASP I	Pandey and Welch 2005
Personnel Red Tape	1, 2, 3, 4	Likert 1–5	NASP II	Pandey, Coursey, and Moynihan 2007
Personnel Red Tape	1, 2, 3, 4, 5	Likert 1–4	NASP I	Rainey, Pandey and Bozeman 1995
Personnel Red Tape	1, 2, 3, 4	Likert 1–5	NASP II	Scott and Pandey 2005
Personnel Red Tape	1, 3	Likert 1–7	English Study of Best Value	Walker and Brewer 2008

but also the ways in which personnel constraints are related to performance (Brewer and Walker 2010a; Pandey, Coursey, and Moynihan 2007), organizational culture (Pandey and Moynihan 2006), and public service motivation (Scott and Pandey 2005).

The items used to measure PRT offer one of the best examples of public administration research reusing and reapplying a measure in multiple contexts with the aim of testing public administration theory (in this case, most prominently the theory of sector distinctions). The PRT Scale has no direct counterpart in organizational behavior, business, or industrial psychology research—perhaps because red tape itself remains the research domain of those interested in the public sector. Numerous studies have shown the important ways in which personnel constraints and flexibilities and the ability to reward and punish employees significantly vary across sectors (Bozeman and Bretschneider 1994; Brewer and Walker 2010a, 2010b; DeHart-Davis and Pandey 2005; Feeney and Rainey 2010; Pandey and Moynihan 2006; Pandey and Welch 2005; Rainey 1983; Rainey, Pandey, and Bozeman 1995; Walker and Brewer 2008, 2009a, 2009b). Not only are these findings consistent and strong, but also they further public administration theory and red tape theory.

Validation of social science measures and constructs is an iterative process (Schwab 1980). The items used for the PRT Scale have the advantage of this iterative process, appearing in multiple instruments that use a variety of response scales (Likert scales ranging from 4 to 7 response categories). Moreover, numerous types of analyses have been applied to these measures, including confirmatory factor analysis, exploratory principal components analysis, correlation analysis, summation, and index creation.

Despite the advances, these various measures and the research using these measures of red tape have shortcomings and omissions. One problem is that little attention has been given to establishing the validity and reliability of these measures and testing or critiquing the methodological strength of particular items. While most red tape researchers show some diligence in explaining their measures and situating them within the general body of red tape research, there is no overarching study or meta-analysis testing variation of these measures or investigating, for example, whether a measure of personnel red tape requires five items, three items, or a single item to best capture perceptions of personnel red tape.

In the cases of the PRT Scale's measurement, if one considers the specific language in the personnel items (see Table 4.2) in relation to the standard definition of red tape as "rules, regulations and procedures that remain in force and entail a compliance burden but do not advance the legitimate purposes the rules were intended to serve" (Bozeman 2000, 12), one sees limited correspondence between the measures and the red tape concept. Instead, these

PRT items ask the respondent about burdensome rules and regulations—thus leading us into the murky waters of distinguishing red tape from formalization and bureaucratic control. While it is true that public organizations, compared to private organizations, have higher levels of personnel constraints and that public managers are more likely than private managers to report that rules and regulations make it difficult to remove a low-performing employee or reward a good employee, it is not clear that there is more *red tape* in public organizations' personnel systems and it is not clear that the items in the PRT scale distinguish sufficiently between burdensome personnel rules and personnel red tape. It is quite possible that personnel rules and regulations, though burdensome, are not red tape, but instead rules intended to protect workers' rights, minority groups, or the organization. This is a particularly worrisome issue with the items used to measure personnel red tape because none of those items include the words "red tape." Instead, the questionnaire items ask about formal rules and structures that might impede action or the ability to reward employees. It would perhaps be more useful for those items to state, for example, "Even if a manager is a poor performer, *red tape* makes it hard to remove him or her from the organization" or "Due to *red tape,* pay raises for managers are based more on longevity than on performance."

Arguably, the slow, bureaucratic hiring process in state and local governments protects employees and institutions from political interference. The sluggish, complicated process for firing managers in the federal personnel system may be the result of efforts to ensure equal opportunity employment. Or the difficulties found in many governments' personnel systems could relate entirely to red tape rather than to any rationale for promoting effectiveness. Unfortunately, the measures currently used by red tape researchers fail to differentiate between burdensome rules that are important and burdensome rules that are red tape. Red tape researchers have made only limited progress validating the PRT Scale or the GRT Scale or determining their test-retest reliability. Indeed, the construct validity of these and other red tape measures remains suspect. Do these scales really measure red tape? When confronted with that question, most red tape researchers are quick to say that theirs are indirect measures or useful surrogate measures rather than claiming that their measures tap into most of the meaning of red tape concepts. Red tape research has by now advanced to the point that empirical research requires a higher commitment to the validation of its measures.

Management Subsystem Red Tape

Brewer and Walker (2006; Walker and Brewer 2008) argue that red tape is best viewed as subcomponents of management subsystems such as personnel, budgeting, and procurement. By measuring red tape related to procurement and purchasing (Chen and Williams 2007; Pandey, Coursey, and Moynihan 2007; Pandey and Garnett 2006; Pandey and Moynihan 2006; Scott and Pandey 2005; Welch and Pandey 2007), information systems (Chen and Williams 2007; Pandey and Moynihan 2006), communication (Chen and Williams 2007; Pandey, Coursey, and Moynihan 2007; Pandey and Garnett 2006) and budgeting (Chen and Williams 2007; Pandey, Coursey, and Moynihan 2007; Scott and Pandey 2005), researchers are able to test a number of propositions and hypotheses about the ways in which red tape affects management and outcomes. Table 4.3 notes the questionnaire items used to operationalize these measures.

Much of the empirical research investigating these subsystem measures of red tape relies on the NASP II dataset or similar measures. One of the advantages of having multiple researchers using the same dataset is that researchers are able to build upon one another's work and confirm and retest propositions. For example, Chen and Williams (2007) developed a red tape model with four constructs: political support, goal clarity, developmental culture, and red tape. This model builds upon Coursey and Pandey's (2007a) measurement model where red tape is measured as a second-order construct reflecting five first-order factors (personnel inflexibility, communication inflexibility, procurement inflexibility, information inflexibility, and budget inflexibility). Chen and Williams (2007) investigate seven hypotheses, of which five are related to red tape. Specifically:

1. Organizations with a higher level of political support from elected officials will tend to have a lower level of red tape.
2. Organizations with a higher level of developmental culture will have a lower level of red tape.
3. Political support indirectly reduces red tape, mediated by developmental culture.
4. Organizations with a higher level of goal clarity will have a lower level of red tape.
5. Political support will reduce red tape through the mediation of organizational goal clarity.

This model supports the first hypothesis listed above, finding that political support is associated with a lower level of red tape, but offers no support for the fifth hypothesis that organizational goal clarity will mediate the relationship between political support and red tape. Chen and Williams conclude that a higher level of support from elected officials is related to lower levels of red tape as reflected in human resource management, communication, procurement, information systems, and budget processes.

Table 4.3

Management Subsystem Red Tape

Procurement/Purchasing Red Tape
1. The rules governing purchasing/procurement in my organization make it easy for managers to purchase goods and services (reversed).
2. Due to standard procedures, procurement is based more on the vendor's ability to comply with rules than on the quality of goods and services.
3. The rules governing procurement make it hard to expedite purchase of goods and services for a critical project.
(Chen and Williams 2007, using items 1 and 3; Pandey, Coursey, and Moynihan 2007; Pandey and Garnett 2006; Pandey and Moynihan 2006; Scott and Pandey 2005; Welch and Pandey 2007)

Information Systems Red Tape
1. Rules and procedures on preparation of information system reports ensure that managers receive timely information (reversed).
2. Procedural requirements for information system requests make it difficult for managers to obtain relevant information.
(Chen and Williams 2007; Pandey and Moynihan 2006)

Budgetary Red Tape
1. Budgetary rules and procedures limit managers' ability to reprogram funds in accordance with agency mission.
2. The budgeting rules and procedures limit managers' ability to deal with unexpected program/project cost overruns.
(Chen and Williams 2007; Pandey, Coursey, and Moynihan 2007; Scott and Pandey 2005)

Communication Red Tape
1. Top managers in this agency are allowed to communicate freely with reporters (reversed).
2. Communication within my agency is restricted by policies and procedures.
3. Communication with other government agencies is restricted by policies and procedures.
(Chen and Williams 2007; Pandey, Coursey, and Moynihan 2007; Pandey and Garnett 2006)

Using the same dataset, Welch and Pandey (2007) investigate the interaction between red tape and intranet usage in state human service agencies, testing a sociotechnical model that takes into account bidirectional causal relationships and an assortment of internal and external influences. The authors operationalize procurement red tape as a summative measure of responses to three survey items about procurement rules. Welch and Pandey test (1) whether higher levels of red tape will negatively affect the level of intranet technology implementation (in terms of reliance and information quality) in public organizations and (2) whether higher levels of intranet implementation (in terms of reliance and information quality) will reduce the level of red tape in public organizations. Using two-stage least squares, the authors are able to test the direction of the relationships between red tape and intranet implementation. They conclude that intranet reliance reduces procurement red tape, but red tape has no effect on intranet reliance or information quality. Moreover, the authors include measures for formalization in their red tape models and find that formalization is positively associated with intranet reliance and procurement red tape, but negatively related to information quality. Thus, although formalization is often associated with organizational red tape, in this case empirical evidence finds that it is not a significant determinant of procurement red tape.

Using measures of information system, budgetary, and communication red tape, researchers have tested a number of hypotheses about the relationships between red tape and public service motivation, organizational performance, developmental cultures, communication performance, and political support from elected officials (Chen and Williams 2007; Pandey, Coursey, and Moynihan 2007; Pandey and Garnett 2006; Pandey and Moynihan 2006; Scott and Pandey 2005). Pandey, Coursey, and Moynihan (2007) find that although red tape has a direct negative relationship with perceived organizational effectiveness and performance, not all red tape has the same effect on performance. They report significant relationships between information systems red tape and organizational effectiveness and performance but no significant relationship between procurement, budgetary, and communication red tape and organizational effectiveness and performance.

Scott and Pandey (2005) find that perceptions of procurement red tape and budgetary red tape, along with general and personnel red tape, are significantly related to public service motivation (PSM). In fact, among the dimensions of PSM, they find that attraction to public policy-making has the strongest relationship to red tape perceptions. Pandey and Garnett (2006) test an exploratory model of public sector communication performance and find that although red tape constrains communication performance, red tape can be overcome by a culture that supports communication and flexible goal clarity. Because these three studies rely on NASP II data, and presumably because they are authored by the NASP II principal investigator Sanjay Pandey, they each use the same measures and classifications for operationalizing and talking about information systems, budgetary, and communication performance red tape—regardless of whether the analysis uses red tape as the dependent variable (Scott and Pandey 2005) or independent variable (Chen and Williams 2007; Pandey, Coursey, and Moynihan 2007; Pandey and Garnett 2006; Pandey and Moynihan 2006).

The measures developed in NASP II have been adopted by other public administration researchers. Researchers using data from the Centre for Local and Regional Government Research at Cardiff University's study of the impact of Best Value and Core Performance Assessment (CPA) on service improvement in local authorities in the United Kingdom offer a different view of management subsystem red tape. Publications resulting from the English Local Government Best Value study describe two types of red tape: internal red tape and external red tape. Walker and Brewer (2008) note that internal red tape "refers to bureaucratic rules and routines that cause task delays and negatively affect the internal operations of a public agency" (1118), while external red tape affects the ability of citizens and external stakeholders "to interact with the agency or comply with legal mandates" (1118).

Internal red tape is measured using four survey items that ask respondents about global, personnel (two items), and administrative red tape. The four measures ask respondents to indicate their level of agreement or disagreement with the following statements:

1. The level of red tape is high in our service/authority. [global measure]
2. Even if a manager is a poor performer, formal rules make it hard to remove him or her from the organization. [personnel red tape]
3. The formal pay structures and rules make it hard to reward a good manager with higher pay here. [personnel red tape]
4. Reorganizing an organizational unit or department can be achieved within two or three weeks in our service/authority. [administrative red tape]

Walker and Brewer (2008) measure external red tape with one global measure of respondents' levels of agreement with the following statement: "administrative rules and procedures are open and responsive, allowing stakeholders (users, businesses, government agencies, etc.) to freely interact with our service/authority." Walker and Brewer (2008) use these measures for internal and external red tape as dependent variables estimated in lagged models and predicted by organizational determinants (devolved management, devolved behavior, target setting, formalization, developmental culture, logical incrementalism, rational planning, and internal political context) and external controls (reducing costs, resource constraints, regulation, direct intervention, external political context, ability to influence, service need, diversity of service need, and change in service need) (Walker and Brewer 2008). They also use the same measures as independent variables predicting government performance (Brewer, Hicklin, and Walker 2006; Walker and Brewer 2008). They conclude that red tape is significantly related to organization performance in areas of information systems, budgeting, and communication, confirming Brewer and Walker's (2005a, 2005b, 2006) argument that red tape has different components and that it is increasingly important to understand how different types of red tape in management subsystems affect outcomes.

Some researchers have tried to develop other methods for understanding red tape in organizations without directly asking respondents about red tape. For example, Kingsley and Reed (1991) do not operationalize red tape, but instead ask respondents about the degree to which they were constrained by unnecessary rules during the decision-making process (Rule Constriction). Bozeman and Kingsley (1998) also aim to understand red tape as rules, asking respondents about their perceptions of rules and the organization's adherence to rules. They ask respondents their level of agreement with the following items:

1. When a situation arises, we have procedures to follow in dealing with it. [procedures]
2. In this organization, conformance to rules and procedures is very important. [rule conform]
3. People here feel as though they are constantly being watched to see they obey all the rules. [rule watch]

While the management subsystem measures of red tape outlined in this section indicate a growing focus on the ways in which red tape shapes managerial systems, the bulk of this research draws from NASP II and the English Local Government Best Value Study. Because NASP II was a survey of state departments of health and human services, we do not find empirical tests of procurement, information systems, communication, and budgetary red tape by sector or function (e.g., across public sector agencies). In comparison, the English Local Government study, focusing on local government, enables hypothesis testing about organizational function, but not sector. There is also no empirical test of the ways in which these types of red tape affect stakeholders who are not public managers (e.g., clients, street-level bureaucrats, private sector contractors, political officials).

Many of these measures of red tape are used to understand organizational levels of red tape, sources of red tape, and the relationship between perceptions of red tape and other organizational values and perceptions, much in the spirit of Bozeman's (2000) conceptualization. These self-assessed measures of red tape are distinct from related concepts such as formalization, and many researchers make a point of noting this distinction (e.g., Bozeman and Kingsley 1998; Bozeman and Scott 1996; Pandey and Bretschneider 1997; Pandey and Scott 2002; Walker and Brewer 2008; Welch and Pandey 2007). Because these measures are based on respondent perceptions, they are conditioned by the respondent's perspective, position, and stakes. Almost all the measures of red tape employed to this point in published studies are typically concerned with red tape internal to the organization.

Red Tape as Delay

Although many red tape studies operationalize red tape as perceptions of red tape, as noted in the preceding section, other studies operationalize red tape as the amount of time required to complete tasks. The earliest description of red tape as a delay comes from Bozeman, Reed, and Scott (1992), who measured red tape as the time required to complete core organizational tasks in 900 research-intensive organizations. In their study comparing 733 public and private national research centers, Bozeman and Bretschneider (1994) operationalize red tape as the amount of time spent in hiring and dismissal of full-time personnel (personnel decisions), the amount of time that research was circulated outside of the organization and until it was published (knowledge flows), and the amount of time to finalize decisions concerning purchases of equipment costing more than $1,000 (purchasing). More recently, West (2004) operationalizes red tape as the (1) length of time to create a rule and (2) the length of time for public comments about that rule. Pandey and Bretschneider (1997) argue that red tape is a residual concept where total procedural delay is the starting point and the appropriate place to begin operationalizing red tape.

Numerous studies have measured red tape as the total number of weeks spent obtaining approval to carry out key organizational tasks, including hiring a person in a new civil service position, purchasing equipment costing less than $1,000, purchasing equipment that costs more than $1,000, contracting for services, enacting major policy changes, enacting major administrative policy changes, and changing major program policies (Bozeman and Kingsley 1998; Bretschneider 1990; Pandey and Bretschneider 1997). DeHart-Davis and Bozeman (2001), in their study of regulatory compliance, asked firms to indicate, for each activity, how much time (in weeks) is typically required between a request made by a unit within the company and the actual approval of the request. The activities included hiring a full-time employee, firing a full-time employee, buying low-cost equipment (under $10,000), buying more expensive equipment (over $10,000), reorganizing a department or unit, starting a minor new project, and starting a major new project. Similarly, Bozeman, Reed, and Scott (1992) measure red tape as the amount of time required (in weeks) to complete the following tasks: purchasing equipment, hiring full-time personnel, hiring part-time personnel, firing full-time personnel, circulating research products outside organizations, receiving approval to publish research findings, receiving approval for new research projects, receiving approval for intermediate research projects, and receiving approval for large-scale research projects. They also include a variable aggregating responses to all the items on delays.

Kaufman and Wei (1999) ask respondents to indicate whether "senior management of your company" spends more or less than "30 percent of its time dealing with government bureaucracy" and use the responses to measure the time that management wastes in dealing with regulation and negotiating tax relief. They conclude that this time wasted is red tape. However, they fail to differentiate between time spent dealing with regulation and negotiating tax relief, which results in benefits to the company (e.g., tax relief), as compared to time that results in no positive outcome for the company, which indeed would be wasted time and could constitute a proxy for red tape, thus differentiating it from direct testing and advancement of red tape theory.

These studies operationalizing red tape as delay draw on a number of datasets, including a national survey of 900 research and development organizations; NASIS—a study of 1,005 data processing managers in public and private organizations; NASP I—a survey of top and midlevel managers from both public and private organizations in Syracuse and Albany, New York; and an Environmental Protection Agency study implementing a cross-sectional mail survey of representatives from Title V-regulated firms in Georgia, Oregon, South Carolina, and Wisconsin (see appendixes for details). Research measuring red tape as administrative delay has consistently found significant differences between public and private organizations.

Bretschneider (1990) finds that, after controlling for organization size and mix of technology, public organizations report significantly longer time delays to complete tasks. Bozeman and Kingsley (1998) find that red tape increases the transaction costs associated with completing tasks and conclude that this red tape may ultimately reduce the organization's risk-taking culture. Pandey and Bretschneider (1997, 118) use data from an administrative delay questionnaire to test the hypothesis that "the greater the red-tape induced administrative delay in an organization, the more interest the organization will display in new information technologies." They conclude that red tape and information technology usage are endogenous and that red tape is correlated with organizational interest in information technology.

Moving away from public administration research, Zhou (1993) takes a rules-based approach to understanding red tape. Although Zhou is not particularly concerned with "red tape" as defined in the public administration literature, he is concerned with the rule birth, foundation, and change associated with it. Zhou uses surveys to understand individual perceptions of the dynamics of organizational rules. Zhou asks respondents to indicate the rate of rule change (age of a rule and the number of times it has been changed), rule birth due to external shocks, the extent to which the organization's agenda is rule-related, rule change related to changes in governmental funding or legislation, and rule foundations and changes related to organizational size. Although Zhou does not adopt an operationalization found in the public administration literature, this work uses a similar self-assessment method for understanding red tape.

Measures of administrative delay as a proxy for red tape raise important questions about measurement, including its relation to Bozeman's theory of red tape. If red tape is viewed as a negative phenomenon impeding organizational objectives and the attainment of a rule's functional object, it is unclear how administrative delay is an acceptable measure of red tape. First, administrative delay may have little to do with rules and more to do with norms and informal behavior in the organization. However, we suspect this is not the case since most purchasing, hiring, and firing decisions do require a significant amount of paperwork and administrative burden. That said, we still have the problem of understanding whether or not measures of administrative delay are measuring the underlying concept of red tape. Unfortunately, there is no public administration research confirming the usefulness of administrative delay measures as a best method for measuring red tape. Perhaps the best construction of a delays-based red tape measure is one developed by Bretschneider and Bozeman (1995) for a little-known paper published in an edited volume on public management. Breschneider and Bozeman examine delays in terms of the median distance of an organization's delays for personnel, hiring, budgeting, and other processes, compared to other organizations with similar missions. While this approach does not clearly distinguish delay and red tape, it at least takes into account the fact that different types of organizations may reasonably be expected to take different amounts of time for core tasks.

General Findings of Empirical Research

Given the widespread use of similar measures in public administration red tape empirical research, we are able to assess some general conclusions and findings from this work. As noted in Table 4.4, red tape has been used as an independent variable to predict a number of dependent variables, such as worker alienation and motivation and organizational goals, effectiveness, and performance. Research has found that red tape is negatively related to organizational characteristics, such as organizational effectiveness (Pandey, Coursey, and Moynihan 2007) and information technology innovativeness (Moon and Bretschneider 2002). Bozeman and Kingsley (1998) find that red tape is a significant predictor of perception of risk culture—organizations with more red tape tend to have a less risky culture. Red tape is also negatively associated with individual characteristics such as job satisfaction, job

Table 4.4

Dependent Variables Predicted by Red Tape

Dependent variables	Citation
Alienation	DeHart-Davis and Pandey 2005
Creativity	
Productivity	Feeney and DeHart-Davis 2008
Risk-taking	
Communication performance	Pandey and Garnett 2006
Cutback decision content	Bozeman and Pandey 2003
Information system decision content	
Goals	Lan and Rainey 1992
Authority	
Interest in new technologies	Pandey and Bretschneider 1997
Organizational effectiveness	Pandey, Coursey, and Moynihan 2007
Organizational goal ambiguity	Pandey and Rainey 2006
Organizational performance	Brewer and Walker 2010a; Pandey and Moynihan 2006; Walker and Brewer 2009a
Public service motivation	Moynihan and Pandey 2007b
Research unit performance (publications, patents, reports)	Bozeman and Loveless 1987
Title V overcompliance	DeHart-Davis and Bozeman 2001
Unbureaucratic personality	DeHart-Davis 2007
Web effectiveness	Coursey, Welch, and Pandey 2005
Work motivation	Baldwin 1990

involvement, organizational commitment (DeHart-Davis and Pandey 2005), risk-taking (Feeney and DeHart-Davis 2009), and public service motivation (Moynihan and Pandey 2007b), but positively related to creativity (Feeney and DeHart-Davis 2008). Additionally, red tape is positively correlated with an unbureaucratic personality (DeHart-Davis 2007), but unrelated to intranet reliance or information quality (Welch and Pandey 2007).

While some models using red tape to predict outcomes produce similar results, others have produced contradictory findings. For example, when predicting organizational or agency performance, Brewer and Selden (2000) find that perceptions of red tape have no effect on agency performance. On the other hand, Pandey and Moynihan (2006), using four regression models, find that red tape negatively effects performance. Walker and Brewer (2008) argue that red tape has both positive and negative effects on government performance, noting that different dimensions of red tape differently affect performance. They find that internal red tape generally lowers governmental performance, especially personnel red tape, but that external red tape does not lower government performance measured as customer satisfaction or value for money. In fact, they find that external red tape can have positive effects on stakeholder views of quality and equity (Walker and Brewer 2008).

These contradictory findings may be related to measurement error, bias, or misuse of definitions. Unfortunately, because public administration researchers are not in the habit of assessing their measures, there is no current research aimed at determining whether the contradictory findings are a result of a gap in theory of measurement error and bias.

Empirical Measurement and Implications

In this chapter we have discussed two common measures used to assess red tape, self-reported assessments and administrative delay. Social science research often involves measuring abstract constructs by assigning numbers and values to the phenomenon under study. In assessing red tape perceptions through scales, either to a single global measure or a set of items used to construct an index, these measures must meet a certain level of reliability and validity in order to advance theory testing and development. Self-reported assessments of perceived red tape and administrative delay seek to operationalize red tape based on Bozeman's theory of red tape defined as "rules, regulations and procedures that remain in force and entail a compliance burden but do not advance the legitimate purposes the rules were intended to serve" (Bozeman 2000, 12). In general, whether using self-reported assessments of perceived red tape or measures of task delays, these methods rely on a shared set of assumptions. First, the measures assume that respondents can accurately assess red tape and delays. Second, the measures assume that respondents are noting red tape and delays that serve no functional purpose for the organization. Unfortunately, without tests of reliability and validity, there is no way to know that these are indeed cases of red tape and not just rules and regulations perceived as inconvenient by the respondent, but useful for some other purpose such as legal compliance, transparency, or oversight.

Reliability refers to the consistency of measures and the degree to which a measure is repeatable. Reliability is estimated through testing and retesting or based on internal consistency. The best method for testing a measure's reliability is to test and retest the measure. By testing correlations between the measure on test one with the measure on test two, researchers can assess change in the underlying condition. There is no evidence of this type of reliability test in the red tape research, most likely because there is no example of red tape empirical research using data derived from a measurement instrument that has been administered in two time periods.

The second method for estimating reliability is internal consistency. Researchers can estimate reliability by grouping questions that measure the red tape concept in a single questionnaire. The researcher then tests the reliability of these questions by correlating the responses to the survey items to determine if the items are reliably measuring the concept. Within the empirical red tape research, measures for the PRT Scale represent one of the best examples of using internal consistency to estimate reliability. A number of research papers have found significant, strong correlations between the items used to capture personnel red tape (see Chen and Williams 2007; DeHart-Davis and Pandey 2005; Feeney and Rainey 2010; Walker and Brewer 2009b). Empirical red tape research regularly uses correlation analysis and Cronbach's alpha to estimate the reliability of questionnaire items measuring red tape concepts. Using internal consistency to estimate measure reliability in red tape research is most likely more commonly used because public administration researchers rely heavily on single-time, self-administered surveys.

Measurement validity refers to the extent to which survey items and indicators actually measure what they aim to measure. In this case, are the General Organizational Red Tape Scale, the PRT Scale, and management subsystem items measuring red tape? How do researchers know, or verify, that respondents indicating red tape levels and perceptions are indeed guided by the underlying concept of red tape? For example, when a respondent indicates that the overall level of red tape in her organization is "3," is she responding with regard to true red tape, the overall level of formalization in her organization, or the amount of red tape in her work unit? It is conceivable that there is unreported red tape in her organization or red tape that she has not encountered and therefore the true level of red tape is "7."

To date, there are no experiments, tests, or methodological studies aiming to assess the content validity of common red tape measures. Similarly, because there is little longitudinal research or study of red tape over time in public administration, there is no research investigating the criterion-related validity of red tape measures, be it concurrent or predictive. This fact might be the result of a lack of interest in measurement refinement among red tape researchers or the result of a dearth of these types of studies in the public administration field (Wright, Manigault, and Black 2004).[3] However, on a more positive note, we do have some level of "consensual validity" for the aforementioned red tape measures, since numerous scholars have accepted these measures as valid and have adopted them in their own work (Kellough 1998; Meier and Brudney 1993). We also know that red tape survey items have a high level of stability as they have been used in a variety of samples and resulted in relatively stable and consistent findings.

As with all research that relies on respondent perceptions, most public administration red tape research assumes that respondents understand the terms to which they are responding. Moreover, self-assessments of red tape and reporting of time delays rely on subjective survey responses (e.g., Likert scale responses of agreement) or respondents' ability to recall time allocations (e.g., time it takes to hire or procure supplies). The reliance on self-reported survey data limits the lens through which red tape is assessed. Employees may view performance reports as red tape, especially if they do not see a direct relationship between their performance and reward systems. However, that performance report may be a useful tool for some other member of the organization. Surveys prevent researchers from understanding how one person's red tape is another person's source of critical information.

One worker's red tape might indeed be another worker's appropriate rule. One employee's administrative delay may be another employee's oversight mechanism. We, of course, accept that one's perceptions of red tape are claims from that person's point of view. After all, social scientists agree that human research subjects (in this case human survey respondents) report their views based on perception, context, and past experiences. Certainly the messiness of social science is no reason to give up trying to measure and understand red tape in organizations. This is why theory development and testing in the social sciences requires extensive testing—enter the *law of large numbers*. "The law of large numbers suggests that when a measurement is too imperfect for our taste, we should not stop measuring. Quite the opposite—we should measure again and again until niggling imperfections yield to the onslaught of data" (Gilbert 2005, 77). We need multiple surveys of rules and red tape and numerous researchers working with a plethora of datasets to run sundry models to test hypotheses about red tape. Large numbers enable us to remedy many of the problems inherent in subjective human experiences.

Red tape research offers one of the best examples of cumulative empirical research in the young field of public administration. As noted in previous chapters, since 1993 red tape researchers have collected data on hundreds of respondents at multiple levels of government and in the private for-profit and not-for-profit sectors in order to test a wide array of hypotheses. Repeated application and testing of red tape measures have furthered the reliability of these measures. Even if the General Organization Red Tape Scale does not perfectly capture the concept of organizational red tape, the repeated application and consistent findings related to this measure demonstrate the reduction of measurement error. Developing reliable social science measures for concepts requires repeated testing. Red tape measures are one of the best examples of repeated empirical testing of public administration theory. For example, if public administration researchers, using multiple instruments, datasets, and modeling techniques (simple cross-tabulations, analysis of variance, ordinary least squares regression analysis, and two-stage least squares), consistently find that public managers report significantly higher levels of organizational red tape, personnel red tape, and administrative delay as compared to private for-profit and private not-for-profit sector respondents, then we see that those consistent perceptions must be indicating some level of reality.

Moreover, despite the limitations of perceptual measures, perceptions, whether or not they are true, realistic, and consistent, affect behavior and individual actions and relationships (Buckley and Chapman 1997; Lord and Maher 1993; O'Connor, Bord, and Fisher 1999). If public managers perceive high levels of red tape in their respective organizations and private managers in comparison perceive lower levels of red tape, does it matter if those perceptions are inaccurate? Surely if managers perceive red tape, their behavior is shaped by that perception. They are either encouraged to develop creative approaches to navigating around those perceived barriers or they are discouraged and make no attempt at all. The law of large numbers, along with the assortment of red tape empirical research published in the last twenty years, leads us to conclude that empirical red tape research, while certainly not perfect nor ideal, has advanced our knowledge and understanding of red tape.

The field of public administration has struggled with measurement and development of empirical research for a few decades. As noted by Wright, Manigault, and Black (2004), a number of studies have raised concerns about the quality of quantitative research in public administration, suggesting that

> the vast majority of students are neither guided by an explicit theoretical or conceptual framework (Adams and White 1994) nor engaged in hypothesis testing or theory development (Houston and Delevan, 1990, 1994; McCurdy and Cleary 1984; Perry and Kraemer 1986; Stallings and Ferris 1988) and, generally, are characterized by an infrequent use of sophisticated research designs (Houston and Delevan 1990, 1991, 1994; Perry and Kraemer 1986) and inappropriate or flawed statistical techniques. (Cozzetto 1994; Wright, Manigault, and Black 2004, 748)

While it is true that public administration has labored with these issues, we believe that red tape is one of the best examples of the field using empirical research to test hypotheses and test theory. Many of the red tape papers reviewed in this chapter do test hypotheses and are situated with reflection on Bozeman's theory of red tape. While there has been a growth in the amount of red tape research published in public administration journals in the past two decades, much of this research is distant from the theory it aims to test. While researchers cite Bozeman's theory and definition of red tape, there are few examples of an instrument specifically designed to test this theory. For example, we find no peer-reviewed publication citing a research design that collected data in order to answer questions about rules born bad and rule-evolved red tape or assessing the origins of red tape through the creation and implementation of rules. It is also true that many of the methods are less sophisticated than ideal, but recent publications have moved toward structural equation modeling and more appropriate methods. We see a great deal of promise for the future of red tape empirical research and theory development.

Understanding red tape is important. Making organizations more efficient, speeding delays, and removing barriers to managers' work are important. Dealing with the challenges that result from red tape requires understanding red tape. Given the importance of understanding red tape, it would be nice to say precisely what red tape is and how we might measure it. We have a theory that outlines what red tape is. Now we need to continue working on how we might best measure red tape. This chapter discusses the wide array of empirical research that has operationalized red tape measures. Now that we are nearing the "onslaught of data" about red tape, it is important to return to the question of how to best measure and account for red tape as it relates to theory.

One of the first steps in moving from lots of surveys and measures to a strong empirical basis for theory development is the pursuit of psychometric studies. For example, red tape measures require a test of reliability, where data are collected over time, with the intent of cross-validating the measures. For example, Kim (2009) recently collected two independent samples of Korean civil servants in order to validate, reduce, and cross-validate Perry's PSM factor structure. Similarly, red tape scales and measures require longitudinal data to test for cross-validation and reliability. Red tape researchers also need to implement red tape scales and measures in more international contexts, to better understand the reliability of red tape measures across cultures and nationalities. Finally, theory development requires research designs that move beyond surveys. Only when we have a stronger sense of the validity and reliability of these empirical measures will public researchers be able to use empirical methods to test, advance, or refute red tape theory.

Notes

1. This is probably less likely the result of a lack of interest in comparative red tape studies, but the result of public administration research being predominantly conducted within national frameworks. A common criticism of the public administration field is the lack of comparative work (Hou 2006; Straussman and Zhang 2001; Tsui 2006; Welch and Wong 1998). One recent publication (Kim 2009) makes a first step in testing whether empirical measurements developed in U.S. public administration (PSM in this case) can be generalized to other nations (Korea).

2. Phase 1 of NASP I: A consortium of researchers at the University of Denver, Florida State University, the University of Georgia, The Ohio State University, and Syracuse University. Data were collected in Colorado, Florida, and New York from both senior and midlevel managers in the public, private, and nonprofit sectors. The NASP projects are discussed extensively in later chapters.

3. Our search for published peer-reviewed journal articles addressing reliability and validity measures in public administration research turned up a handful of such papers: Kellough's "Reliability, validity, and the MV index: Toward the clarification of some fundamental issues" (1998); Perry's "Measuring public service motivation: An assessment of construct reliability and validity" (1996); Kim's "Revising Perry's measurement scale of public service motivation" (2009); and Coursey and colleagues' "Psychometric verification of Perry's public service motivation instrument: Results for volunteer exemplars" (2008).

5

Contracting and Performance

In the 1996 State of the Union address, when President Bill Clinton declared the end of "the era of big government," he failed to note that he and others had ushered in the era of "government by contract." As Presidents Bush and Obama executed the Iraq War (Feeney 2008), we began to see that the single policy realm most often cited as a "pure public good," national defense, was no less subject to privatization and contracting than were other government functions.

According to Paul Light, although there were just under 4.3 million full-time permanent civilian federal workers in the federal government in 1996, there were approximately 6 million jobs created through federal contracts, 2.4 million jobs by federal grants, and nearly 4.7 million jobs through state, county, and municipal government mandates (Light 1999, 1). Light argues that governments throughout the United States have engaged in strong efforts to push jobs and activities outside of government and into the "shadow of government," creating "illusions of capacity and accountability" (2).

As a research field tied closely to practice, public administration scholarship often responds to trends in government practice. During the past two decades, public administration research has taken a growing interest in understanding contracting and performance management. As federal, state, and local governments become more and more experienced with contracting out goods and services, public administration scholars have responded by engaging in research to understand the ways in which contracting trends affect nearly all aspects of public management, including human resources (Fernandez, Rainey, and Lowman 2006; Hays and Sowa 2006), politics and patronage (Feeney and Kingsley 2008), efficiency, effectiveness, and service quality (O'Toole and Meier 2004; Provan and Milward 1995, 2001a; Sclar

2000), managerial capacity (Agranoff and McGuire 1999, 2001a; Brown and Potoski 2003, 2006; Chinowsky et al. 2003; Donohue and Selden 2000; Ponomariov and Kingsley 2006), policy processes and implementation (Hall and O'Toole 2000), and interorganizational networks (Isett and Provan 2005; Provan, Isett, and Milward 2004).

Accompanying contract trends has been a spate of management reforms adopted in government and studied by public administration scholars. While managing for results, performance-based budgeting, and other performance-based management trends are certainly not new, the more recent performance trend in the United States finds its roots in the Government Performance and Results Act (GPRA) of 1993. Under the leadership of then Vice President and former U.S. Senator Al Gore, GPRA aimed to improve the effectiveness, efficiency, and accountability of federal programs by requiring agencies to focus their management practices on results, outcomes, and goal achievement. Essentially, GPRA sought to enable the Office of Management and Budget (OMB), Congress, and the executive agencies to tie government achievements to spending. GPRA required that agencies develop a strategic plan, outline missions, long-term goals, and objectives, and formulate strategies for achieving these goals. Moreover, as of 1999, GPRA required that agencies produce publicly reported annual performance plans that measured progress toward annual and long-term goals.

As noted in government reports (U.S. GAO 2001) and academic research (Moynihan 2006), GPRA came with a number of challenges, including instilling a culture of results orientation; ensuring that agency operations contribute to results; understanding the performance consequences of budget decisions; coordinating cross-cutting programs; and building capacity to gather and use performance information. GRPA represented the start of sweeping changes in the federal government and later state and local governments and managers, and in return academic researchers sought to understand the ways in which this new emphasis on performance would alter public administration and management. New research has investigated the outcomes of pay for performance (Kellough and Nigro 2002), performance in the age of contracting (Milward 1996), and the affects of performance standards (Heckman, Heinrich, and Smith 1997).

Thus, as government management and administration have shifted toward concern with contracting, performance measurement, and accountability, public administration research agendas have followed along. The study of red tape is one of the many fields affected by "government by contract" as researchers have sought to understand the ways in which red tape impedes, facilitates, and moderates government contracting activities and performance and the ways in which contracting either reduces or exacerbates red tape. This chapter reviews recent red tape research on contracting and performance.

Contracting

Since 1980, one of the primary shifts in public administration in the United States, Europe, Australia, and Asia has been the growth of privatization and, more specifically, contracting out. In this era of contracting out, there is a growing need to understand the relationship between contract management and red tape and how contracting may serve to reduce or increase red tape. It is conceivable that contracting out of services lowers red tape as it shifts management to a private or nonprofit organization that is free from the personnel constraints of public organizations—a primary source of red tape. For example, in the United States, the political right argues that remedies to red tape include deregulation, asset sale and leases, and competitive contracting and privatization of public services. On the other hand, it is possible that contracts add an additional layer of reporting, accountability, and paperwork to public organizations and the provision of public goods and services and thus serve to expand red tape.

E.S. Savas's *Privatizing the Public Sector* (1982) provides a good introduction to prescriptions that flow from privatization and the alleged benefits of privatization that influenced the policies of the Reagan administration and subsequent efforts to outsource public services in the United States. Since 1982, as the movement to privatize and outsource has moved from the federal government to state and local governments, public administration research on privatization and contracting out has expanded to test the efficiency of privatization (Brown and Brudney 1998; Donahue 1989; Osborne and Gaebler 1993; Vickers and Yarrow 1991), the ethics of outsourcing public goods and services (Beck Jorgensen 1993), the challenges and effects of managing contracts (DeHart-Davis and Pandey 2005; Meier and O'Toole 2002), the personnel effects of outsourcing (Fernandez, Rainey, and Lowman 2006; Hays and Sowa 2006; Walters 2002), and the transaction costs associated with outsourcing (Agranoff and McGuire 2001a; Brown and Potoski 2003, 2006; Provan 1993; Williamson 1999). Suffice to say, the privatization movement of the past three decades has resulted in a growing interest in efficiency, contracting, and performance measurement among public administration scholars.

Despite the near geometric growth in public sector contracting literature, only a small fraction addresses the issue of red tape. Johnston and Romzek (1999) note that contracting out to nonprofit organizations may not only reduce the size and scope of government, but ensure that service delivery occurs through organizations that have less red tape and fewer hierarchical accountability relationships as compared to larger government organizations. Johnston and Romzek go on to note that "contracting with nongovernment entities has important implications for accountability because such a process may increase services but dilute government control and accountability" (387) because some government rules and regulations, though often perceived as red tape, are intended to ensure control and accountability. But, of course, inappropriate accountability relationships (Johnston and Romzek 1999) and incorrect rule forecasts and misguided overcontrol (Bozeman and DeHart-Davis 1999) might be the basis for red tape, in particular rule-inception red tape.

The red tape studies that deal with contracting often do so as part of other foci. Although some red tape studies mention contracting (Bozeman and Kingsley 1998), interview contractors (Bozeman and DeHart-Davis 1999), and control for levels of contracting in the organization (Welch and Pandey 2007), only a handful focus directly on red tape associated with contracting (DeHart-Davis 2000; Feeney and Bozeman 2009).

It is not difficult to see the relation of red tape scholars' core concerns to contracting. If we return to Bozeman's (2000) theory of red tape (see Figure 3.1 in Chapter 3), we can identify some propositions about the ways in which contracting trends might affect red tape and vice versa. In fact, it is easy to see how contracting out can result in both rule-inception red tape and rule-evolved red tape. Rule-inception red tape may occur because of privatization efforts and outsourcing of government functions and service delivery. We can easily imagine how the process of developing a call for proposal, sifting through applications, choosing a contractor, and finalizing a contract could lend itself to the creation of rules that are counterproductive or do not advance the interests of the public agency. Second, red tape can emerge from efforts to implement rules and regulations about contracting and adjust those rules to address specific cases and instances. Third, contracting red tape may differently affect organizational members and stakeholders.

Bozeman's theory of red tape notes the importance of understanding red tape and the ways in which it may or may not differently affect organizational clients, leadership, members, and affiliates. Bozeman proposes that stakeholders—clients, public managers, and the contractors with which they work—will hold divergent views of red tape and its consequences.

The modest literature on red tape and contracting falls into one or both of two categories: (1) research that investigates red tape associated with procurement and contracting processes (e.g., paperwork and time delays) and (2) red tape associated with contracting relationships (e.g., relationships between principals and agents). The first set of research relies on measures of red tape associated with procurement and contracting activities. Bozeman and Kingsley's (1998) tests of risk culture and red tape do not directly test relationships between contracting and red tape, but they do note that contracting can result in increased time spent completing tasks, which can contribute to red tape. Bozeman and Kingsley test a model of the relationship between the dependent variable, risk culture, and the following independent variables:

1. Total Time   Time in weeks taken by the organization to complete core managerial processes, including hiring, firing, buying equipment, reorganizing, starting a new project, and contracting out

2. Procedures   "When a situation arises, we have procedures to follow in dealing with it."
Scale: 1 = strong agreement, 4 = strong disagreement

3. Rule Conform   "In this organization, conformance to rules and procedures is very important."
Scale: 1 = strong agreement, 4 = strong disagreement

4. Rule Watch   "People here feel as though they are constantly being watched to see they obey all the rules."
Scale: 1 = strong agreement, 4 = strong disagreement

5. Red Tape   "If red tape is defined as burdensome administrative rules and procedures that have negative effects on the organization's effectiveness, how would you assess the level of red tape in your organization?"
Scale 1–10; 1 = strong disagreement, 10 = strong agreement

Although Bozeman and Kingsley do not discuss the red tape and the delays specifically associated with contracting out, they do include a survey item that recognizes that contracting out is a task that can be associated with delays in organizational managerial processes.

Another red tape study acknowledges the growing role of contractors in public administration and the red tape they may experience interacting with public agencies. In their analysis of the red tape associated with rule-inception in Title V of the 1990 Clean Air Act Amendments, Bozeman and DeHart-Davis (1999) interviewed multiple stakeholders, including private contractors. Bozeman and DeHart-Davis note that industrial consulting firms are contracted to compile "turnkey" permit applications and that these contracts, since they are awarded based on market competition among consultants, provide a valid reflection of the true costs of the regulations. Although Bozeman and DeHart-Davis were not focused on red tape associated with contracting or the role of contractors in creating or reducing red tape, this paper is one of the few that notes the role of these important stakeholders. More detail is provided in DeHart-Davis's dissertation (2000), "Environmental Permit Costs: The Roles of Red Tape, Communications, Experience and Subcontracting," which directly assesses the role of red tape in subcontracting.

In their study of e-government and bureaucracy, which tests the bidirectional relationships between intranet usage and the reduction of red tape, Welch and Pandey (2007) include two control variables that account for contracting influences as exogenous variables to the model. The variables are "Government Contracting Influences" and "Business Contracting Influences," indicating the percentage of total budget spent on contracts for goods and services with government and private organizations, respectively. Welch and Pandey hypothesize that higher levels of contracting will be related to higher reliance by organizations on intranet technologies and to manager activities associated with procurement. The models tested in this paper do not support the hypothesis. Welch and Pandey conclude that business and government contracting has no effect on intranet reliance or quality. It is possible that these findings are the result of a lack of relationship or data limitations, since the National Administrative Studies Project (NASP II) relies on responses from similar agencies, which are less likely to have varying levels of contracting.

Cardiff University's Centre for Local and Regional Government Research administered a survey in 2004 asking authority employees about their organization's performance, factors affecting the authority, the authority's approach to Best Value reforms, and individual respondent characteristics. This survey asked respondents about red tape in their organizations, including the General Red Tape (GRT) Scale, rules associated with removing poorly performing employees and rewarding good managers, and the responsiveness of administrative rules and procedures to stakeholder interaction. Although the study did not ask specifically about red tape associated with contracting, the survey did ask if contracting out and outsourcing were a major part of the approach to organization adopted in the respondent's authority (see Appendix 6 for more detail about the English Local Government study of Best Value).

The second research approach investigates red tape in contracting relationships. Feeney and Bozeman (2009) present this work using survey data from public managers and the contractors with whom they work. Feeney and Bozeman's analysis of red tape in contracting was the result of a study of contracting at the Georgia Department of Transportation (GDOT). The researchers asked both sets of respondents about red tape in their respective organizations and about red tape associated with their interactions. The researchers proposed the following hypotheses:

H1: Public managers will perceive higher levels of organizational red tape in the government agency compared to private managers' perceptions of red tape in private consulting firms.
H2: Compared to public managers, private consultants will perceive higher levels of contracting red tape.

Their results support the first hypothesis, but not the second. They conclude that public managers perceive significantly higher levels of organizational red tape as compared to private managers, but that the two groups report similar levels of red tape in their contracting relationships. In addition to this simple comparison of the ways in which contractors and public managers perceive general organizational and contracting red tape, the authors also investigate the ways in which red tape perceptions vary across contracting relationships, by testing hypotheses about the amount of time spent communicating, doing paperwork, and working with government contracts. They find that public managers' red tape perceptions are related to the amount of time they spend managing and communicating with consultants, while consultants' red tape perceptions are associated with the number of years the firm has worked with the agency and the proportion of cost-plus contracts at the firm.

Performance

As noted in the introduction to this chapter, the performance movement in the United States and abroad gathered momentum in the 1990s under the leadership of the Clinton-Gore administration. One might argue that the dominant theme in public administration in the 1990s was performance; certainly performance measurement was one of the core components of public management reforms, in particular what became known as New Public Management (Behn 2001; Kettl and Diulio 1995; Pollitt and Bouckaert 2000). Subsequent to the GPRA and the shifting culture of performance management in the United States, although little research focused specifically on understanding the connections between red tape and performance, researchers did note that rather than freeing managers to concentrate on results, many of the GPRA requirements increased constraints on managers (Mintzberg 1996; Radin 2006). Radin (2006) argues we are in a "performance movement" and that this movement is not relegated to the U.S. experience alone (Forbes and Lynn 2005; Grossi and Mussari 2008).

Because performance management is a multilevel and cross-level phenomenon (DeNisi 2000) and programs are increasingly administered through complex decentralized governance structures, including networks and collaborations (Lynn, Heinrich, and Hill 2008), it is easy to see how red tape can emerge from these types of reforms.

At the organizational level and at the individual level, performance is a key component of public administration and public management scholarship and practice. For scholars, performance is critical for understanding the mechanisms that make organizations and individuals effective and efficient. For practitioners, monitoring performance is dictated through legislation such as the GPRA of 1993, the National Performance Review, the more recent Program Assessment Rating Tool (PART), and the numerous evaluations and reviews individuals encounter throughout their working careers.

The performance literature spans numerous topics in the public administration literature and includes different terms and foci in its many guises, including organizational performance, performance budgeting, public service performance, performance management, government performance, performance indicators, bureaucratic performance, job performance, performance-based accountability, performance-based budgeting, performance-contingent pay, and performance auditing. Boyne (2002) identifies five themes of performance in public organizations: outputs, efficiency, effectiveness, responsiveness, and democratic outcomes. Public management and public managers help to shape organizational performance, and therefore the delivery of public services and organizational performance is one of the four most important themes in public administration and public policy communities, along with public management practice, acceptance of a distinction between public and private organizations, and a focus on multiorganizational issues (Pitts and Fernandez 2007, 4).

In their review of conference papers presented at the Sixth, Seventh, and Eighth Public Management Research Conferences (PMRC), Pitts and Fernandez (2007, 15) find that although there is a "*practical* emphasis on performance issues at all levels of government, the [public management] research literature does not appear to be too narrowly focused on this area." They find that one-third (32.4 percent, $N = 61$) of PMRC papers focused primarily on performance and that one-third of those performance-focused papers were presented at the 2001 conference. The authors suspect that the decline in performance-focused papers after 2001 is a sign of fatigue with the "strong emphasis on Reinventing Government and New Public Management in the late 1990s and early 2000s" (14). They also note that this decline in performance-focused research might be associated with measurement problems. However, when we expand our search from the narrow field of public management research to public administration research, including personnel research, we find an abundance of performance literature, including a journal dedicated to the study of performance, *Public Performance and Management Review*.

Another indicator of the influence of the performance literature is citation rates. By this measure, performance studies are more influential than most other areas of public administration scholarship. We searched major public administration journals in the ISI Web of Science, using the search term "performance" and limiting the findings to only those papers that explicitly name performance in the title of the paper and are published in journals classified as "Public Administration."[1] We found that between 1994 and 2009 there were

Table 5.1

Public Administration Publications With "Performance" in the Title, 1994–2009

Year	Count	Year	Count	Year	Count	Year	Count
2009	36	2005	26	2001	20	1997	15
2008	36	2004	25	2000	24	1996	19
2007	36	2003	20	1999	12	1995	23
2006	30	2002	25	1998	19	1994	4

Source: ISI Web of Science. Search criteria of: TI = Performance, Years 1994–2009, Public Administration. Search conducted on August 17, 2009.

370 research papers published that have "performance" in the title. Between 2000 and 2005 alone, there were 140 research papers published (see Table 5.1). This is a conservative estimate, since we did not consider papers that may name "performance" in the abstract or focus on performance within the analysis and text of the paper.

In summary, performance is a key topic of public administration research and an important focus in public management research. However, we note that although many real government reforms have aimed to reduce red tape, both in the United States (Gore 1993; Osborne and Gaebler 1993) and abroad (Blair 2002; Gershon 2004; Office of Public Service Reform 2002), there is little theory aimed at understanding the relationships between red tape and performance. This disconnect is so important that Rainey and Steinbauer (1999) refer to the lack of tests on red tape on organizational performance as the elephant in the room.

One might well expect that red tape research and theory should be intimately entwined with the performance of both individuals and organizations. Red tape may impede individual success within an organization or force individual employees to spend time working on excessive paperwork and tasks that serve no functional purpose but to delay efficiency and reduce performance. High levels of red tape in organizations might result in systemic negative effects on performance. Furthermore, performance-centered reforms and policies such as performance-based budgeting may create additional layers of red tape. Unfortunately, the scholarly work connecting red tape research and performance research is limited and overwhelmingly comes from the side of red tape research (e.g., Pandey, Coursey, and Moynihan 2007; Pandey and Moynihan 2006), rather than the performance literature (e.g., Brewer and Selden 2000).

Within the red tape literature, Pandey, Coursey, and Moynihan (2007) offer one of the only models for testing the effects of red tape on organizational effectiveness—an important model that brings together two significant areas of research in the public management literature. They argue that red tape is directly related to organizational effectiveness and that the organization's culture can moderate the impact of red tape on performance. The authors assert that the lack of empirical research testing the relationships between red tape and performance is the direct outcome of the focus on red tape research testing for sector differences. They propose that red tape research and theory has reached a maturity level that warrants shifting "from whether public organizations have more red tape" than private organizations, which research supports, to understanding "how organizations might overcome red tape" (400). Other researchers (Brewer and Walker 2010a; Walker and Brewer 2009a) have joined Pandey and his colleagues' call for additional research focusing on red tape and performance.

Recent work by Brewer and Walker (2009a, 2010a) has aimed at understanding the relationships of red tape to government performance and service delivery. Walker and Brewer (2009b) note that the United Kingdom (UK), like the United States, has targeted red tape as a prime source of inefficiency in public organizations. Leadership in the UK, first the Conservative Party and then the Labour Party, has defined red tape, respectively, as the state and institutional controls that prevent efficiency and warrant the introduction of market mechanisms and as "bad rules" that prevent street-level bureaucrats from delivering services effectively and thus advancing public service.

In an effort to reduce these "bad rules," under the leadership of the Labour administration in 1997, the national government created the Better Regulation Executive (BRE) to work "with government departments and regulators to scrutinize new policy proposals; achieve effective new regulations; make it easier to change or remove regulation, where beneficial; reduce existing regulatory burdens affecting business, the third sector and frontline staff in the public sector; improving transparency and accountability for regulation; effectively communicate regulatory changes; and drive forward the better regulation agenda in Europe."[2] This mission statement clearly aims to prevent what Bozeman (2000) calls "rules born bad" by scrutinizing new regulations and to eliminate rules gone bad by making it easier to change or remove ineffective or inefficient regulations. The efforts of the BRE also aim to address red tape external to government agencies (e.g., regulatory requirements) and internal red tape (e.g., unnecessary and wasteful bureaucracy and internal reporting rules and regulations) as the means to improving public service and performance.

The British government argues that reducing regulation and red tape will benefit businesses, public servants, and the public. The BRE serves businesses by reducing the administrative burden of filling out forms, reporting activities, and complying with inspections, improves the work life of public servants by enabling them to serve the public with reduced demands for reporting and unnecessary paperwork, and enables consumers (citizens) to better consume, process, and understand information generated through government regulation and reporting requirements (e.g., food and drug safety information). As these reforms have begun to take effect in the UK, public administration researchers have taken a particular interest in understanding the impacts of such reforms. Specifically, a team of researchers at the Centre for Local and Regional Government Research at Cardiff University was commissioned by the Office of the Deputy Prime Minister to evaluate the impact of Best Value and Core Performance Assessment (CPA), an effort of the English government to measure perfomance and reward and punish local authorities, on service improvement in local authorities. The study began in 2001 and included administering electronic surveys to English local authorities through 2004. The survey explored informants' perceptions of organization and management, notably culture, structure, strategy-making, and strategy content, together with drivers of service improvement, background variables, and "Best Value." As a result of this commissioned work, researchers have published several interesting academic papers proposing and testing hypotheses about the relationships between red tape, efficiency, and organizational and managerial performance.

Using data from this English study, Walker and Brewer (2009b) find that public managers in different services and program areas report variance in their perceptions of red tape, thus supporting the idea of stakeholder red tape and the role of service area as a determinant of red tape perceptions. They also find that changes in the external environment affect levels of reported red tape. These two findings, taken together, reinforce the relationship between red tape and performance and point to the importance of understanding how red tape in varying situations can differently affect service delivery. Walker and Brewer (2009b) test a series of hypotheses to understand how policies, programs, and managerial behavior can reduce red tape and thus improve performance and service delivery. They find that integration programs that aim to change an organization's internal structures and procedures are an effective means for reducing red tape. They note that integration (e.g., National Performance Review in the United States and Best Value in the UK) is one of the easiest reform tools available to public organizations seeking to reduce red tape and improve service delivery.

In addition to their research on red tape and service delivery, Brewer and Walker (2010a) take on the larger performance issues of quality, efficiency, customer satisfaction, and citizen perceptions of value for money. Brewer and Walker argue that the relationships between red tape and quality, efficiency, effectiveness, responsiveness, and equity are five key components of the multidimensional concept of government performances. The authors surveyed corporate and service-level respondents working in English local government delivering multiple services to develop aggregated data at the authority level. The unit of analysis is the authority—a representative sample of local governments—not the individual respondents. This approach has the advantage of providing responses that are an organizational mean of corporate and service officers. One of the most interesting findings of Brewer and Walker's analysis is that "external red tape measure is positive, suggesting that some degree of external red tape has a positive effect on performance" (2010a, 15). If the external red tape (or whatever external regulations and rules are being captured in this measure of red tape) is in fact improving the performance of the organization, one is left to wonder if this is indeed red tape.

Some studies examine the relation of red tape to particular types of performance. Welch and Pandey (2006), testing for relationships between red tape and intranet reliance and quality, find that neither general red tape nor procurement red tape affects intranet reliance or intranet information quality. In contrast, they also find that higher intranet reliance leads to lower red tape, thus pointing to an important prescription for reducing red tape and ultimately, one would hope, improving performance. Furthering the hypothesis that reduced red tape improves performance, Pandey, Coursey, and Moynihan (2007) find that red tape in information systems negatively affects organizational effectiveness.

Pandey, Coursey, and Moynihan (2007) present a series of hypotheses about the relationships between organization effectiveness and five dimensions of red tape, including procurement red tape, budgeting red tape, personnel red tape, information systems red tape, and red tape in communication. The research investigates how the relationships between these types of red tape and organizational effectiveness are mitigated by organizational culture, if at all. The authors offer some qualitative data and elements of their interview data in order to capture a detailed understanding of how respondents define red tape and thus develop a starting point for parsing out the exact rules, regulations, and red tape to which respondents refer. For example, the respondents describe information systems and procurement red tape when there is a "lack of uniformity in the contracting process" (412) or when divisions within an agency have "different standards" and "don't talk with one another" (413). Are these mismatches in systems really red tape, or do the differing systems serve an administrative purpose of which the respondent is unaware? The inability of an agency to create a relational database or share client or contractor information across units may be a barrier that is intended to protect individuals or groups. The use of interviews to decipher the meaning in respondents' use of terms such as "red tape," "performance," and "efficiency" are important, but also it is indicative of Kaufman's maxim that "one man's red tape is another's treasured procedural safeguard" (Kaufman 1977). While Pandey, Coursey, and Moynihan (2007) offer an important finding about the negative effect of human resources red tape and information systems red tape on organizational effectiveness, it remains important for researchers to aim to understand if perceived red tape is indeed red tape, a barrier to effectiveness, or a service to some other important public goal or value not perceived by the respondent. This dilemma relates to the investigation of stakeholder red tape.

Stakeholder Red Tape

One important area of red tape research that ties performance to Bozeman's red tape theory is research investigating stakeholder red tape. However, very little research focuses on stakeholder red tape. Bozeman (2000) defines stakeholder red tape as a " rule that remains in force and entails a compliance burden, but serves no objective valued by a given stakeholder group" (83) and notes that stakeholder red tape "assumes that a rule may be red tape for one set of stakeholders, but functional for another" (82). Bozeman proposes that red tape is important to understand as subject-dependent because this approach can enable researchers to understand the complex relationships within organizations that might lead to red tape, run up against red tape, or oppose red tape. Unfortunately, our ability to understand and empirically test hypotheses about stakeholder red tape is complicated by the nature of measuring subject-dependent concepts. It is obvious why measuring and assessing subject-dependent red tape is a daunting task for researchers. First, it is virtually impossible to predict the outcomes of rules on diverse sets of stakeholders (Bozeman 2000, 83). Second, when stakeholders are asked to rate the level of red tape in the organization or a particular task within the organization (e.g., hiring new employees, managing contracts), it is difficult or impossible for social scientists to truly know if the internal stakeholders (agency employees) and the external stakeholders (clients or contractors) are accurately assessing the level of red tape or even if their relative assessments are valid and reliable.

The validity and reliability of red tape assessments is one of the fundamental challenges of this work and of much of social science research assessing perceptions. For example, Feeney and Bozeman (2009) asked public managers at the GDOT the following question:

Q. If red tape is defined as "burdensome administrative rules and procedures that have negative impacts on the organization's effectiveness," how would you assess the level of red tape in the contracting relationships between GDOT and private firms? (Please circle the appropriate response.)

Almost No Red Tape										A Great Deal of Red Tape
0	1	2	3	4	5	6	7	8	9	10

The researchers then asked the private consultants that work with GDOT contract managers the following question:

Q. If red tape is defined as "burdensome administrative rules and procedures that have negative impacts on the organization's effectiveness," how would you assess the level of red tape in the contracting relationships between your consulting firm and GDOT? (Please circle the appropriate response.)

Almost No Red Tape										A Great Deal of Red Tape
0	1	2	3	4	5	6	7	8	9	10

These two survey items asking respondents to assess the level of red tape in a contracting relationship suggest that all respondents understand red tape to mean the same thing and that they are equally capable of ranking red tape perceptions on this scale. But if GDOT employees work in an environment in which organizational red tape is extremely high and consultants work in firms where organizational red tape is extremely low, will they be equally able to assess red tape in their contracting relationships? Will the different baselines lead to different responses? Will consultants, with their free-from-red-tape firms, view the contracting relationships as overwhelmed with red tape? Will GDOT employees, oppressed by red tape in their daily work lives, view the contracting relationship as just a normal level of red tape or even possibly a lower level of red tape? Or maybe GDOT employees who have never worked in the private sector do not know what it is like to work in a place free from bureaucratic control and personnel restrictions and paperwork; therefore, they rank the red tape in their organization and in their contracting relationships as quite low—they just do not know anything different. Does it matter that stakeholders have opposing views of the same relationship? Is it important for us to know if one stakeholder has a more reliable or valid response than another? Clearly, relying on respondents' perceptions of a phenomenon or experience makes stakeholder red tape a difficult concept to measure. However, despite this difficulty, it is a useful enough construct to warrant attempts at measurement.

Despite the challenges of operationalizing and measuring stakeholder red tape, some researchers have worked to develop constructs. In one of the earliest attempts to understand whether or not red tape is dependent on one's perspective and if perceptions of red tape vary significantly within and among stakeholders, Bozeman and DeHart-Davis (1999) interviewed numerous stakeholders, including state government officials responsible for designing and implementing Clean Air Act Title V programs, industry personnel, environmental professionals, and firm compliance officers, in order to assess red tape from multiple perspectives. Based on the interview data, they concluded that red tape is more prevalent in complex policy networks. Unfortunately, Bozeman and DeHart-Davis did not empirically test whether red tape is more or less prevalent because of the varying interests of stakeholders or the conflicting perceptions of stakeholders. Furthermore, the researchers did not ask about specific rules, which would have been an opportunity to test for variance in stakeholder perceptions of red tape aimed at the same functional object.

Brewer and Walker (2010b) and Bozeman and Scott (1996) assert that stakeholders' perceptions matter when assessing red tape and that, in some cases, it is important to measure stakeholder red tape. Brewer and Walker (2010b) offer an example of empirical research aimed at testing variance across stakeholders within organizations using a survey of managerial perceptions in English local government. In this case, "stakeholder" is defined as a manager within the agency. The study asks agency respondents at multiple levels of the organization to indicate their perceptions of rules and procedures in the organizations. Unfortunately, the study of English local government focuses on government employees within the organization and does not assess external stakeholders' perspectives (e.g., clients, elected or appointed officials). Like so much of the red tape research discussed in this book, there is no operationalization of survey items that get at specific examples of red tape and stakeholders' experiences navigating that red tape.

Feeney and Bozeman (2009) offer the only example to date of red tape research that tests complementary stakeholders' perceptions of red tape. First, they consider the clear distinctions of organizational culture and function between a public agency and the private firms with which they contract. Second, they consider the strategic motivations and incentives that bring public agencies and private firms into these relationships. The contract between the principal and the agent is laden with threats of information asymmetry, shirking, and challenges to developing and ensuring confidence and trust. In classic, principal-agent relationships, the principal (in this case the agency) develops rules, regulations, and oversight mechanisms to ensure compliance and efficient work of the agents (the contractors). Meanwhile, private firms balance their desire for large state contracts and their ability to suffer under and navigate burdensome rules and regulations. With the case of the GDOT and its consultants, Feeney and Bozeman investigate stakeholder red tape associated with contracting relationships. The authors measure agency managers' perceptions of organizational and contracting red tape and compare those assessments with contractor perceptions of organizational and contracting red tape. Feeney and Bozeman offer one of the only empirical tests comparing red tape perceptions across stakeholders, but still fall victim to the empirical challenges of accurately measuring red tape.

Given the limitations with understanding how stakeholders perceive red tape and if those perceptions are valid and reliable, some researchers have taken a different approach to the concept of stakeholder red tape. Rather than think of stakeholders as the victims of red tape or the agents possibly being ill served by a rule, Welch and Pandey (2007) test the role of stakeholders as creators or enablers of red tape. In their paper examining the effects of intranet implementation on red tape, Welch and Pandey investigate the extent to which external stakeholders, measured as twelve institutions (clients, public opinion, media, business, the state governor, state legislature, agency head, federal courts, state courts, federal agencies, the president, and Congress), influence red tape in the organizations being studied. This study is an important empirical test of stakeholder red tape because it offers one of the first empirical tests of relationships between external stakeholders and red tape and because it is one of just a few studies providing an empirical test of stakeholder effects on "objectively measured" organizational red tape.

In summary, a qualitative study of stakeholder red tape (Bozeman and DeHart-Davis 1999), a study of internal stakeholders' perceptions of red tape (Brewer and Walker 2010b), a study of external stakeholders' perceptions of red tape in contracting (Feeney and Bozeman 2009), and a study of the effects of external stakeholders on red tape (Welch and Pandey 2007) constitute entirely the efforts of public administration and management scholars to test empirically red tape as it is perceived by and affects or is affected by stakeholders. Given the widespread acceptance of the importance of understanding the role of interest groups and competing interests, networks, and stakeholders within the public administration community at large, operationalizing stakeholder red tape is an important task. We propose a simple first step toward better testing respondent conceptions of red tape. First, if red tape is defined as having no benefit, when we ask stakeholders about red tape in their organizations or relationships, are they responding to truly useless rules? Maybe it would be more useful to ask respondents:

Q. If red tape is a rule that remains in force and entails a compliance burden for the organization but makes no contribution to achieving the rule's functional object, is there red tape in your organization? (Check one)

____ No

____ Yes. If yes, please give an example: _____.

Second, researchers can then take the examples provided by respondents and return to the stakeholders in the case and ask them about a set of examples of red tape. Do leaders of the organization and street-level bureaucrats rank each example as red tape? Do minority stakeholders or disadvantaged stakeholders rank the examples as red tape? Do policy-makers, who may have legislated the rule or regulation, perceive it as red tape? Do clients of the organization perceive these items as red tape? Here is one qualitative means of assessing stakeholder red tape. Unfortunately, the empirical research on red tape has failed to test red tape theory in a systematic manner that would elucidate components of the theory, such as rule-inception, rule-evolved, and stakeholder red tape, and their relationship to individual, managerial, and organizational performance.

Concluding Remarks

As described in this chapter, there is a growing interest among red tape researchers in understanding the connections between red tape and contracting and red tape and performance. While there have been important strides in understanding the ways in which red tape affects individual and organizational outcomes, performance, and interactions with contractors, more research is needed. Given the popularity of contracting and performance research in public administration, it is surprising there is not more work investigating the ways in which contracting and performance management are related to red tape and bureaucracy.

Current efforts to understand the relationships between red tape and contracting and performance rely heavily on red tape researchers and their methods and draw less from the wide, more developed performance literature. For example, in their work investigating red tape and performance, Brewer and Walker (2010a, 2010b) have altered the GRT Scale to test for red tape associated with performance. They define red tape as "burdensome rules and procedures that negatively affect *performance*" and then ask respondents their level of agreement (Likert scale of 1 = disagree and 7 = agree) with the following five items:

1. The level of red tape is high in our service/authority.
2. Even if a manager is a poor performer, formal rules make it hard to remove him or her from the organization.
3. The formal pay structures and rules make it hard to reward a good manager with higher pay here.
4. Reorganizing an organizational unit or department can be achieved within two or three weeks in our service/authority.
5. Administrative rules and procedures are open and responsive, allowing stakeholders (users, businesses, government agencies, etc.) to freely interact with our service/authority.

Similarly, Feeney and Bozeman's (2009) assessment of stakeholder red tape in contracting relationships revised the GRT Scale to query respondents about their contracting relationships. To the best of our knowledge, there is no current red tape research that starts from the vantage point of contracting or performance scholarship and seeks to understand red tape from that theoretical perspective. While red tape researchers work to expand their assessments of red tape to understand its effects on and relationship to contracting and performance, it is equally important that public administration scholars and other experts in performance management and contracting research expand their research agendas to test for the role of red tape.

Notes

1. This category includes the following journals (among others): *Administration and Society*; *Journal of Public Administration Research and Theory*; *Journal of Policy Analysis and Management*; *Public Personnel Management*; *Australian Journal of Public Administration*; *International Review of Administrative Sciences*; *Public Management Review*; *Policy Sciences*; *Policy Studies Journal*; *Public Money and Management*; *Public Administration and Development*; *Public Administration*; *Local Government Studies*.

2. National Archives, "About the Better Regulation Executive," August 4, 2008. www.berr.gov.uk/bre/about/page44014.html.

A Research Agenda for Red Tape

What Has Gone Before

Reviewing and synthesizing red tape research has become pleasantly laborious. In the first systematic review of the red tape literature, Bozeman and Scott (1996) cited only twelve empirical research papers, and most of these were concerned not with red tape but with formalization. In previous chapters we have examined nearly 100 empirical studies of red tape, a remarkable growth considering the generally slow pace at which empirical public administration research accumulates. However, as we see in this chapter, previous research is neither deep nor rich enough as to preempt new work. Quite the contrary: red tape research has proved incremental and somewhat repetitive, often examining new variants of old questions. Indeed, the vast majority of red tape research studies can be grouped into just two categories: (1) comparisons of public and private organizations' red tape, and (2) perceptions of red tape and their relation to work attitudes. While these two categories cover a great deal of organizational and management territory, they are far from exhaustive.

One reason for the comparatively narrow range of red tape research is that almost all studies (exceptions include Scott and Pandey's experiment [2000] and Bozeman and DeHart-Davis's [1999] case study) employ survey research and questionnaires, an approach especially amenable to analysis of attitudes and motivation but not as well adapted to examining multiple organizations, networks, organizational groups and coalitions or long-term behaviors of individuals. Arguably (we take up this issue in the concluding chapter) the predominance of questionnaire-based data is one of the reasons why red tape theory and red tape empirical research have not converged to the degree we might have anticipated. Indeed, many components of red tape theory remain virtually unexamined, including stakeholder red tape, red tape origins, pass-through red tape, red tape and rule density, and red tape in interorganizational and intersector relations.

Although red tape empirical research has come a long way in only twenty years, the topic now seems at risk of slow growth. We suggest in this chapter a research agenda that could spur a new phase of red tape research and theory, especially if red tape researchers can complement the many fine questionnaire-based studies with alternative approaches. Then, in the final chapter, we are emboldened to discuss the ways in which public administration research and theory may take more than a passing notice of each other, illustrating with past and potential red tape studies.

In the section below we consider a research-theory issue that is in part related to the predominant methods in the red tape literature, namely the separation between *concepts* of red tape and the *constructs* employed to examine red tape. We refer to this as the problem of "real red tape." We use this term not in the Platonic sense—we are not searching for essential forms—but rather in the critical realists' sense (see Archer 1995) of understanding that there are actual phenomena available for study even if the phenomena are mediated by observer response or social construction. The key in the observer response is to come as close as possible to capturing the actual, the *real* phenomena. In general, we are not confident that red tape researchers' constructs are exactly on target.

In later sections of this chapter we discuss the need to expand methodological approaches to red tape, especially using qualitative methods. Then we note some ways in which current streams of red tape research might be improved, a topic to which we return, in full force, in the final chapter.

"Real Red Tape": Concepts, Constructs, and Explanation

The chief rationale for systematic study of red tape is that red tape affects lives, routinely and universally. Red tape often creates great and even grievous harm. Some of the harmful effects of red tape are not well known or publicized. For example, Bozeman (2000) discusses the case of red tape delaying the installation of a traffic light at an intersection in a small Illinois town, a traffic light that might have prevented the traffic deaths that occurred at that intersection just a few days before the traffic light finally received approval. In other instances, the harm caused or abetted by red tape is much more visible and highly publicized. For example, the recovery efforts from Hurricane Katrina were stalled by red tape, leaving thousands of people homeless even as the trailers developed for temporary residences were stored nearby (Waugh 2006).

The empirical red tape literature has thus far paid lip service, at best, to the notion of the harm done by red tape. Red tape has been measured indirectly, in terms of employees' perceptions of red tape in their organization (a judgment not in most cases grounded or anchored in particular instances) or as the time required to fulfill basic tasks. While these two approaches have advanced red tape research and proved quite useful in some respects, no one really feels that the concept of red tape has been nailed by these particular constructs and their associated measures. Thus, the red tape research performed to this point describes the well-being of individual respondents and, possibly, their organization more often than it explains the experiences that clients and customers have with organizations. It focuses more on nuisances, inefficiency, and vexation than on actual pernicious harm or manifest bureaucratic pathology. To be sure, red tape *is* a considerable nuisance (see bulleted list below if that point needs any reinforcing), but it is not *only* a nuisance. In some instances, the repeated experience of red tape is a sort of organizational "death by a thousand cuts," and in the most unfortunate cases, red tape can even lead to organizational disasters.

Developing additional, stronger constructs of red tape can help the advance of red tape research in at least three important ways. In the first place, applied and clinical research on red tape, quite scarce at present, will not likely thrive until red tape constructs tap more of the experience of citizens and organizational members affected by dysfunctional rules and regulations. Second, new constructs will permit red tape researchers to build on past methods and approaches but take these to new research topics. Third, significant new advances in empirically based red tape theory require constructs closer to the theoretical concepts developed thus far. Extant concepts seem to signify the red tape that people actually experience; it is the constructs generally employed that fail to capture these experiences fully.

Before discussing "real red tape" and possible approaches to capturing it, let us take a brief departure to provide examples of red tape that differ quite a bit from the behavior and attitudes captured by most red tape constructs and the research built upon them. It takes little space to show how citizens experience red tape. Consider the following examples posted as electronic comments to a *New York Times* article about red tape (Malkin 2009).

- I am a salaried employee, but I have to turn in a timesheet every two weeks.—Doreen, Bar Harbor, Maine
- I remember flying to the USA from the UK and being required to sign a form stating that I was not a terrorist. The bureaucratic assumption, I suppose, was that terrorists may be wicked—but still honest.—John Rawlins, United Kingdom

- When a graduate student at Michigan State University, in order to drive university vehicles, my British driver's license had to be translated—from English into . . . English!—Terry Podmore, Fort Collins, Colorado
- Being told that I needed a new copy of my birth certificate because the one I had was twenty years old and out of date.—John C., Portugal
- In the Department of Social Services in Virginia Beach, a form that I submitted was refused by a supervisor because it was typed and not hand-written.—Foxfire, Orange, California
- When I received a parking ticket in the mail for a vehicle that wasn't mine, I fought the ticket by mail. The DC DMV responded with a letter saying I had 30 days to prove the vehicle was NOT mine. I wasn't sure how to prove the negative, so I sent them a photo of me NOT driving it.—Jason Pier, Washington, DC

Over the past thirty years, red tape researchers have developed some knowledge of the characteristics of red tape and ways in which managers can and do navigate red tape. Unfortunately, little research captures what we mean by "real red tape" and few studies are grounded in concrete examples of red tape. In this section, we outline what the contemporary research literature tells us about red tape, we discuss some of the challenges in bridging the gap between research and the application and use of red tape research, and we examine a few red tape field studies for clues about advancing red tape research and developing additional constructs.

Attacking Real Red Tape

In our view, red tape is not a figment in the minds of disgruntled employees and clients but rather a real phenomenon related to the burdens and bad outcomes of rules and procedures. Contemporary researchers embrace this notion, at least to some extent. Researchers overwhelmingly treat red tape as a negative phenomenon, usually focusing on the delays or conflicts it is presumed to cause and which in many studies serve as a surrogate indicator of the red tape phenomenon. Research indicates that red tape is more prevalent in cases with complex policy networks (Bozeman and DeHart-Davis 1999) and that perceptions of red tape are dependent on the respondents' positions within an organization (Feeney and Bozeman 2009; Walker and Brewer 2008). Researchers have shown that red tape can originate both within an organization (internal red tape) and from the external environment (Brewer and Walker 2010b; Coursey and Pandey 2007a; Walker and Brewer 2008) and that red tape is negatively related to performance outcomes (Brewer and Walker 2010a; Walker and Brewer

2009a) and employee alienation, public service motivation, communication, and performance (Moynihan and Pandey 2007b; Pandey and Garnett 2006; Pandey and Kingsley 2000). The past thirty years of empirical research have concluded that red tape is a real problem in organizations with real affects on outcomes.

Almost all approaches to research examine just a few concepts of red tape and most do not capture what we mean by real red tape. As noted in previous chapters, the preponderance of red tape research in public administration relies on the same measures for red tape: the General Red Tape Scale and similar agree/disagree items about personnel red tape. A smaller set of red tape studies (Bozeman, Reed, and Scott 1992; Bozeman and Scott 1996; Kingsley and Bozeman 1992; Lan and Rainey 1992; Pandey and Bretschneider 1997) have operationalized red tape as delays and time to complete tasks such as purchasing, hiring, and firing. These measures, while contributing to measurement validity and consistency across research studies, fail to capture some aspects of red tape. Generally, red tape research has relied on broad concepts, although it is unclear whether respondents are thinking about red tape or about rules they simply do not care for (but that achieve an organizational or policy goal). One important note for red tape researchers is to assess the extent of red tape; is there minimal red tape and extreme red tape? When does a rule go from being a nuisance to being red tape? Is there an assessment between costs and benefits that makes a rule red tape?

We can look to real-life attempts to reduce or rectify red tape for clues about developing additional constructs. In the United States and especially in other nations, there are some attempts to solve the real problem of red tape, although there is little attempt to generate or use applied research to solve red tape problems. The most publicized U.S. effort to attack red tape is the National Performance Review (NPR; Gore 1993), but despite the *From Red Tape to Results* title, the NPR is actually a broad set of reforms, only some of which deal in any but the remotest way with red tape (for a red tape interpretation of the NPR, see Bozeman [2000]).

Red tape remedies are more common in Europe. The European Commission (EC) and the High Level Group of Independent Stakeholders on Administrative Burdens offered an award at the 2009 European Enterprise Award ceremony in Prague to the best idea for originality, feasibility, and overall potential to reduce red tape in government relationships with small and medium-sized enterprises. The EC aims to reduce red tape by one-quarter from 2007 to 2012. The award in 2009 went to the German Confederation of Skilled Crafts, which developed a proposal to exempt additional craft businesses from being required to use a tachograph when traveling distances less than 150 kilometers (93 miles). The obligation to record speed and time for distances beyond 50 kilometers (31 miles; the previous rule) was considered overly burdensome for craftsmen. Revising the rule enables small businesses to work more efficiently and reduces a large compliance burden. According to the EC, "The Best Idea for Red Tape Reduction Award aims at identifying innovative suggestions for reducing unnecessary bureaucracy stemming from European law."[1] Awards are granted based on originality, the degree of innovation, feasibility, burden reduction potential, and transferability to other member states or areas.

In Mexico, in response to citizen's complaints about excessive red tape, President Felipe Calderón's government organized a competition to identify the nation's worst cases of red tape, inefficiency, and corruption and make suggestions for improving the process or problem. The competition, held by an anticorruption group, Transparency Mexico, attracted about 20,000 submissions. The winner was awarded a cash prize and the promise that the government would fix that specific problem (Malkin 2009). These examples highlight the important problems and challenges that red tape poses for governments and practitioners.

While it is clear that red tape is a problem in governments around the world, it is not clear that holding competitions to identify individual examples of red tape is the best means of resolving pathological rules. In most cases, governments are not equipped with the resources or theoretical models to effectively identify and reduce red tape. Rather than hold competitions for red tape solutions, governments might be better served by theoretically informed clinical research on red tape. However, it is difficult to know since so little clinical research exists. One avenue for revitalizing red tape research is to take it seriously as a problem-solving enterprise. The prospect might spur quality research and theory at the same time as it helps solve the problems created by real red tape.

Prospects for Clinical Research on Red Tape

There are a number of possible explanations for the lack of academic research on real red tape problems, including the lack of research funding and resources, the lack of access to data sources, and the lack of a willing organization, since many organizations find the study of red tape inherently threatening. Below, we use proposed examples of red tape to discuss the barriers to developing academic research, including clinical research, on real red tape problems.

To consider the possibilities as well as the need for clinical research on red tape, let us consider a simple, actual example from the above-mentioned *New York Times* article (Malkin 2009):

> In St. Thomas, at the Internal Revenue Bureau, you have to make out a form requesting forms to file your taxes. They have the forms right there in the office for various taxes, but won't give you any unless you make out this request form.—Lonnie Willis, U.S. Virgin Islands

Mr. Willis considers the requirement to fill out Form A in order to get a tax-filing form as red tape. However, despite Mr. Willis's frustration, the rule's status as red tape is an empirical question, one possibly edified by clinical research. There are a number of resources required to test whether or not this requirement is red tape, and if it is red tape, to identify the best method for dealing with this red tape. First, the researcher would need to know the time burden for filling out Form A, the cost of producing Form A, and the amount of resources dedicated to ensuring compliance with the use of Form A. The researcher would then need to evaluate the efficacy of the rule. Does Form A result in more accurate distribution of the tax filing forms? Does Form A save tax filers from wasting time on the wrong tax form? Is Form A being tracked by the tax agency and serving an evaluative function for the agency? Answering these questions and assessing whether Form A is red tape or not would require resources from the researcher/evaluator, the agency, and the users of the forms.

We can see that an assessment of Form A as red tape will require access to the tax agency and its rules, processes, and managerial capacity. We would need to know the cost of producing and processing Form A. We would need access to both clients and agency members in order to survey or interview individuals about Form A and its purposes and possible wastefulness. While it is easy to imagine that this particular tax agency would give a researcher access to determine the level of red tape associated with Form A, it can be extremely difficult for researchers to access other agencies and organizations when assessing the efficacy of rules and the presence of red tape in real problems.

A third barrier to conducting research on real red tape problems is that a useful assessment of red tape within an organization or in a set of programs requires a long-term commitment from both the organization and the researcher. Not only is time required to do a proper historical and current assessment of the rule, but the researcher must take the time required to assess the rule from the perspective of multiple stakeholders, determining if the rule is red tape for some or for all.

Fourth, as with all managerial and organizational evaluations, there is the threat of finding unpopular results. When a researcher is asked to assess a poorly designed rule, red tape born bad or red tape gone bad, the researcher is being asked to investigate an organizational problem or pathology. This type of research is often sensitive and controversial. What happens when the researcher finds that much of the red tape is being created by insecure, overcontrolling managers? Even more troublesome, what about red tape that has its origins in self-aggrandizement or corruption? The challenge of doing research on real red tape is convincing an organization that it is in its interest to employ researchers and evaluators to assist in the identification and possible elimination of red tape. Researchers must build trust with organizations so that organizations will support professional, honest research; in turn, researchers must be sufficiently sensitive to help the organization without creating embarrassment or blame games. While this situation is not, of course, different from some other topics of clinical research in organizations, the fact that the research begins with a search for possible pathology can easily set everyone on edge.

Finally, the continual challenge in bridging academic research to real problems is timeliness. Just as policy-makers require information in a timely manner in order to guide and influence policy development, organizations require timely research to prevent and reduce red tape. Especially when we consider research aimed at preventing red tape or identifying red tape in its inception, red tape researchers and experts need to be engaged in identifying and solving red tape problems as they are being created. The identification of red tape and solving of red tape problems should occur at the same time as organizations are committed to reducing red tape.

Solving the problems of real red tape and bridging the gap between red tape research and application, practice, and reform present difficult challenges. Researchers face the challenges of earning support for this research (both monetary and nonmonetary), gaining access to organizations, making the long-term commitment to the research required for in-depth work, managing the possibility of finding negative results and presenting those results to the organization, and finally, ensuring that the research results are accessible and presented in a timely fashion. Although difficult in many ways, clinical research on real red tape can advance the empirical and theoretical development of the field while at the same time producing important benefits to the practitioner or client.

Origins, Tracking, and Evolution

Whereas most of the research on red tape has focused on a rules-based concept of red tape, very little has actually focused on any specific rules or sets of rules. Most of the rules questions employed in questionnaires do not ask respondents to identify particular bad rules. Even the few case studies that have been developed have focused on very general, sweeping rules (such as aggregated air quality regulations). Studies focusing on specific rules and sets of rules can do much to advance research and theory.

Rule-based studies could take numerous forms, such as a comprehensive study of a set of rules within a single organization, an analysis of the manner in which a federal policy or rule is interpreted and implemented in multiple institutions, or an examination of how state personnel rules and regulations differently affect agencies. Then, with a particular rule or set of rules, the researcher could assess stakeholder views of the rules and ways in which those stakeholders alter or navigate red tape.

While we envision a number of ways in which researchers could do a rule history or rule audit, in 2000 Bozeman developed a proposal for a rule audit that has yet to be embraced by public administration researchers. The rule audit, outlined in Table 6.1, entails six phases: (1) identifying the rule or universe of rules to which the organization is subject, (2) distinguishing between the rules under the control of the organization and those under the control of external authorities, (3) identifying internal and external stakeholders to the rule, (4) assessing and measuring the intended and unintended impact of the rules, (5) assessing the need to reform or revise the rules, and (6) implementing the rule changes.

There is one study in the public administration literature that aims to understand rules from an origins perspective. Using the case study of rule creation at the Environmental Protection Agency (EPA), Bozeman and DeHart-Davis assess the ways in which rules are created and their relationships to the functional objects (Bozeman and DeHart-Davis 1999; DeHart-Davis and Bozeman 2001). With the exception of Bozeman and DeHart-Davis's research on Title V at the EPA, there is no public administration red tape research testing hypotheses about the inception of red tape.

While red tape research has given little attention to the origins of rules, the related field of rules research (as discussed in Chapter 2) provides signposts. For the purpose of red tape research, the task would be to conduct a history of red tape. Rules-focused red tape research could proceed expeditiously by first identifying red tape and then backtracking through document analysis and possibly interviews to identify the points at which red tape emerged from changes in rules implementation or red tape originated in rules. Alternatively, researchers might look to a newly developed program or organization and monitor the creation of rules, seeking out instances of red tape that is created or that evolves from rules.

Clearly research investigating red tape origins, tracking rules and red tape, and mapping the evolution of red tape would require extensive resources and commitment from researchers. Unfortunately, many public administration researchers lack the resources or the job security that would allow them to engage in this type of research. That said, it is not impossible to imagine an evaluation

Table 6.1

Rule and Red Tape Audit Methodology

Process phase	Activities	Techniques
1. Rule identification	Identify the universe of rules and regulations to which the organization is subject.	a. Employee interviews or focus groups b. Back-tracking rules through administrative process paper trail
2. Rule source	Separate the rules and regulations under the control of the organization from those under the control of external authorities and focus on the former.	a. Informal consultation b. Legal interpretation
3. Stakeholder identification	Identify stakeholders to the rule, both internal (employees, managers) and external (clients, oversight agencies).	a. Focus groups b. Documentation through back-tracking rules c. Rule "tracer"
4. Stakeholder process	Develop data from stakeholders for the purpose of (a) assessing the current impact of the rules and regulations; (b) measuring the impact against intended and preferred outcomes.	a. Surveys b. Panels and focus groups c. "Avoidee" assessment
5. Rules assessment	Require a stakeholder delegate panel to categorize each rule and regulation as either (a) acceptable as is; (b) in need of modification; (c) a candidate for abolition. Then, issue red tape audit and recommendations.	a. Open panel b. Anonymous Delphi-like panel c. Measure convergence
6. Rules reformation	Implement rules changes.	a. Managerial action or executive order b. Legislative request

Source: Adapted from Bozeman (2000, 177).

program or contract that might allow a researcher to track red tape and rules in addition to the other programmatic results being tracked in the research. For example, Ken Meier (evaluating the Texas public school system), Kim Isett (investigating state mental health departments), and Gordon Kingsley (evaluating the Georgia Department of Transportation) are examples of public administration scholars who have developed long-term research relationships with organizations that might benefit from the rules and red tape assessments. It is conceivable that researchers engaged in evaluation work or with close relationships with government clients might be in the best position to develop a research agenda centered on conducting a rules and red tape history.

The empirical research on red tape overwhelmingly investigates general perceptions of red tape. Even when these perceptions are narrowed to types of red tape such as personnel, organization, contracting, and procurement red tape, they are still general scales about the "level of red tape in the organization," the "level of red tape in contracts," or the "amount of time to make a purchase," as compared to particular instances of red tape created through legislation or inappropriate rule-making, red tape as the result of misinterpretation of a rule's intent, or red tape as an outcome of an outdated, outmoded rule. Red tape research is lacking in measures that are anchored in instances of real red tape. Indeed, there has been a dearth of research operationalizing the rule or rules as the unit of analysis. In order to assess the rule (or red tape) as the unit of analysis, research must supplement surveys and questionnaire items asking about perceptions of red tape and move to cases and instances of rule-evolved, rule-inception, and stakeholder red tape. This type of research will require extensive resources and a commitment to rigorous qualitative methods, perhaps used in tandem with quantitative research.

Public administration researchers interested in red tape research based on the rules' life cycles have some good starting points in research based in sociology and industrial psychology. Reynaud's (2005) assessment of routines and rule-following in the Paris Metro Workshop is one example of the ways in which qualitative research can advance understanding of red tape and strengthen ties between theoretical frameworks and concepts and empirical measurement and research. Understanding the detailed components and underlying factors affecting rule-evolution into red tape will require a commitment to tracking rules and assessing the multiple factors that might influence their shifting from rules to red tape. Similarly, understanding the inception of red tape will require access and knowledge of a particular organization or program that is not likely to occur through single-event surveys.

In summary, empirical work has tested some components of red tape theory, in particular the ways in which red tape and perceptions of red tape vary across sectors. There remains a great deal of empirical work to be done in testing red tape theory. We suggest that future red tape research focus on red tape and rules as the unit of analysis. We recommend that researchers develop a more comprehensive understanding of the origins of red tape and the ways in which different stakeholders affect red tape and the ways in which red tape differently affects stakeholders.

On Doing What We Are Doing, But Doing It Better

Of course, while there are limitations to the current red tape research orientation, it has contributed much and can continue to do so. Continuing to study perceptual red tape and the ways in which perceived red tape is related to performance and motivation is an important contribution to the study of public administration. As we continue to collect larger data sets, with better samples, and more thorough administration, we are able to improve support for findings. Theories are not tested and proven with single studies; rather, social science theories require extensive research in numerous environments. Thus, it is important for current survey-based empirical research to continue on its trajectory—with important suggestions for how to enhance that trajectory. First, red tape researchers require longitudinal data. Second, empirical researchers must take more responsibility for engaging in confirmatory analysis and conducting tests of reliability and validity.

If we look at the history of surveys of perceived red tape and red tape as task delays, we see that surveys administered to managers in public, private, and nonprofit organizations in New York were followed by NASP II, a survey of managers in departments of health and human services across the nation, which was followed by NASP II, a survey of public and nonprofit managers in all fields in two states, and then NASP IV, a survey of a national sample of senior managers in local government jurisdictions. These U.S. surveys, each building on the previous ones either through shared items, knowledge, or the training of junior researchers, also set the stage for items to be shared across national borders. For example, the English Local Government Best Value Study draws its red tape and personnel flexibility items directly from the work of the NASP projects, while offering improved measures of its own.

Similar to most public administration research (indeed, most research in the social sciences), red tape research suffers from a paucity of longitudinal study. While many new researchers in the field are trained in empirical methods analyzing longitudinal data, there is a dearth of longitudinal data available to answer important public administration questions. Most analyses in the field using time series data are derived from national datasets such as the U.S. Census, Federal Human Capital Survey, and the International City/County Management Association longitudinal data on service delivery, economic development, e-government/technology, and police and fire personnel and expenditures. These large datasets enable researchers to investigate hypotheses about general change. Although these data are collected at the individual level, they are not panel data, or repeated surveys of the same individuals with the individual's responses in year one being matched to each subsequent year. Thus researchers can use these federal datasets to investigate average change in the national population over time, but not detailed shifts in individual or organizational motivation and work life. To fully advance empirical research on red tape, public administration scholars need to develop a research agenda that includes collecting time series data that will enable the testing of red tape theory and the ability to develop predictive (causal) models.

The second important task not yet taken up by red tape researchers is systematic study of the reliability and validity of red tape measures. Reliability, the extent to which repeated experiment, test, or measurement produces the same results, is critical to advancing understanding of red tape. Current efforts in red tape research have made important strides in this direction. The question of construct validity—does the measuring device do what it is intended to do—has been less tested in public administration research. Construct validity is critical to understanding the connection between the concept of red tape and the indicator (e.g., scale or survey item used).

An important step has been taken toward testing validity of red tape measures through the use of anchoring vignettes. This method, developed by King and colleagues (2004), uses anchored vignettes to assess the validity of individual reports of general perceptions. By anchoring general perceptions to reality-based vignettes, researchers are able to make comparisons across respondents and vignettes to identify the differential item functioning (DIF), or the degree of variance in respondents' perceptions of red tape. DIF occurs when respondents differently understand a survey question or item.

Pandey and Marlowe (2009) present an analysis of anchored vignettes from the recent fourth phase of the National Administrative Studies Project (NASP IV) study conducted in 2008. NASP IV was an Internet survey administered to a national sample of senior managers in U.S. local government jurisdictions with populations over 50,000, drawn from the population of International City/County Management Association and publicly available data. From the sample of 3,316 managers, 46.4 percent responded. Anchoring vignettes about personnel red tape were included in surveys sent to a randomly chosen proportion of the sample. Three hundred and seven of the respondents completed the vignettes. A summary of the vignette design is in Table 6.2.

In their paper analyzing previous and current public administration approaches to using survey-based measures of personnel red tape, Pandey and Marlowe (2009, 18) find that although there is DIF between the perceptions and reporting of these three human resources red tape items, the differences do not have a material effect. By comparing the results from the traditional personnel item about promotion and the vignettes, the authors are able to show that "survey questions measuring red tape are viewed as intended by researchers and that respondents do not necessarily invoke other values in answering these questions." This research marks an important effort toward confirmatory analysis in public administration red tape research.

Cronbach (1971, 447) argues that "one validates, not a test, but an interpretation of data arising from a specified procedure." Thus, it is possible that red tape

Table 6.2

NASP IV Personnel Red Tape Vignette Design

The survey asked respondents the standard red tape perception measure with respect to their organization:

1. Personnel rules on promotion make it hard for a good employee to move up faster than a poor one.

• Response categories: 1 = strongly disagree; 2 = somewhat disagree; 3 = neutral; 4 = somewhat agree; 5 = strongly agree.

Respondents were presented with the following three vignettes about promotion and asked to assess the level of human resources red tape experienced by the manager.

1. Gene would like to promote a highly effective young employee. The city's personnel rules provide managers broad discretion in hiring and promotion. Within one month Gene requests a promotion for the employee, that request is approved, and the new employee begins in the new position.
2. Chris would like to promote an excellent employee. Chris is advised to nominate a more experienced employee because the city's personnel system rewards tenure. The excellent employee is nominated, the promotion process takes nine months, but the promotion is approved. Chris is advised to "play by the rules" next time.
3. Terry would like to promote an excellent, but relatively new employee. Personnel rules require that experienced employees should be promoted first, but those rules allow for exceptions. Terry requests such an exception, and that request is denied. Terry repeats the request six months later and is denied again. Terry gives up on the idea of rewarding the excellent employee through early promotion.
4. Leslie has identified an employee for a promotion. Leslie is instructed to promote a different employee who is a member of a protected demographic category. Leslie promotes the protected employee. The nonprotected employee is promoted nine months later.

Following each vignette, the respondent was asked, "For the above scenario, please indicate your level of agreement with the statement that personnel rules on promotion make it hard for a good employee to move up faster than a poor one."

• Response categories: 1 = strongly disagree; 2 = somewhat disagree; 3 = neutral; 4 = somewhat agree; 5 = strongly agree.

According to Pandey and Marlowe (2009), these vignettes were carefully crafted to make certain they speak only to the efficiency dimension of human resources red tape.

measures are valid measuring instruments for one concept or phenomenon, but not for another. The current empirical public administration red tape research does not sufficiently parse out the distinction between valid red tape measures and their relationships to particular concepts. It is entirely plausible that personnel red tape measures are a valid indicator of personnel red tape concepts, while general red tape measures are not a valid indicator of organizational red tape—or vice versa. Each measure presented in the red tape research must be a valid measure of the concept it purports to measure. While research has found that public managers report higher levels of red tape in their organizations as compared to private managers, researchers have not assessed the validity of these reports by showing that managers' perceptions of red tape accurately predict the volume or mass of red tape in their respective agencies.

Carmines and Zeller (1994) note that "it should be clear that the process of construct validation is, by necessity, theory-laden" (23) and that it is impossible to validate measures without developing sufficient theoretical frameworks to support them. They note that construct validity comes through "different researchers using different theoretical structures across a number of different studies" (24). Current red tape research is being conducted by a growing number of different researchers through a number of studies. The key will be to develop better theoretical structures for advancing this research. As empirical researchers seek to test and verify the reliability and validity of empirical red tape research, this advancement cannot be done without strong consideration of red tape theory and development.

Theory Testing and Development

Bozeman's (1993, 2000) theory of government red tape proposes a number of concepts for understanding, measuring, and researching red tape. If we return to that theory development, we see definitions of formalization, rule sum, compliance requirement, compliance burden, functional objects, and rule efficacy. When thinking of examples of red tape, we can see that in some cases the problem is a compliance burden problem or a missed functional object. For example, requiring a permanently disabled person to reapply annually for a disabled parking sticker seems like red tape to the individual citizen. However, we can see that the city probably requires annual reapplication to prevent fraud and theft—the functional object being the prevention of permit fraud. Temporary permits, requiring reapplication, enable the city to ensure that individuals are not selling their parking passes or that a family member is not using the pass after the intended recipient has died. There is a functional object here. But is the compliance burden for users too high? Are there more efficient rules to address the functional object? Can we expect a government organization (or any organization for that matter) to assess the level of compliance burden as compared to the efficacy of the rule?

Similarly, there are examples of conflicting rules—for example, requiring picture identification (ID) in order to get a birth certificate and requiring a birth certificate in order to get a picture ID. Both rules have the functional object of verifying identity and preventing fraud. Together, the two rules create a compliance burden for some citizens. How does an agency determine whether or not the compliance burden warrants rule change?

Some rules are simply poorly conceptualized. For example, a posting to a recent article about red tape notes, "I was required to take an ESL (English as a Second Language) class when I first started college in the U.S. because I was from a foreign country—England" (Malkin 2009). Had the rule been that students who do not speak English must take an ESL class, English-speaking foreign students would not be subject to this rule. The rule missed its functional object, which presumably was to provide ESL to students who were not native English speakers; because the "dilemma of the scientist is to select models that are at the same time simple enough to permit him to think with the aid of the model, but also sufficiently realistic that the simplifications required do not lead to predictions that are highly inaccurate" (Blalock 1961, 8), solving real red tape problems will require researchers to develop models that do a better job connecting the theoretical concepts of functional objects, rule efficacy, compliance burden, and red tape to accurate application.

In addition to revisiting key concepts in red tape theory, it is important for researchers to develop more tests of the conceptual such as Bozeman's (2000) and, perhaps more important, to formulate and test new conceptual models. For example, Bozeman's (1993) early work on red tape theory introduces the idea of pass-through red tape. To date, researchers have not investigated the ways in which red tape passes through an organization to another organization or to clients. There is no research on pass-through red tape. Many of our students, when introduced to Bozeman's (1993) red tape theory and considering his typology relating origin and impact of red tape (see Figure 6.1), note that there is little development and discussion of the idea of pass-through red tape. For practitioners, pass-through red tape is very real. For example, one student noted that while working at a nonprofit organization that delivered mental health services, he was often required to enforce or pass on red tape to clients who were recipients of federal funding or state programs. The student explained that sometimes one group of clients would be subject to more red tape than a second group because services to the first group were funded through a federal contract while the second group's service were funded from another source. He said that his organization often passed external red tape to clients and stakeholders. This and other examples of red tape in action remain unstudied.

Because Bozeman's typology of origin and impact of red tape was generated in work prior to 1993, we might conclude that the prevalence of contracting, outsourcing, and interorganizational management and governance has likely increased the amount of red tape that would qualify as pass-through red tape, or red tape generated from external origins and having external impacts. If we look to Bozeman's typology (Figure 6.1), we see that current

Figure 6.1 **Typology Relating Origin and Impact of Red Tape**

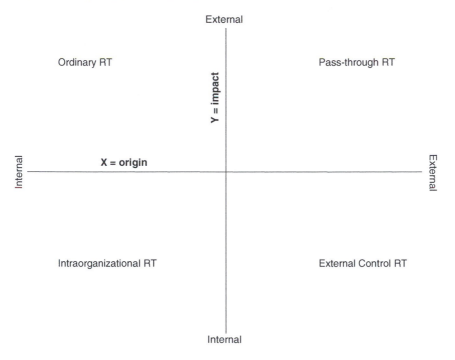

Source: Adapted from Bozeman (1993, 290).

red tape empirical research gives a lot of attention to quadrant II, ordinary red tape. Surveys enquiring about an organization's red tape or the time to deliver services to clients could be used to test hypotheses about ordinary red tape. Similarly, because most of the current research focuses on managerial perceptions of red tape, we know a lot about intraorganizational red tape (quadrant III). For example, personnel red tape is internal to the organization and primarily affects organizational members. External control red tape, shown in quadrant IV, has also received some attention from empirical researchers. For example, Walker and Brewer (2009b) find that, according to government employees, external control (and the external environment) and uncertainly are the primary causes of red tape, while internal managerial skills and discretion can reduce the impact of red tape. Meanwhile, there is no research investigating red tape that is external in origin and impact. One might expect that pass-through red tape is actually quite prevalent, given the inability and disincentives to combat externally created red tape that affects external stakeholders. For now, we can only speculate; advancing this area of research would certainly improve our overall knowledge of red tape, our ability to develop simple models for predicting outcomes, and could tie red tape research to the larger public administration research questions related to inter- and intraorganizational management and governance.

Perhaps the most important item for a research agenda is to press forward with the refinement and testing of the multidimensional red tape concept. This task is formidable. It requires researchers and theorists not only to deal with multiple perspectives on rules' impacts (as with stakeholder red tape), but also to develop measures that tap a wide variety of criteria of rules' effectiveness.

Concluding Remarks

In this chapter we have outlined a number of items for the red tape research agenda. Perhaps the most important of these is focusing on particular instances of red tape, including documenting that the rules are, in fact, real red tape. While we do not call for academic researchers to transform themselves into practitioners, we do emphasize the need for academic researchers in this professional field to engage in research that draws on real problems and to anchor empirical red tape research in actual rules and measured red tape. Clinical research on red tape enables such a focus and, at the same time, benefits from it.

The preceding chapter indicates that there is little connection between actual, tangible organizational problems and red tape research and theory. If we agree that red tape is a "real problem," it is critical that public administration researchers develop research agendas aimed at real red tape, particular instances of red tape, rather than generalized perceptions of red tape or indirect, albeit useful, indicators such as delays, number of layers of authority, or number of signatories to a decision.

Public administration researchers can benefit from learning from and drawing from important research tool applications from other disciplines. In particular, we highlight the importance of drawing on sociological research on rules and rules histories to develop more in-depth qualitative approaches to understanding government red tape. Taking cues from the rules history work of Schulz and Beck (2002) and Zhou (1993), we can see the value of more detailed, qualitative approaches to understanding red tape and the ways in which rules can constrict decision-making, managerial discretion, and organizational efficiency.

We encourage red tape research employing the tradition and orientation set by previous questionnaire-based studies, but with additional emphasis on tests of reliability and validity, breadth of empirical analysis, and efforts to collect longitudinal data. We expect that public administration red tape research, while setting the groundwork for theory development and empirical testing of theory, requires better integration into the other areas of research and theory in public administration. Red tape may not only hinder managing people, budgets, and processes in public organizations, but also affect managing public service provision and advancement of collective purposes. Red tape is a critically important factor in understanding public sector work and worker motivation and organizational efficiency and efficacy.

While we think there are a few more "big questions" in public management research than the three posed by Behn (1995, 362), we can examine his three to consider just how red tape research can be of use to a variety of core issues in public administration and management.

1. How can managers break the micromanagement cycle?
Clearly red tape is an important factor in the micromanagement cycle. On the one hand, red tape might cause micromanagement by providing requirements to which managers must submit but which do not advance any organizational purpose. On the other hand, attempts to reduce micromanagement could result in the development of red tape or rules that eventually become red tape.

2. How can public managers motivate people to work energetically and intelligently toward achieving public purposes?
Red tape research can contribute to this big question as it aims to understand the relationships between red tape and motivation. For example, does red tape frustrate and hinder highly motivated, energetic public employees? Or does red tape encourage highly motivated and energetic people to behave in more creative and entrepreneurial ways and seek methods to navigate around obstructing rules?

3. How can public managers measure the achievements of their agencies in ways that help to increase those achievements?
Identifying red tape in public organizations and making recommendations to reduce red tape, conducting red tape histories and audits, and developing simple, straightforward models for identifying and eliminating red tape are ways in which red tape research can help to answer this final, big question in public management. Reduction of red tape would be a clear means for public managers to measure achievement in their agencies, while incentives for managers to reduce red tape would increase those achievements. Thus, a research agenda for red tape theory and research should aim not only at the detailed suggestions outlined in this chapter, but also at the larger questions of public administration and management.

Note

1. European Commission, "Better Regulation: Best Idea for Red Tape Reduction Award." http://ec.europa.eu/enterprise/policies/better-regulation/administrative-burdens/award.

7

Red Tape as Token

The tradition of criticizing public administration and public administration research is a long and venerable one (e.g., Adams 1992; Box 1992; Kraemer and Perry 1989; McCurdy and Cleary 1984) and shows no sign of waning (e.g., Luton 2007; Lynn, Heinrich, and Hill 2008; Meier 2005; Wright, Manigault, and Black 2004). Using red tape research and theory as a case in point, this chapter adds to the critical tradition, but from a somewhat different vantage point.

More than a few active and, indeed, renowned public administration researchers have been among the field's critics. But a greater proportion of the criticism has come from persons who are hostile to empirical research generally and who bring their antipathy to their views of public administration research and theory. Or, to avoid imputation of motive, we can alternatively observe that many critics, regardless of their personal taste for empirical research, do very little of it.

Most extant criticism of public administration research, regardless of the epistemological persuasion of the respective critics, has this in common: criticisms presented are as applicable to any branch of social science research as to public administration. Our aim is to develop criticisms a bit more tailored to the peculiar problems of public administration research (though we cannot entirely avoid tying these public administration peculiarities to overarching problems with social science research and theory-building). Our approach is at least a bit different from others, not only because we use a particular case, red tape research, to exemplify problems with public administration research and theory-building, but also because we are criticizing a body of work to which we have actively contributed. We refer to this as an "embedded approach" to criticism. The approach strongly relies on our experiences as researchers focusing on the topic criticized and employs personalized commentary not only on the intellectual and theoretical aspects of work, but also on the history and sociology of knowledge development.

The embedded approach is expressed in two different ways here, in different sections of this chapter. The first part of the embedded approach provides a social and intellectual history of red tape research and theory, from a participant-observer perspective. This is to a large extent a history of group research projects and network building. The analysis takes care to distill lessons from the various projects. The second part of the embedded approach, after reviewing this history, is an attempt to distill broad lessons from the entire course of red tape research and theory, apart from any particular work or project, and to suggest how the successes and failures of red tape research relate more generally to developing public administration research and theory. In a section below, we consider further the underlying assumptions of the embedded approach and assess its strengths and weaknesses.

Before taking up an embedded critical perspective and applying it to red tape research and theory, we review briefly some previous works criticizing public administration research and theory. This is *not* a comprehensive review of this literature, much of which is familiar, but a distillation of a few particularly relevant works. We consider this literature in large part in order to understand where our own critical effort might fit within it or relate to it. We consider criticism in two very different categories: "postmodern" and "data-driven."

We include in the postmodern category a bit more than card-carrying postmodernists would likely approve. We include virtually any criticism in this category if the critic articulates a deep suspicion about the value of quantitative research or the testing of explicit, generalizable hypotheses and wishes to substitute an epistemology based on an entirely different way of knowing. While we well understand that postmodernists may engage in desperate philosophical struggles with naturalistic epistemologists and that critical theorist do not necessarily embrace hermeneutics and that phenomenology and deconstruction are not really the same thing, we are not (at least for present purposes) interested in these nuances.

Our primary interest is in data-driven critical perspectives. Whereas we provide a cursory review of postmodern perspectives, we give greater consideration to the data-driven perspectives since these critics clearly have objectives in line with ours.

Critical Perspectives on Public Administration Research

In our view, both the critical approaches reviewed below have value, especially when blended into a multimethod, epistemological cocktail. After reviewing these approaches, we present our embedded approach, which is the focus of this chapter.

Brief Commentary on Postmodernist Perspectives

The postmodernist critical perspective is particularly popular these days. Postmodernists[1] use (or more often prescribe) a wide variety of analytical approaches, including symbolic interactionism (Burnier 2005), phenomenology (White 1986a), deconstructionism (Luton 2007), hermeneutics (Balfour and Mesaros 1994), and narrative inquiry (Dodge, Ospina, and Foldy 2005), just to name a few.

After having reviewed many of the papers we are lumping together as postmodern approaches to public administration, we think it fair to say that they more often *advocate* these approaches than actually *apply* them. When postmodernist approaches are applied rather than just prescribed, they are as often used for criticizing others' original research as for setting out on new substantive topics. In almost every case, postmodernist criticisms are not aimed at other postmodernists but at those who are doing more traditional social science inquiry. At the risk of some oversimplification, we suggest that postmodernists tend also to think that public administration research is wanting—but for nearly opposite reasons given by the data-driven critics. Postmodern critics tend to feel that public administration has *too much* focus on mainstream hypothesis-testing social sciences, quantitative methods, and model specification.

Many postmodernist critiques of public administration research and theory have undisguised disdain for quantitative approaches to the study of public administration or, related, to the application of conventional scientific methodology in public administration research. In our view, quantitative, hypothesis-testing social science (let us use the term "conventional" social science) is a legitimate way of knowing about social phenomena, including public administration. It can be just as useful, if in very different ways, as narrative inquiry, historical analysis, qualitative research, and philosophical and conceptual analysis. However, since we do accept conventional social sciences as an entirely legitimate and often quite useful research approach, we almost necessarily disqualify ourselves as translators of postmodernism, much of which rejects an approach that we do not reject. We do feel it is incumbent on us to make one observation: we suggest that there is very little in the postmodernist approach that has any *particular* relevance to public administration research and theory or, more importantly, to *advancing* public administration research and theory. Almost all the postmodernist arguments are general ones that apply as well to political science or sociology as to public administration.

More important, the arguments that seem to be addressed chiefly to public administration research often seem to us to focus on a construction of public administration research that bears little resemblance to the work that we have read and to the research that we have reviewed in this book.

Finally, we reiterate that none of the above is intended to discount sensible cautions offered by postmodernist and deconstructionist critics of public administration. Certainly there is a core truth to most postmodernist perspectives: conventional, quantitative social science is not all-powerful but rather one of several ways of knowing. In particular it is premised on aggregating phenomena that some would prefer to treat as unique.

Data-Driven Perspectives

Data-driven approaches to criticizing public administration research develop data about public administration research, analyze the data, and report on it. Almost all studies in the data-driven category find egregious problems with public administration research (Adams and White 1994; Cozzetto 1994; Houston and Delevan 1990, 1994; McCurdy and Cleary 1984; Perry and Kraemer 1986; White 1986b).

Naturally, those who develop and use data in their criticisms tend to think data are useful, to embrace "mainstream social science" and its methods, and to use "mainstream social science" criteria such as statistical and methodological rigor,[2] external validity, model specification, and progress in explanatory theory. An early data-driven study that engendered some controversy was McCurdy and Cleary's (1984) assessment of research in public administration or, in their words, "the feeble state of research in public administration" (49). Searching the 1981 *Dissertation Abstracts International*, they examined 142 doctoral theses in policy analysis, administrative theory (36), comparative public administration (21), organizational theory (14), and organizational development and human resources management (12) and found them wanting on methodological, theoretical, and technical standards. They assessed the dissertations on six measures of impact (testing a theory and causal relationships), validity, and importance (central to public administration and cutting-edge topics) and concluded that only 42 percent tested a theory or reached a conclusion containing a causal statement, 21 dissertations used a research design with some validity, and only 9, or 6 percent, dealt with a major public administration topic that could be considered "cutting-edge."

McCurdy and Cleary concluded that their findings pointed to a "relatively weak status accorded research in graduate public administration programs" (52) and that "most public administration dissertations are not set up in such a way that they can make much of a contribution to the development of our conceptual base or even to our base of information" (54). Their interpretation of the dissertation data was met with considerable criticism from those who objected to their using the standards of "mainstream social sciences" instead of standards emphasized in more applied fields and fields focused on practice and practitioners (e.g., Box 1992).

In 2000, Cleary published a second study of public administration doctoral dissertations, reporting marked improvements since the 1984 study. He assessed 168 dissertation abstracts from 1998 and found that 89 percent conducted basic research, 34 percent met the criterion for methodological validity, 97 percent tested at least one cause-effect relationship, and 19 percent tested an existing theory. He concluded that in the sixteen years since the initial study there was a large decline in the percentage of doctoral dissertations that were purely descriptive and based on single case studies. In a bit of public administration methodological irony, Cleary reported changes in the percentage of dissertations ranked on research purpose, rigorous research design, testing an existing theory, including causal statements, and topic of importance, but failed to apply even a basic test as to whether or not these changes were statistically significance. Thus, we know that a larger percentage of dissertations outline a research purpose and causal relationships, but we do not know if these differences are significant, or if the causal relationships outlined in these 1998 dissertations were accurately inferred, which is an important note considering that the bulk of these dissertations surely used self-administered surveys and cross-sectional data.

In another data-driven critical review, Perry and Kraemer (1986) examined a decade's worth of articles in *Public Administration Review*. In their review of 289 articles, Perry and Kraemer coded twelve variables, including research stage, problem delineation, variable identification, establishment of causality among variables, evaluation of alternative policies and programs, research methodology, method of empirical analysis (if applicable), and focus on theory-building or problem resolution. They concluded that public administration research was not cumulative, in part because of a greater attention to application rather than generalization, and that public administration research lacks adequate institutional support. They noted that of the 289 articles, 238 indicated "no" external funding, and 25 reported "other" sources of funding, such as faculty or university-based research funds. Perry and Kraemer concluded that "relatively few public administration scholars pursue research actively or pursue research issues to advanced stages of development" (220). Given the lack of institutional support and applied nature of public administration research, it is not surprising that advanced empirical research has been slow to develop.

More recently, Wright, Manigault, and Black (2004) examined a random sample of 143 empirical articles from six public administration journals over three years (1996, 1997, and 1998). The authors coded the 143 articles according to the presence or absence of information regarding number of measures, type of measures, method of measurement, source of measures, and "whether they [authors] provided direct or indirect evidence that could be used to establish the measurement properties of the research data" (753). Wright and colleagues noted that more than half of the empirical studies in the sample use self-administered surveys. They also note that only 7.5 percent of the articles provided evidence of measure reliability, less than 4 percent provided evidence of measure validity, and only 34 percent offered a description of measurement error or bias. They concluded that there are a number of weaknesses with quantitative research in public administration, in particular that too much empirical work relied on surveys and that the source of measures was often unclear. They argued that theoretical progress in the field was thwarted in part by researchers' failure to provide sufficient detail about their findings and methods to either allow accumulation of research or even accurate interpretation of results.

The results of data-driven analyses of public administration research can be summarized quite succinctly: critics have found that public administration research leaves much to be desired. While we do not entirely disagree with these critics, we note that two of the best known data-driven critiques, McCurdy and Cleary (1984) and Perry and Kraemer (1986), are now more than twenty years old and were criticizing a literature in which quantitative research and conventional social science were still scarce. The more recent critique, Wright, Manigault, and Black (2004), while important in understanding methodological limitations in the field, focuses on the reporting quality in journals: not necessarily the abilities and preferences of researchers and authors, but a lack of demand for rigorous reporting on the part of editors and reviewers or the authors response to demands to save space.

An Embedded Assessment of Research and Theory

The embedded critical perspective is based on the self-reflection and direct experience of persons actually working in the field of research being criticized.[3] The perspective is somewhat of a departure in research criticism. Most critics understandably prefer to take broad shots across the bow, aiming at no particular individuals, and complaining generally about the sorry state of affairs in the field they criticize. Some bolder critics (e.g., Luton 2007) take aim at particular researchers' work. But research critics do not customarily take aim at themselves, using their own work experiences as "data." In a sense, the embedded perspective is an amalgam of the other two approaches inasmuch as it employs data (as does the data-driven), makes observations based on personal experience, and retains skepticism (as does the postmodern) about the connection of findings revealed by secondary data to actual events in a phenomenological world.

Most of the analysis criticism in previous chapters focuses on the content of red tape studies, technical issues in research, and problems in middle-range theory-building. In this chapter, the embedded assessment focuses more deliberately on personal experiences and observations and tries to distill lessons from red tape research and theory that apply more generally to public administration research. The question, then, is this: "If we take red tape research not as exemplary but as *representative* public administration research, what do we conclude?" We are asking the same question as others—"What is wrong with empirical research in pubic administration?"—but in a more reflexive way, considering necessarily what has been wrong with our *own* research. We focus on our own direct research experiences not because they are superior to others' but because they are quite literally the only ones we have. We focus on red tape not out of a sense that red tape research is more important than others, but rather because we feel the obstacles and problems encountered by red tape researchers and theorists are quite similar to and representative of those confronted by other public administration researchers. Before launching into the embedded criticism, let us consider some of the strengths and weaknesses of this approach.

Strengths and Weaknesses of the Embedded Approach

The most obvious disadvantage of the embedded approach to criticism is that the subject/author cannot claim to be impartial or objective. This is a problem but perhaps not a severe one. How many wholly impartial criticisms can be identified? At least no one expects impartiality or objectivity with the embedded approach. A related disadvantage is the threat of intellectual hyperopia. The embedded critic may be so caught up in the minutiae of research, theory, and their social and psychological context as to obscure their larger meaning. This seems a greater problem, but by its very nature we cannot determine just how great a problem it is in the present case. Others will have no difficulty making this determination.

Perhaps the greatest disadvantage of embedded criticism is that it runs the danger of "financial crisis logic": turning to the same incompetents who caused the problem and asking them to prescribe a fix. Doubtless, we, along with our red tape research colleagues, are culpable with respect to many of the shortcomings of red tape research—but not all of them. Some obvious flaws with research are structural or institutional rather than straightforward human mistakes. Most obvious are problems with sample design that often owe more to an absence of research funds than to blockheaded research strategies.

While we are not willing to suggest that the advantages of the embedded approach outweigh the disadvantages, we are willing to say that the three advantages of the approach suffice to at least encourage us to give it a try. Advantage one: the embedded approach provides insight into the social psychology of research. Most intellectual histories provide no consideration of motive and intent.[4] How could they? Unless one is criticizing one's own research or research issuing from a research team or network in which one has been embedded, any comments about motive are speculative. True, not everyone feels that motive and social psychological context are important in the course of knowledge development, but we shall argue otherwise. (Here, at least, the postmodernists are likely to agree with us).

Advantage two: in the embedded approach the critic often knows about specific choices, including not only the ones leading to published work, but also dead ends and circuitous routes to knowledge that can never be fully comprehended by critics outside the research domain. Increasingly, sociologists of science have shown that decisions not manifest in published work often are vital determinants of research outcomes and accepted knowledge (Knorr-Cetina 1999; Lynch 1994). For example, the phenomenon of "data editing" (Leahey 2008; Leahey, Entwisle, and Einaudi 2003) has begun to receive some attention. The focus of data editing, a somewhat misleading term, is not on coding data but on the many discrete, unreported decisions that researchers make in determining approaches to analysis and, particularly, which data results to present. Naturally, an embedded approach permits, at least in principle, a researcher to provide more information about "scientific practice as ordinary action" (Lynch 1994) than would be possible for even the most penetrating external critic.

Red Tape as Token: What Are Its Bona Fides?

In seeking to understand the problems and prospects of public administration research, why choose as a focus red tape theory and research? We feel there is a simple but excellent justification for focusing on red tape. In red tape research, unlike many topics in public administration, there *is* theory and there *is* research and sometimes the research is informed by theory and sometimes the theory is informed by the research. These seem modest accomplishments but, as critics of every stripe acknowledge, they are ones we cannot necessarily expect in public administration. Second, as a fellow critic (Luton 2007, 530) notes, "it would be difficult to identify a concept that is more identified with the field of public administration than red tape."

The quantity of red tape research recommends it as a focus. As seen in the foregoing chapters, there is plenty of red tape research and theory, but, just as important, the development of red tape research and theory is sufficiently recent that any active researcher who has worked on the topic for several years has witnessed its growth from virtually nothing to such an estimable position it gives rise to both literature reviews (e.g., Pandey and Scott 2002) and critical potshots (Luton 2007).

Another argument for focusing on red tape research is that, like so much of public administration research, it is for the most part grounded in data obtained from questionnaires administered in surveys. We argue below and elsewhere that this is a serious limitation. But it is a *representative* limitation in that survey research is certainly the single most common type of quanti-tatively oriented research published in public administration research. For decades, public administration research was shaped strongly by its predomi-nant method—the case study—and the strengths and weaknesses of public administration research were then, as now, tied strongly to the method.

Finally, we feel that red tape research resembles other fields of public administration research in that it is neither entirely feckless nor particularly potent. Some might dispute this assessment, from one direction or the other. In our view, however, red tape research, like so much of public administration research, has provided incremental improvements in knowledge, improve-ments accruing largely from the convergent validity of separate research studies rather than any research-based breakthrough in theory (or any theory-based breakthrough in research).

Embedded in Red Tape: Prehistory

Red tape research came late to public administration, beginning to flourish only in the 1990s as several excellent researchers began to probe the topic. Before the 1990s, a few important works were available, especially related topics by sociologists (see Chapter 2 of this book), but red tape did not exist as a research field in public administration. There were several important public administration essays that at least discussed red tape (see especially Waldo 1948) and excellent books examining various forms of bureaucratic pathology (e.g., Thompson 1961), but no one (with one possible exception, noted below) had actually conducted empirical research on the topic.

In the 1990s, when empirical research on red tape was first being published, the best known work on red tape was still Herbert Kaufman's book *Red Tape: Its Origins, Uses, and Abuses* (1977)—a small (about 100 pages), accessible, interesting work still widely read. Until recently (2009), it was the most cited scholarly work on red tape.[5] While the book includes useful ideas, many are not fully developed. The book occupies territory somewhere between academic work and popular management, as its cartoons and aphorisms make clear enough. Indeed, Kaufman himself was a little taken aback at how seriously some people viewed his book (Kaufman, personal communication, 1993).[6]

Red Tape Studies, Pre-1990

Before the 1990s there was but a single empirical study published using as its primary focus a variable termed "red tape." Bruce Buchanan (1975) produced the study and its title was "Red Tape and the Service Ethic" (seemingly presaging both red tape research and public service motivation research). In retrospect, the title of this noteworthy study was in one important respect misleading. Upon examination one finds that the measure Buchanan was using as red tape was identical to the measure that several other organization researchers had used as an index of formalization. It is perhaps more accurate to say that this is the first published work in the public administration literature to focus on formalization. As we noted in preceding chapters, the differences between formalization concepts and the most familiar red tape concepts might seem small but, in fact, have great import in explanation.

By the 1980s, organizational formalization studies were extensive and perhaps the most important intellectual resource available to those who set out to develop a research program on red tape. At the time almost all the well-known formalization studies were in the organizational sociology literature (e.g., Hall 1968; Hall, Johnson, and Haas 1967; Pugh et al. 1969). One representative definition of formalization is "the extent to which rules, procedures, instructions and communications are written" (Pugh et al. 1969, 75). If we consider the ordinary use of the term "red tape," it was as clear to us in the mid-1980s as it is today that formalization did not capture much of the meaning of the red tape concept. As we noted in earlier chapters, in common usage red tape is a negative aspect about organizations, typically implying inefficiency, delay, or wasted effort. No one complains much about written rules if they are effective.

Red Tape Research and Data Opportunism

The first systematic, empirically based published study focusing chiefly on red tape (Bozeman, Reed, and Scott 1992) as a concept distinct from formalization was published seventeen years after the Buchanan study. However, in the period 1975–1992, papers that included red tape variables, though *not* as a primary focus, were published in the public administration literature. One such paper was Bozeman and Loveless's (1987) study of performance in public and private organizations, a study using red tape measures as independent variables predicting performance. The origins of that study are worth discussing, not only because it was the senior author's first foray into red tape research of any sort, but also because it provides a key lesson about the course of public administration research: that much of its development has been opportunistic, rather than following theory-based cues or a systematic research trajectory.

Bozeman's involvement with red tape research began in his collaboration with the late Steve Loveless. In the early 1980s, Loveless was a doctoral student planning his dissertation (with Bozeman as adviser). Loveless, an accomplished and published researcher before beginning his dissertation, had a long-standing interest in red tape. It is not clear just where this interest originated, but perhaps from his earlier work as a research assistant to Waldo. Loveless had read all of Waldo's work and was particularly taken with Waldo's writings about red tape. However, Loveless's research orientation was strongly empirical and his theoretical background, while broad, included an interest in organizational sociology, particularly studies of organizational structure and formalization. Knowing that empirical researchers in sociology had made considerable progress in studying structural features of organizations, he was both disappointed and motivated by the fact that no one had really conducted research explicitly on the topic of organizational red tape. Red tape seemed to Loveless such a pervasive phenomenon that it made no sense that there would be such a void in the organizational literature.

Loveless sought to write a dissertation on red tape. However, there were no data explicitly focused on red tape. Thus, after a fruitless search for data on red tape, he decided to focus on performance data that happened to incorporate a few questions (among hundreds) on red tape. His thesis adviser, Bozeman, was conducting research not only on public organizations but also research and development (R&D) policy and had access to one of the most extensive and, at that time, underutilized databases about R&D organizations, a multinational study developed by organizational sociologist Frank Andrews (1979) and his colleagues. The Andrews study was on R&D unit performance and while it was not primarily concerned with sector comparisons, it nonetheless included data on whether organizations were government-based or industry-based. This material permitted Loveless to do a dissertation examining the relation of sector to performance. His work (Loveless 1985) ultimately won the prize awarded by the National Association of Schools of Public Affairs and Administration for best dissertation of the year. As part of that work, Bozeman and Loveless began a collaboration that resulted in an article (Bozeman and Loveless 1987) comparing public and private organizations.

The key point here is that one focus (not the primary one) of the Bozeman and Loveless paper (and to some extent the Loveless dissertation) was the effect of red tape on performance. Andrews (1979) had included a battery of questions asking explicitly about red tape, but had never really used these items. Bozeman and Loveless, after controlling for a wide variety of possible conflating factors such as organizational size and resources, found that red tape remained a major factor in determining performance differences between public and private R&D organizations (Bozeman and Loveless 1987). While this study is not often cited as a work on red tape, given that its focus is more on public and private sector comparison, it is probably the first work published in the empirical public administration literature that includes a measure of red tape as an important component of its model (at least if one considers Buchanan's work as focusing on formalism). The developer of the database, Andrews (1979), did not focus on red tape per se and had no particular interest in public sector organizations. But the red tape measure they employed was not dissimilar to those employed later by others.

It is worth noting that the availability of the Andrews data, with its large number of observations and its measures of red tape, could be construed as having played an important role in the early history of public administration research on red tape. Without the Andrews data, Bozeman and Loveless would have had no other relevant data and no support for developing data related to red tape. Further evidence of the role of idiosyncrasy in research trajectories: While Bozeman was on leave from his home institution (then Syracuse University) and visiting Virginia Tech, he obtained the data from Professor Joe Cheng, a faculty member at Virigina Tech. Cheng, who had recently graduated from Michigan and whose adviser was Frank Andrews, was one of only three or four people who had full rights and access to the data.

The course of much red tape research, and perhaps much public administration research, depends on such "accidents" and on opportunism. The reason idiosyncrasy plays such a major role is there are so few general databases related to public administration and so little research funding for developing new ones. Much empirical research on red tape (and, more generally, public administration research) is the story of databases: data sponsored by grants and foundation gifts focused on public administration (very rarely!); public administration data developed ("bootlegged") from sponsored research studies that do not have public administration as their chief focus (more common); and databases developed on the modest resources put together by researchers themselves (e.g., NASP I, II, and III).

This sort of opportunism is true for many topics and many social sciences fields, but in most instances the causation is bidirectional: researchers are attracted by data and data attracts researchers. In public administration research, there is a great deal of researcher "push" and only limited data "pull."

Embedded in Projects: The Role of Team-Based Research Projects in the Development of Red Tape Research

We see above how research projects can play an important role in the advance of research, even when the projects are not specifically about the topic of the research. The above example was an instance, frequently replicated, of red tape researchers using someone else's data and bending it to their own purposes. However, most empirical research published by red tape researchers has been based on data developed by themselves or by colleagues, sometimes from studies designed expressly to address red tape and sometimes from studies where red tape is only a component and perhaps not a major one. Since we feel there are important lessons to be learned about the interaction of projects and research trajectories, we focus on several here.

It is difficult to overemphasize the role of research projects and data development in the social history of red tape studies. In fact, the role is so prominent that we organized this research history based on these project experiences. We have already discussed the role of the NASP projects in red tape research, but we consider them here from a different perspective, an embedded one.

NASP I: Lessons From a Participative Research Project

Beginning in 1990, several colleagues (including Bozeman, David Coursey, Hal Rainey, Dennis Wittmer, Sanjay Pandey, Patrick Scott, and Stuart Bretschneider, among others) developed the first of the public organization data projects that are now called the National Administrative Studies Project (NASP). This first NASP was a multiuniversity effort that began at Syracuse University's Maxwell School.[7]

This first NASP study was largely self-financed, using small amounts of money available from academic departments and individual research accounts. The goal of this project was, from the beginning, development of a multipurpose database that would not only include questions developed by several individuals but also address a variety of organizational research topics. Since this was the approach used, at least to some extent, for all three NASP projects, the peculiarities of the approach are worth some attention, especially since this design element affects not only red tape research possibilities, but also public administration research generally.

It is important to understand the motives underlying the first NASP study, especially since they were to some extent motivating factors in the two later ones as well. In 1990, there was no public administration database that had all the characteristics of being (1) widely available, (2) created by public administration researchers, (3) multitopic, and (4) oriented to fundamental research. The absence of such databases was due in part to a lack of funding but also, just as important, to a lack of understanding of their importance. Even today, there seems to be no awareness, or at least no concern, among research funding agencies about the need for general-purpose public administration databases. To be sure, there are many sources of funding for public administration researchers, but in nearly every case, the funding is available for a specific applied problem (e.g., improving communication with public agency clients) and within a particular policy domain (e.g., social services). For most funding agents, the term "fundamental public administration research" likely has no meaning or seems an oxymoron. Public administration scholars have done such a good job convincing others of the utility of their work that it is difficult to assess public administration research on any basis other than its immediate utility.

Circa 1990 it was perhaps also the case that not many public administration scholars saw a strong need for multipurpose public domain datasets. In the first place, public administration was not in general an empirical research field at that time. Most persons who referred to themselves as public administration scholars were oriented to strategy and focused on case studies and what later came to be referred to as "best practices" (for an analysis of epistemological orientations of public administration in the decade of the 1990s and before, see Bozeman 1993). Those few 1990s-era scholars who were focused on public administration and were active empirical, quantitative researchers tended to rely on general federal government databases (e.g., the General Social Survey), external funding of focused research topics (e.g., the URBIS project centered on information technology and located at University of California–Irvine), or small-scale datasets, often from a single organization, developed by individual researchers using limited or no institutional funds.

At least some of the scholars involved in NASP I had considerable experience developing large-scale databases for sponsored research projects aimed at focus research topics. For example, Bozeman had experience with large-scale databases funded by the National Science Foundation (NSF) and focused on R&D laboratories. Similarly, Stuart Bretschneider, also closely involved in NASP I, had experience in large-scale energy- and environment-focused projects. Thus, some of the NASP I architects had seen firsthand the value of team-oriented databases developed in multiperson projects. However, the chief substantive concern of NASP I was one that no mission-oriented, applied funding agency was likely to sponsor. The primary research interest of NASP I was comparing public and private organizations and their management, a topic too broad to be of interest to any mission-oriented public agency and too diffuse to be of interest to a private foundation. That primary interest (and limited funds) dictated the sampling strategy for the study: matched functional groups in public and private organizations in the state of New York (with subsequent administration of the same questionnaire to smaller samples in Florida by David Coursey and in Colorado by Dennis Wittmer).

A second important motivation was the presence in the early- and mid-1990s of a large number of high-quality Syracuse University doctoral students (e.g., David Coursey, Gordon Kingsley, Gerald Lan, Jae Moon, Sanjay Pandey, Patrick Scott, Eric Welch, Dennis Wittmer) shopping for dissertation topics related to organization studies or public administration. While most of these doctoral student participants in NASP I had paid research assistantships, some of which were directly associated with NASP tasks, the more important point is a strong set of aligned incentives. Even students who were not committed to producing a NASP-based dissertation were interested in developing publications from the database.

Given the incentive structure and motives for NASP I, the project directive was straightforward: (1) all work on NASP I should support the general objective of developing a database that could be used for the central theme of comparing public and private organizations and (2) all participants could submit a set of questionnaire items that would be evaluated by all other project participants. All those participating in NASP I at the outset submitted items. The list was about four times the length that could be accommodated in the questionnaire. Several rounds of open discussion were followed by a rating process, with all participants submitting defenses and rationales for their items and all participants rating everyone else's items. The project director (Bozeman) was responsible for continuity, thematic consistency, and methodological issues (such as ensuring the ability to develop scales from the items), and some other project members had special duties (e.g., Rainey was responsible for the relation of NASP I items to ones used previously in the organization research literature). Ultimately, the list was winnowed until a suitable pretest questionnaire was developed, and the final cuts were made based on the results of the pretest (e.g., items that had insufficient response variance were eliminated). The final NASP I questionnaire was the proverbial elephant: put together by a committee. But it was in some respects a handsome elephant. The questions were not disconnected and while the questionnaire had several themes, none were isolated or jarring to the flow of the questionnaire. *An important element of the first NASP, and all later ones, was compromise. But the reward for compromise was the sustained interest by a cadre of disparate but highly productive public administration researchers.*

The results from the NASP I project were considerable (see Table 7.1), especially considering that many key contributors had (at that time) limited research experience. While NASP I resulted in a number of papers on the core topic, comparing public and private organizations (e.g., Lan and Rainey 1992), most papers used the comparative framework in connection with some set of organization behaviors, including organizational ethics (Wittmer and Coursey 1996), decision process models (Kingsley and Reed 1991), organizational risk (Bozeman and Kingsley 1998), managerial perceptions (Pandey and Welch 2005), entrepreneurship (Moon 1999), and information technology (Moon and Bretschneider 2002). However, the NASP I data also provided the first in a series of studies of public and private differences in red tape (Bozeman and Rainey 1998; Bozeman, Reed, and Scott 1992; Pandey and Kingsley 2000; Rainey, Pandey, and Bozeman 1995). Red tape was one of the major "themes" included in the NASP I questionnaire, with about 25 percent of the original questionnaire being devoted to these items, chiefly because a majority of the original team professed interest in red tape research.

The first NASP paper focusing on red tape was the Bozeman, Reed, and Scott (1992) paper (and the first multiorganization study of red tape as apart from formalization). As such, this study, and the "lock-in" effect of the NASP I questionnaire, set the tone for several later studies of red tape. An important lesson from the NASP I experience, one that goes beyond red tape research, is that *the development of measures often has a lock-in effect that creates a sort of research path dependency.* The NASP I red tape measures (reviewed earlier in this book) were employed in nearly every published red tape study (and any other study using red tape as one of its variables) during the 1990s. Moreover, some of these same measures, or ones quite similar, are employed today in recent research on red tape (e.g., Feeney and Bozeman 2009; Feeney and Rainey 2009; Walker and Brewer 2008).

Red tape research is not unusual in its potential for lock-in. There are few instances of empirical public administration research where extant databases do not substantially affect the course of research (think of the Texas schools data). Whether we think of researchers as being indebted to or prisoner to the constructs and measures developed in public databases, the point is important. If the designers of questionnaires and other data instruments do not get it right at the outset, the ability of other researchers to correct deficiencies is usually quite limited.

Another lesson from the NASP I project (and it pertains equally to later NASP projects) has to do with the effects of project-based research in developing research and training networks. Doctoral students play the pivotal role in this case. When projects include a large number of junior researchers and doctoral students, the ideas migrate: doctoral students take jobs at other universities or research institutions and, if interests are sustained and data are public domain, take the data and their research ideas with them. In turn, they influence their own doctoral students and new colleagues, often providing the public domain data in a convenient form. In a memorable phrase, "participa-

Table 7.1

NASP I Papers

Bozeman, B., and G. Kingsley. 1998. Risk culture in public and private organizations. *Public Administration Review,* 58(2), 109–118.
Bozeman, B., and H.G. Rainey. 1998. Organizational rules and the "bureaucratic personality." *American Journal of Political Science,* 42(1), 163–189.
Moon, M.J., and S.I. Bretschneider. 2002. Does the perception of red tape constrain IT innovativeness in organizations? Unexpected results from a simultaneous equation model and implications. *Journal of Public Administration Research and Theory,* 12(2), 273–291.
Pandey, S.K., and G.A. Kingsley. 2000. Examining red tape in public and private organizations: Alternative explanations from a social psychological model. *Journal of Public Administration Research and Theory,* 10(4), 779–799.
Pandey, S.K., and P.G. Scott. 2002. Red tape: A review and assessment of concepts and measures. *Journal of Public Administration Research and Theory,* 12(4), 553–580.
Pandey, S.K., and E.W. Welch. 2005. Beyond stereotypes: A multistage model of managerial perceptions of red tape. *Administration and Society,* 37(5), 542–575.
Rainey, H.G., S.K. Pandey, and B. Bozeman. 1995. Research note: Public and private managers' perceptions of red tape. *Public Administration Review,* 55(6), 567–574.
Wittmer, D., and D. Coursey. 1996. Ethical work climates: Comparing top managers in public and private organizations. *Journal of Public Administration Research and Theory,* 6(4), 559–572.

tive public projects pollinate." *A fundamental sign of a project's success is that persons not known to the originators of the project are publishing good work based on the project's data*—a good example of university-based public administration researchers contributing to the public domain and the pool of knowledge.

The National Comparative Research and Development Project: Lessons in "Backdoor" Public Administration Research

The NASP I project was the quintessential bottom-up, participative project. In many cases, however, public administration research is a by-product of large research projects focused on entirely different topics. For this reason, among others, we consider the role of the National Comparative Research and Development Project (NCRDP) in promoting red tape research—the project illustrates a "backdoor" means of supporting public administration research.

The NCRDP was typical of projects funded by government agencies or, more accurately, typical of projects funded by the NSF. The NCRDP studies (for an overview, see Crow and Bozeman 1998) were conducted at Syracuse

University's Center for Technology and Information Policy and were sponsored by the NSF and the Department of Energy. This effort to profile and assess the performance of the research system of the United States gathered case study, historical, and questionnaire data (in three different rounds and in Japan as well as the United States) from thousands of R&D managers.

As we noted above, the idea of funding fundamental research on public administration is a concept still looking for a government sponsor. Of course, the NSF's chief mission is funding fundamental research, including social science research and, as in this case, science and technology policy. The chief goal of the four-year, well-funded projects encompassed under the NCRDP rubric was to provide a theory-based inventory and classification of the U.S. research and development enterprise (see Bozeman and Crow 1990; Crow and Bozeman 1987, 1998).

The NCRDP is a good illustration of building public administration research through a backdoor strategy: addressing public administration concerns in a specific policy context or including public administration research questions as ancillary to the chief concern of a much larger project. The backdoor strategy involves giving the sponsor results on all that has been contracted . . . and more. The "more" quite often includes low-demand (by public policy-makers) questions pertaining to public administration. Thus, the NCRDP provided a great deal of information about research organizations and their effectiveness in the United States, including more than twenty articles on the topic and four dissertations. But these same data were employed for research on a variety of public administration topics (see Bozeman and Crow 1990; Bozeman and Bretschneider 1991), *including* red tape (Bozeman and Crow 1991).

One obvious public administration lesson from the NCRDP case is the usefulness and "production efficiencies" entailed in bringing public administration research objectives to other project foci. Public administration theory and research can often improve the primary focus. Just as important, *backdoor resources are often the only available resources for much public administration research*. But this is an obvious lesson and one that many have already applied with considerable success.

A less obvious lesson is that *public administration learning is almost always abetted by grounding in a particular institutional and policy setting.* In the case of the NCRDP, red tape research was ancillary to this project, but the grounding of red tape studies in a particular policy domain yielded insights that could not easily have been obtained in a less focused study (see Bozeman and Crow 1991). For example, Crow and Bozeman (1998) found that R&D laboratory directors reported extremely high levels of perceived red tape, but by every objective measure (sign-offs, authority levels, delays in core functions) their organizations had unusually low levels of red tape compared to organizations studied previously. This led us to examine the variable "red tape tolerance," not unlike a previous construct, "tolerance for bureaucratic structure," developed by Baker and colleagues (1973). Similarly, later project-based studies, ones focused on different policy domains, showed that policy-focused studies could lead to new and different questions.

Consider another backdoor project related to red tape. Feeney and Bozeman (2009) studied state transportation agencies. Their work on dyadic red tape, matching contractors' red tape assessments against those of agencies, flowed directly from the fact that state transportation policy is a domain characterized by an unusual degree of reliance on contractors. The general point is that *particular policy settings, essentially necessitated by projects funded for applied work, provided insights that probably would not have emerged from studies that are context-free.*

The NCRDP case provides good illustrative material, but it is not unusual in its ability to spawn public administration research from purposes oriented to particular policy domains. For example, studies of organizational performance have benefited from funding agents' interests in financing studies of schools (O'Toole and Meier 2004), and studies of networks have benefited from grants to study mental health (e.g., assorted work of Milward, Provan, and Isett). *Public administration researchers who have large grants to support their research often find ways to satisfy sponsors' requirements and, at the same time, build additional research agendas not directly pertaining to the grants' topics.*

The NYSERA Project: Lessons From Digging Deep

Each of the NASP projects has contributed to some degree to empirical work on red tape. A very different project made a very different contribution. In 1990, Syracuse University's Center for Technology and Information Policy (the research unit housing the faculty and doctoral students beginning a focus on red tape research) was awarded a large, two-year grant to perform a thoroughgoing evaluation of the New York State Energy Research and Development Authority (NYSERDA), the nation's largest state government energy research organization, seeking to improve management, focusing particularly on management information systems. The grant supported a number of individuals, some public administration researchers (including Bozeman, Gordon Kingsley, and Stuart Bretschneider), as well as engineering professors.

The NYSERDA research team had unprecedented access, including access to all documents for the history of the organization and the ability to interview anyone ever affiliated with the organization (and the organization was of sufficiently recent vintage that it was easy to interview those present at the creation). The focus of the work was intense, so much so that the research team had a suite of offices located in the organization's headquarters and a project townhouse in Albany, three blocks from the Rockefeller Plaza location of NYSERDA.

Naturally, the team began to develop a deep knowledge of the organization and its history. Most NYSERDA activities, as is the case for almost all government R&D funding agencies, involved contracting. Where contracting goes, red tape is almost sure to follow (see Feeney and Bozeman 2009). While NYSERDA was in general very well managed, it was subject to an extremely dense latticework of rules and regulations, many of its own devising and many imposed externally. During the project, the research team began to focus on the causes of red tape and possibilities for reducing red tape. We felt that almost all the management problems encountered at NYSERDA, a highly competent organization with high-quality leadership, were owing to the regime of rules and regulations that it labored under.

To make a long story short, the work on the NYSERDA project yielded knowledge that would make any phenomenologist proud. Direct reflection and discussions about NYSERDA rules and regulations showed us that there was an inadequate language for even discussing red tape, that few useful concepts were available, and that what literature was then extant provided few interesting hypotheses but was, rather, oriented to suggesting that red tape really is not so much of a problem—that is, as Kaufman (1977) put it, "One man's red tape is another's treasured procedural safeguard"—or seemed to make no distinction between formalization (the number of rules) and the *effectiveness* of the rules. However, by intense observation of the day-to-day activities of one organization operating under dense rules and regulations, we were able to invent needed concepts about various types of red tape (e.g., "stakeholder red tape") and red tape origins (e.g., "pass-through red tape") and, perhaps most important, to develop hypotheses about the red tape generated by the organization, including those who no longer worked there ("organizational phantoms"). We were also able to see how very bright, well-intentioned people could, due to the complexities of contingent social forecasts ("rules forecasts"), create and implement rules that did not serve the purpose intended (the "functional object of the rule"). By observing a variety of attributes of the organization's rules (e.g., "rules density," the "rules ecology"), we were able to develop still more hypotheses about how red tape emerged.

The experience with the project was vital to developing the systematic theory first published in Bozeman's "A Theory of Government 'Red Tape'" (1993). Many of the concepts that emerged from this phenomenological understanding of one complex organization to which we had unlimited access are used routinely in today's red tape research.

It is important to understand that the only thing exceptional about the NYSERDA project was that this well-managed organization was willing to open its doors to visiting academic researchers for no reasons other than the hope of improving the organization. Contracting organizations may be especially good sites for red tape theory development, but *any* large, complex organization that had afforded the same access would have probably proved an excellent "red tape laboratory."

While many public administration research lessons could be drawn from the NYSERDA project, one is obvious and recognized by almost all public administration researchers. *Case studies provide an excellent means of developing theory and hypotheses; the greater the access and the more intense the focus, the more likely those case studies will prove fruitful. However, case studies, even multiple, interrelated case studies, have only limited utility for testing or validating theory and hypotheses.* With respect to red tape, we can perhaps see the relevance of case studies to theory development. But to what extent has theory development led, in turn, to research aimed at validating theory?

NASP II

It is fair to say that NASP II, perhaps more than any of the other projects discussed here, was the creation of one person, Sanjay Pandey.[8] Although he was involved with NASP I and consulted many public administration scholars in the design of the items for his instrument, NASP II was more the result of one person's enterprise. The focus of NASP II was a nationwide sample of individuals involved in information management in state government health and human services agencies. What is of interest for present purposes, however, is that it included more red tape indices that any previous or subsequent project. Most of the red tape papers published between 2004 and 2008, more than eighteen papers, either focusing specifically on red tape (Chen and Williams 2007; DeHart-Davis and Pandey 2005; Pandey, Coursey, and Moynihan 2007; Pandey and Moynihan 2006; Scott and Pandey 2005; Turaga and Bozeman 2005; Welch and Pandey 2007) or including a red tape component (Coursey, Welch, and Pandey 2005; Garnett, Marlowe, and Pandey 2008; Moynihan and Pandey 2007a; Pandey and Garnett 2006; Pandey and Rainey 2006; Pandey and Wright 2006; Yang and Pandey 2009), used NASP II data.

Table 7.2 lists the NASP II papers that deal with red tape, either as a central concern or as one of several independent variables.

According to Pandey, he spent about seven months developing content for NASP II and its associated questionnaire. He drafted an initial question-

Table 7.2

NASP II Papers

Chen, G., and D.W. Williams. 2007. How political support influences red tape through developmental culture. *Policy Studies Journal*, 35(3), 419–436.

Coursey, D.H., and S.K. Pandey. 2007a. Content domain, measurement, and validity of the red tape concept: A second-order confirmatory factor analysis. *American Review of Public Administration*, 37, 342.

DeHart-Davis, L., and S.K. Pandey. 2005. Red tape and public employees: Does perceived rule dysfunction alienate managers? *Journal of Public Administration Research and Theory*, 15(1), 133–148.

Moynihan, D.P., and S.K. Pandey. 2007b. The role of organizations in fostering public service motivation. *Public Administration Review*, 67(1), 40–53.

Pandey, S.K., D.H. Coursey, and D.P. Moynihan. 2007. Organizational effectiveness and bureaucratic red tape: A multimethod study. *Public Performance and Management Review*, 30(3), 398–425.

Pandey, S.K., and J.L. Garnett. 2006. Exploring public sector communication performance: Testing a model and drawing implications. *Public Administration Review*, 66(1), 37–51.

Pandey, S.K., and D.P. Moynihan. 2006. Bureaucratic red tape and organizational performance: Testing the moderating role of culture and political support. In *Public Service Performance*, ed. G.A. Boyne, K.J. Meier, L.J. O'Toole, and R.M. Walker. Cambridge, UK: Cambridge University Press.

Pandey, S.K., and H.G. Rainey. 2006. Public managers' perceptions of organizational goal ambiguity: Analyzing alternative models. *International Public Management Journal*, 9(2), 85–112.

Pandey, S.K., and P.G. Scott. 2002. Red tape: A review and assessment of concepts and measures. *Journal of Public Administration Research and Theory*, 12(4), 553–580.

Pandey, S.K., and B.E. Wright. 2006. Connecting the dots in public management: Political environment, organizational goal ambiguity, and the public manager's role ambiguity. *Journal of Public Administration Research and Theory*, 16(4), 511–532.

Scott, P.G., and S.K. Pandey. 2005. Red tape and public service motivation: Findings from a national survey of managers in state health and human services agencies. *Review of Public Personnel Administration*, 25(2), 155–180.

Turaga, R.M.R., and B. Bozeman. 2005. Red tape and public managers' decision making. *American Review of Public Administration*, 35(4), 363–379.

Welch, E.W., and S.K. Pandey. 2007. E-government and bureaucracy: Toward a better understanding of intranet implementation and its effect on red tape. *Journal of Public Administration Research and Theory*, 17, 379–404.

Yang, K., and S.K. Pandey. 2009. How do perceived political environment and administrative reform affect employee commitment? *Journal of Public Administration Research and Theory*, (2), 335–360.

naire and solicited three rounds of evaluation from more than fifteen people (including Rainey, Bretschneider, Bozeman, and others long involved in red tape research). Like all NASP projects, NASP II was chiefly funded by modest university funds. As Pandey wryly notes in his communication with us, "it is possible to be bold, ambitious and inclusive and let the 'force' guide you—once you give up on the idea of [external] research funding." Pandey goes on to give a sense of both the esprit and the difficulties of low-budget NASP projects:

> The administration of the project had all the NASP hallmarks: painful, un-derstaffed, and under-resourced. [In addition to a modest level of university funds] I used some of my own money. Sheela [Pandey's spouse] took pity on me and did the database programming, along with a really good, part-time MPA student. But the implementation turned out to be top-notch; people with much more money are not able to do this as well.

Pandey told us that his chief concern for NASP II was "pushing red tape research in all kinds of new arenas" and that his primary plan was to connect red tape research to the traditional research themes in public administration. Thus, the NASP II work linked red tape to performance (Pandey, Coursey, and Moynihan 2007; Pandey and Moynihan 2006); to organizational com-munication (Garnett, Marlowe, and Pandey 2008; Pandey and Garnett 2006); to goal ambiguity (Pandey and Rainey 2006; Pandey and Wright 2006); to public service motivation (Coursey and Pandey 2007b; Scott and Pandey 2005); and to classic organizational behavior concerns such as job satisfaction and commitment (DeHart-Davis and Pandey 2005; Scott and Pandey 2005; Moynihan and Pandey 2007a). Pandey summarizes his NASP II experience: "it is a little like planning a camping trip with friends, where you do some scouting, take care of some strategic and logistical issues, have a rough plan for all the fun that is possible once you reach the campsite and then just enjoy the party."

In the other projects discussed in this section, one or both of the coauthors were deeply involved. However, we were not "embedded" in NASP II but, rather, were more or less peripheral actors who made a few comments on early instruments and then used the data (e.g., Bozeman and Pandey 2004). We shall leave to Pandey the task of drawing embedded lessons for NASP II. Let us simply observe that NASP II was similar to other NASP projects (as Pandey notes), but was quite different in that it focused even more on red tape, developing additional measures, and made a valuable contribution by connecting red tape to other public administration and organization stud-ies' research questions that had not previously been viewed as particularly related to red tape concerns. In these ways, the empirically based theory and research on red tape was expanded beyond its previous boundaries and red tape was used often as an independent variable (DeHart-Davis and Pandey 2005; Moynihan and Pandey 2007b; Pandey and Garnett 2006; Pandey and Moynihan 2006; Pandey and Rainey 2006), whereas previous studies, espe-cially the several studies comparing public and private organizations (e.g.,

Bozeman and Bretschneider 1991; Bozeman, Reed, and Scott 1992) had generally employed red tape as a dependent variable.

NASP III

NASP III is the least red tape–oriented of any of the NASP projects, including only one questionnaire item directly related to red tape and rules. NASP III closely resembled the two NASP projects preceding it in the following respects: (1) it was a team effort involving scholars from several institutions (in this case, Georgia Tech, University of Georgia, University of Illinois–Chicago); (2) it was funded by small university-based funds (less than $10,000 total); and (3) it relied heavily on doctoral student researchers (Mary K. Feeney, a doctoral student at the time, was project manager). Just as important, the data were used in several dissertations (five and counting) and in a significant number (thirty-seven and counting) of papers published in the public administration literature.

The explicit objective of the NASP III project was to focus on areas different from NASP I and II. While yet another elephant built by committee, with contributions from at least ten faculty and doctoral student researchers, the primary foci of NASP III were mentoring relationships and career trajectories (especially job choice factors and the effects of switching sectors). A primary red tape implication was the folly of not following through. Bozeman made the decision to exclude many of the previous NASP red tape measures, ones that would have shed light on several of the human resources issues examined in NASP III.

The limitation of a single red tape measure (in this case and many others, the General Red Tape Scale) has not stopped researchers from using NASP III for red tape–focused research (see Feeney and Rainey 2010), even with all the usual admonitions about single-measure organizational constructs. For example, Feeney and Rainey (2010) used the General Red Tape Scale and a set of items they call "personnel flexibility" but which Pandey in numerous NASP II papers called "personnel red tape" to test for differences in perceptions of red tape and personnel rules among managers in the nonprofit and public sectors. Feeney (2008) also used the General Red Tape Scale as an independent variable for understanding perceptions of the public sector. Ponomariov and Boardman (in press) investigated the relationships between job characteristics and career trajectory and perceptions of general organizational red tape, and Feeney and Boardman (2010) note relationships between perceived general organizational red tape and organizational confidence.

Benefits of Team-Based Public Administration Projects

We have presented short histories of several *very* different projects, all of which resulted in empirical research in red tape. We examined the three

NASP projects, examples of poorly funded but extremely productive public administration–focused projects relying almost exclusively on questionnaires. Together, they drew information from literally thousands of organizations throughout the United States and from all sectors. The NASP projects contrast sharply to the NYSERDA project, which employed relatively abundant resources but focused exclusively and intensely on a single organization. The NCRDP project was included to show the importance of backdoor means of developing public administration research data, using a well-funded project focused on a set of public policy questions.

Figure 7.1 provides a summary of the lessons from the various projects.

We conclude with a couple of broader points. First, let us emphasize, we are *not* implying that advancing public administration research depends on projects. Clearly, most published work in public administration (though not red tape), especially conceptual work, has had no particular relation to team-based projects. However, we should note that team-based projects do present some important secondary benefits only alluded to above. The most important of these, perhaps, is the building of a research and training network. We feel that public administration research has benefited a great deal over the decades from the continued contact, communication, and collaboration of people who were involved in the various projects discussed above and ones much like them. In this, public administration research has much in common with work in the sciences, almost all of which is developed in a team project mode.

As in the sciences, the public administration research projects discussed above have been fruitful in large measure because several doctoral students were involved in each of them and the projects necessarily provided strong educational and socialization opportunities. For example, the first NASP project included graduate students such as Gordon Kingsley, Sanjay Pandey, and Patrick Scott. NASP II, which was largely the product of Sanjay Pandey, enabled the collaboration of numerous public administration scholars on research papers, including David Coursey, Leisha DeHart-Davis, Patrick Scott, and Eric Welch. The NASP III project included support from Julia Melkers, Hal Rainey, Barry Bozeman, Gordon Kingsley—all faculty members who worked on earlier NASP projects—and was managed by a graduate student, Mary Feeney, who is now a professor at University of Chicago at Illinois managing graduate students on a similar national survey. The history of red tape research in public administration, in some ways, is a history of research training in the field. There is an entire cohort of scholars who have worked on and around these national studies of red tape and who have worked together to publish results from these datasets. For example, if we consider the thirty or so researchers who publish public administration red tape research, most of them have coauthored with another researcher in that group, either a student or a faculty member, and in many

---

Figure 7.1

Lessons Learned From Team-Based Public Administration Research Projects

An important element of the first NASP, and all later ones, was compromise. But the reward was sustained interest by a cadre of somewhat disparate researchers.

The development of measures often has a lock-in effect that creates a sort of research path dependency.

Doctoral students play a critical role in team-based PM projects. When projects include a large number of junior researchers and doctoral students, the ideas migrate. Participative public projects pollinate. A fundamental sign of a project's success is that persons not known to the originators of the project are publishing good work based on the project's data.

Just as important, backdoor resources are often the only available resources for much public administration research.

A less obvious lesson is that public administration learning is almost always abetted by grounding in a particular institutional and policy setting. The general point is that particular policy settings, essentially necessitated by projects funded for applied work, provided insights that probably would not have emerged from studies that are context-free.

Public administration researchers who have large grants to support their research often find ways to satisfy sponsors' requirements and, at the same time, build additional research agendas not directly pertaining to the grants' topics.

Case studies provide an excellent means of developing theory and hypotheses; the greater the access and the more intense the focus, the more likely those case studies will prove fruitful. However (and there is perhaps less agreement here, at least among public administration researchers), case studies, even multiple, interrelated case studies, have only limited utility for testing or validating theory and hypotheses.

---

cases both. It is through the development of instruments, the implementation of research studies, and analysis and dissemination of results that faculty members have built ties with each other, trained graduate students, and prepared the next generation to engage in similar types of research projects.

While we certainly do not claim that the formation of viable research networks requires team projects, we do contend that such projects are quite beneficial for building the "scientific and technical human capital" (Bozeman, Dietz, and Gaughan 2001) required to stimulate and sustain knowledge development. Such projects provide a strong degree of shared purpose and, usually, social cohesion, which can be invaluable to the long-term health and well-being of research and theory.

Concluding Thoughts

If we take red tape research as a case in point for public administration theory, several lessons emerge (as we note above). But if there is a single, overarching implication, it is an optimistic one: that a few friends and colleagues can take it on themselves to create a new research field from whole cloth. While it is easy enough for we-the-embedded to find significant flaws and limitations in red tape research (and probably much easier for other informed critics to do so), we can make an important and consequential claim: not long ago there was no red tape research, and now there is. The body of work produced by the hundred or fewer researchers involved in the study of red tape remains poorly anchored, it is a bit too reliant on just a few limited measures, and it is rife with fragmented empirical induction. However, many of the findings of red tape research seem to have both convergent validity and face validity. Even if red tape research represents some of the characteristic weaknesses of public administration knowledge, it represents also the more important legacy of empirically grounded, theory-seeking work emerging in a field that not too long ago could claim very little as its own.

Notes

1. We are aware that we are painting with a broad brush, lumping together postmodernist, critical theory, and hermeneutics approaches under the general heading "postmodern." We argue below that postmodern perspectives, while worthy of acknowledgement, have no strong relevance to the peculiar problems of red tape research or public administration research. In general, postmodern arguments seem to us to apply to any social science endeavor intent on developing theory by employing quantitative data to test explicit hypotheses. Our excuses: first, we doubt that we are qualified to provide an adequate sorting; second, scholarly taxonomy is not a major concern of this paper. We are chiefly concerned about providing our opinions rather than classifying those of others. For anyone whom we may have placed in undesired company, please take this as a blanket apology and please accept our invitation to set us straight.

2. Obviously, nonmainstream approaches can certainly make claims to rigor, but with different criteria than those of traditional scientific method.

3. While both Bozeman and Feeney contributed substantially to each of the chapters in this book, including the present one, it should be noted that the personal perspectives presented in this chapter are primarily Bozeman's. When Bozeman first began as an "embedded" red tape researcher, Feeney was not yet ten years old.

4. The best exception to this generalization: James Watson's *The Double Helix* (1968), in which the author is fearless about describing the research-as-it-happened, including in ways that are clearly not self-flattering. We shall not be so revelatory as Watson.

5. In 2010, a paper by Rainey, Pandey, and Bozeman (1995) surpassed the Kaufman book in Google Scholar and Web of Science citations. This is an extremely rare case in public administration research in which an empirical research study is more cited than books or conceptual papers on the same topic. But augury seems unlikely. What is much more telling is that the paper is one of the most highly cited empirical public administration research papers even though it has only 108 Google Scholar citations. The most cited paper is a conceptual work on the new public administration. Christopher Hood's (1991) paper in *Public Administration* registered 2,707 Google

Scholar citations as of June 1, 2010. By contrast, at the same time a paper needed only fifty Google Scholar citations to be on the "top 10" list in empirical public administration research.

6. As Bozeman was becoming more committed to red tape research, he took Kaufman out to dinner in fall 1993 to discuss Kaufman's book, its origins, and, in general, why other scholars had not paid more attention to red tape as a focus for their work. Regarding the latter question, Kaufman said that he had no idea but that he considered his own book neither scholarly or theoretical in its intent, but rather a whimsical book that he wrote in between two more serious projects.

7. A trial run project, referred to as the Syracuse Metropolitan Organization Theory Project (SMOT), was conducted by a doctoral seminar Bozeman taught at Syracuse University with the help of Hal Rainey.

8. We communicated with Pandey about the origins and motivations of NASP II and we appreciate the information he has provided. The description here is not, however, his description, and any errors or omissions are ours, not his. However, all the quotes below are directly from Pandey, from private communications. We have, of course, received his permission to use these quotes in this book.

Appendixes

Since such a large proportion of the empirically based studies of red tape employed just a few data sources, it is useful to review in these appendixes some of the history and procedures associated with the primary data sources mentioned in this book and the articles reviewed.

Appendix 1
National Administrative Studies Project (NASP I)

The data for the National Administrative Studies Project (NASP I) were collected by a consortium of researchers at Syracuse University, Ohio State University, the University of Georgia, the University of Denver, Florida State University, and the Georgia Institute of Technology. The goals of NASP I were to develop a public administration database that had all the characteristics of being (1) widely available, (2) created by public administration researchers, (3) multitopic, and (4) oriented to fundamental research. The primary research topic for NASP I was comparing public and private organizations and their management.

Data were collected in Colorado, Florida, and New York from both senior and midlevel managers in the public, private, and nonprofit sectors. The purpose of the data collection effort was to develop a better understanding of bureaucratization, red tape, personnel systems, and other dimensions of public, private, and hybrid organizations. The NASP I data appear in numerous studies comparing red tape across public and private organizations (Pandey and Welch 2005). Extensive information regarding data collection methods is available in a number of publications (e.g., Bozeman 2000; Bozeman and

Kingsley 1998; Pandey 1995; Pandey and Kingsley 2000; Pandey and Scott 2002; Rainey, Pandey, and Bozeman 1995).

- Overall sample frame of 877 top managers; 341 responded (39 percent).
- The public subsample consisted of 386 top managers; 161 responded (42 percent).
- The private subsample consisted of 284 top managers; 79 responded (28 percent).
- The nonprofit subsample consisted of 207 top managers; 101 responded (49 percent).

Appendix 2
National Comparative Research and Development Project (NCRDP)

The National Comparative Research and Development Project (NCRDP) was conducted at Syracuse University's Center for Technology and Information Policy. The research was sponsored by the National Science Foundation (NSF) and the U.S. Department of Energy and aimed to profile and assess the performance of the research system of the United States. The project gathered case study, historical, and questionnaire data (in three different rounds) from thousands of research and development (R&D) managers in the United States and Japan. The chief goal of the four-year project was to provide a theory-based inventory and classification of the U.S. R&D enterprise (see Bozeman and Crow 1990; Crow and Bozeman 1987, 1998).

The NCRDP questionnaires were mailed to research directors from a sample pool of 1,341 research centers, with a total of 733 responses.

The NCRDP provided a great deal of information about research organizations and their effectiveness in the United States, supplying more than twenty articles on the topic and four dissertations. These data also were employed for research on a variety of public administration topics (Bozeman and Crow 1990; Bozeman and Bretschneider 1994), including red tape (Bozeman and Crow 1991).

Source: Bozeman and Bretschneider (1994).

Appendix 3
New York State Energy Research and Development Authority (NYSERDA)

In 1990, Syracuse University's Center for Technology and Information Policy was awarded a large, two-year grant to perform a thoroughgoing evaluation of the

New York State Energy Research and Development Authority (NYSERDA), the nation's largest state government energy research organization, seeking to improve management, focusing particularly on management information systems.

The NYSERDA research team had unprecedented access to the organization, including access to all documents for the history of the organization and the ability to interview anyone ever affiliated with the organization (which was of sufficiently recent vintage that it was easy to interview those present at the creation). Naturally, the team developed a deep knowledge of the organization and its history. During the project, the research team focused on the causes of red tape and possibilities for reducing red tape in the organization.

Appendix 4
National Administrative Studies Project II (NASP II)

The second National Administration Studies Project (NASP II), led by Dr. Sanjay Pandey, was a mail survey sent to 570 information managers in state-level primary health and human services agencies in the fifty states and Washington, DC, in 2002. At the conclusion of the project (winter 2003), there was a total of 274 responses (response rate 53 percent). The survey included a variety of rules and red tape items. The NASP II data provided a robust approach to assessing multiple types of red tape and enabled researchers to test red tape perceptions and concepts across the states (Chen and Williams 2007; Coursey and Pandey 2007a; Moynihan and Pandey 2007b; Pandey, Coursey, and Moynihan 2007; Pandey and Moynihan 2006; Pandey and Rainey 2006; Scott and Pandey 2005; Welch and Pandey 2007; Yang and Pandey 2009).

Appendix 5
National Administrative Studies Project (NASP III)

The third version of the National Administration Studies Project (NASP III) was conducted in 2004. The principal investigator was Barry Bozeman, and Mary K. Feeney, a doctoral student, was the project manager. The research was supported by university and individual funds from Barry Bozeman, Hal G. Rainey, Julia Melkers, and Eric Welch. Additionally, the instrument was developed with input from multiple researchers. NASP III asked respondents about (1) job motivations, (2) work environment, (3) organizational rules and procedures, (4) sector comparisons, (5) civic and political activity, (6) mentoring, (7) job history, and (8) demographic characteristics. The survey included only a few items related to rules and red tape.

Surveys were sent to 1,849 full-time public managers and 1,307 full-time nonprofit managers in Georgia and Illinois. Respondents represented organizations and agencies of numerous functions. NASP III was closed in January 2006 with a total of 1,200 responses (overall response rate 39 percent).

- Public managers = 790 (43 percent)
- Nonprofit managers = 430 (33 percent)

Appendix 6
English Local Government Dataset: Best Value and Core Performance Assessment (CPA)

The Centre for Local and Regional Government Research at Cardiff University was commissioned by the Office of the Deputy Prime Minister in 2000 to undertake a "Long Term Evaluation of Best Value and Its Impact." The study resulted in a dataset of survey responses from local government officers, measures on the organizational environment from the UK Census, and performance data from central government and its agencies.

The survey was conducted from 2001 to 2004. At the core of the study was a survey of 100 local authorities that are representative of all authorities in England. In 2001 and 2004, these 100 local government authorities were supplemented with a census of all upper-tier English local governments. The study implemented an electronic multiple informant survey strategy, surveying up to thirty-six officers per authority. These officers came from the corporate center and from service offices in seven policy areas. The survey explored informants' perceptions of organization, management, and environment, notably culture, structure, strategy, and drivers of service improvement together with the organizational environment, performance, and the Best Value regime.

Measures of red tape were included in the 2004 round of the survey. The 2004 survey was administered to 175 authorities (the basic 100 plus all upper-tier local governments). Responses were received from 166 authorities, which included 785 service areas and 1,232 officers. The papers examining red tape typically draw upon the context Census data that provides information on the characteristics of the local population and on performance using the Core Performance Score from the Comprehensive Performance Assessment. Some of the analysis has also included data from the 2003 survey.

The survey instrument is available from the Economic and Social Research Council's data archive (www.data-archive.ac.uk).

Appendix 7
Public Sector Workplace Survey: Kansas Data

The Public Sector Workplace Survey was led by Leisha DeHart-Davis at the University of Kansas. The survey was mailed to all employees of four cities from June 2005 to December 2006 and resulted in an overall response rate of 49 percent (n = 645). The four cities were a small agricultural community (n = 36; 61 percent response rate); a small city with a light industrial economic base (n = 90; 83 percent response rate); a mid-sized city located near a military base (n = 136; 43 percent response rate); and an affluent metropolitan city (n = 383; 45 percent response rate). The survey was preceded by ninety in-person interviews with city employees from a range of hierarchical levels and departments.

Appendix 8
Syracuse Metropolitan Organizational Theory Project (SMOT)

This project was a survey of organizations and managers in the Syracuse, New York, area. The sampling frame included managers at public, private, and hybrid organizations with more than ten employees (six or more in the case of school districts). The public organizations included local, state, and federal government agencies. The sampling frame included manufacturing firms and banks as representatives of the private category. The hybrid organizations included schools and hospitals. The surveys asked top and midlevel managers about decision-making.

For the sample of business firms, 96 manufacturing firms were randomly selected from among the 231 business firms in the area listed in Macrae's Industrial Directory for 1986. Because of their limited numbers, the sample included all the banks, schools, hospitals, and governmental agencies in the area that met the inclusion criteria. Researchers phoned the 120 organizations in the sample (17 public, 77 private, and 26 hybrid). Respondents from these organizations provided a list of 323 managerial employees (134 public, 111 private, and 78 hybrid) for the written survey. Questionnaires were then sent to the 313 respondents in a three-step procedure: alert letter, survey questionnaires, follow-up letter and second copy of the mail survey. Respondents returned a total of 220 usable responses for a 67 percent response rate. The final sample included 92 responses from public managers, 62 from private organizations, and 66 from hybrid organizations.

Source: Lan and Rainey (1992).

Appendix 9
National Administrative Studies Project IV (NASP IV)

The fourth National Administrative Studies Project (NASP IV) was conducted in 2008 by a group of researchers from several universities. NASP

IV was a multimethod study that included an Internet survey administered to a national sample of senior general (city manager and assistant/deputy city managers) and functional (managers of key departments such as Finance/ Budgeting, Public Works, Human Resources, Economic Development, Parks and Recreation, Planning, and Community Development) managers in U.S. local government jurisdictions with populations over 50,000, drawn from the population of the International City/County Management Association and publicly available data.

From the sample of 3,316 managers, 46.4 percent responded ($n = 1,538$). Anchoring vignettes about personnel red tape were included in surveys sent to a randomly chosen proportion of the sample. Three hundred and seven of the respondents completed the vignettes.

Source: Pandey and Marlowe (2009).

Appendix 10
The Staatsblad

The Staatsblad is a source of national regulations in The Netherlands. The Staatsblad publishes all formal laws, together with all accompanying changes. Many Dutch university libraries have a complete archive of Staatsblad editions. Researchers used the hard-copy archives of the Staatsblad to compile a list of all amendments in Dutch higher education acts. The coding process included using the acts themselves, as published in the Staatsblad, and minor amendments that appear in subsequent editions of the Staatsblad. All coded acts and amendments were confirmed with the Schuurmans and Jordens educational editions (an important source for information on Dutch educational acts).

Source: A. van Witteloostuijn and Gjalt de Jong. 2007. The evolution of higher education rules: Evidence for an ecology of law. *International Review of Administrative Sciences,* 73(2), 235–255.

Appendix 11
Public-Private Organization Studies Project at Syracuse (PPOSP)

A stratified probability sample of managers with sectoral status as the stratum was drawn from the Syracuse and Albany metropolitan areas in New York. The public organizations are state government agencies in Albany and Syracuse and city and county governments in Syracuse. The range of functions carried out by these organizations includes education, law enforcement, health services, welfare, economic development, and environmental protection. The private sample is made up of manufacturing organizations (metalworking, plastics, ceramics, chemicals, electrical, and electronic products), health services, elderly services, charitable social services, financial service, and engineering services. $n = 566$; public = 269; private = 297.

Sources: Coursey and Bozeman (1990); Kingsley and Reed (1991); Pandey and Kingsley (2000).

Appendix 12
Environmental Protection Agency Title V Study (EPA)

This study was an investigation of the extent of red tape involved in regulartory permitting for major federal air quality policy, specifically Title V of the Clean Air Act Amendments of 1990. Barry Bozeman, the principal investigator, and Leisha DeHart-Davis, then a doctoral student, collected data using a cross-sectional mail survey of representatives from Title V-regulated firms in Georgia, Oregon, South Carolina, and Wisconsin. These states were chosen because a review of standard industrial classifications revealed that they were home to a mixture of industry types and sizes.

The researchers used a random sampling process to draw 498 Georgia companies, 414 South Carolina companies, and 441 Wisconsin companies. Because Oregon had a small Title V-regulated community, all 242 sources were sampled. The response rates were 35 percent (Georgia), 40 percent (Oregon), 43 percent (South Carolina), and 31 percent (Wisconsin).

References

Aaronson, D., L. Barrow, and W. Sanders. 2003. *Teachers and Student Achievement in Chicago Public High Schools*. Chicago: Federal Research Bank of Chicago.

Abramson, Susan. 2005. Statewide smoking ban approved. *Atlanta Journal-Constitution*, March 31. www.ajc.com/metro/content/custom/blogs/georgia/entries/2005/03/31/statewide_smoking_ban_approved.html.

Adams, G.B. 1992. Enthralled with modernity: The historical context of knowledge and theory development in public administration. *Public Administration Review*, 52(4), 363–373.

Adams, G.B., and J.D. White. 1994. Dissertation research in public administration and cognate fields: An assessment of methods and quality. *Public Administration Review*, 54(6), 565–576.

Agranoff, R., and M. McGuire. 1999. Expanding intergovernmental management's hidden dimensions. *American Review of Public Administration*, 29(4), 352–369.

———. 2001a. Big questions in public network management research. *Journal of Public Administration and Theory*, 11(3), 295–326.

———. 2001b. American federalism and the search for models of management. *Public Administration Review*, 61(6), 671–681.

Andrews, F.M., ed. 1979. *Scientific Productivity: The Effectiveness of Research Groups in Six Countries*. Cambridge, UK: Cambridge University Press.

Andrews, R., G.A. Boyne, and R.M. Walker. 2008. Reconstructing empirical public administration: Lutonism or scientific realism? *Administration and Society*, 40(3), 324–330.

Apgar, W., and H.J. Brown 1987. *Microeconomics and Public Policy*. Glenview, IL: Scott, Foresman.

Archer, M. 1995. *Realist Social Theory: The Morphogenetic Approach*. Cambridge, UK: Cambridge University Press.

Argyris, C. 1957. The individual and organization: Some problems of mutual adjustment," *Administrative Science Quarterly*, 2(1), 1–24.

Arnold, P.E. 1976. The first Hoover commission and the managerial presidency. *Journal of Politics*, 38(1), 46–70.

Bagozzi, R.P., and Y. Yi. 1990. Assessing method variance in multitrait-multimethod matrices: The case of self-reported affect and perceptions at work. *Journal of Applied Psychology*, 75, 547–560.

Bailey, M.T. 1992. Do physicists use case studies? Thoughts on public administration research. *Public Administration Review*, 52(1), 47–54.

Baker, S., A. Etzioni, R. Hansen, and M. Sontag. 1973. Tolerance for bureaucratic structure: Theory and measurement. *Human Relations*, 26(6), 775–786.

Baldwin, J.N. 1990. Perceptions of public versus private sector personnel and informal red tape: Their impact on motivation. *American Review of Public Administration*, 20(1), 7–28.

Balfour, D.L., and W. Mesaros. 1994. Connecting the local narratives: Public administration as a hermeneutic science. *Public Administration Review*, 54(6), 559–564.

Ballou, D., and M. Podgursky. 1997. *Teacher Pay and Teacher Quality*. Kalamazoo, MI: W.E. Upjohn Institute for Employment Research.

Baron, J.N., F.R. Dobbin, and P.D. Jennings. 1986. War and peace: The evolution of modern personnel administration in U.S. industry. *American Journal of Sociology*, 92(2), 351–383.

Bayer, C.W. 1990. Maintaining optimum indoor air quality. *Journal of Property Management*, 55(1), 37–39.

Bayer, R., and J. Stuber. 2006. Tobacco control, stigma and public health: Rethinking the relations. *American Journal of Public Health*, 96(1), 47–50.

Beck, N. 2006. Rationality and institutionalized expectations: The development of an organizational set of rules. *Schmalenbach Business Review*, 58, 279–300.

Beck Jorgensen, T. 1993. Rescuing public services: On the tasks of public organizations." In *Quality, Innovation and Measurement in Public Sector Organizations*, ed. H. Hill, H. Klages, and E. Loffer, 161–182. Frankfurt: Peter Lang.

Behn, R.D. 1995. The big questions of public management. *Public Administration Review*, 55, 313–324.

———. 2001. *Rethinking Democratic Accountability*. Washington, DC: Brookings Institution Press.

Benveniste, G. 1983. *Bureaucracy*. San Francisco: Jossey-Bass.

———. 1987. *Professionalizing the Organization: Reducing Bureaucracy to Enhance Effectiveness*. San Francisco: Jossey-Bass.

Blair, T. 2002. *The Courage of Our Convictions: Why Reform of the Public Services Is the Route to Social Justice*. London: Fabian Society.

Blalock, Hubert M. 1961. *Causal Inferences in Nonexperimental Research*. Chapel Hill: University of North Carolina Press.

———. 1962. Further observations on asymmetric causal models. *American Sociological Review*, 27(4), 542–545.

———. 1966. The identification problem and theory building: The case of status inconsistency. *American Sociological Review*, 31(1), 52–61.

Blau, P.M., and W.R. Scott. 1962. *Formal Organizations: A Comparative Approach*. San Francisco: Chandler.

Blumenthal, R. 2009. *NYTimes* City Room Blog.

Box, R.C. 1992. An examination of the debate over research in public administration. *Public Administration Review*, 52(1), 62–69.

Boyne, George A. 2002. Concepts and indicators of local authority performance: An evaluation of the statutory framework in England and Wales. *Public Money and Management*, 22(2), 17–24.

Bozeman B. 1987. *All Organizations are Public: Bridging Public and Private Organization Theory.* San Francisco: Jossey-Bass.

———. 1993. A theory of government "red tape." *Journal of Public Administration Research and Theory,* 3(3), 273–303.

———. 2000. *Bureaucracy and Red Tape.* Upper Saddle River, NJ: Prentice-Hall.

Bozeman, B., and S. Bretschneider. 1994. The "publicness puzzle" in organization theory: A test of alternative explanations of differences between public and private organizations. *Journal of Public Administration Research and Theory* 4(2), 197–223.

Bozeman, B., and M. Crow. 1990. Bureaucratization in the laboratory. *Research/Technology Management,* 32(5), 30–32.

———. 1991. Red tape and technology transfer in U.S. government laboratories. *Journal of Technology Transfer,* 16(2), 29–37.

Bozeman, B., and L. DeHart-Davis. 1999. Red tape and clean air: Title V air pollution permitting implementation as a test bed for theory development. *Journal of Public Administration Research and Theory,* 9(1), 141–177.

Bozeman, B., J. Dietz, and M. Gaughan 2001. Models of scientific careers: Using network theory to explain transmission of scientific and technical human capital. *International Journal of Technology Management,* 22(4), 716–740.

Bozeman, B., and G. Kingsley. 1998. Risk culture in public and private organizations. *Public Administration Review,* 58(2), 109–118.

Bozeman, B., and S. Loveless. 1987. Sector context and performance: A comparison of industrial and government research units. *Administration and Society,* 19, 197–235.

Bozeman, B., and S. Moulton. 2011. The publicness puzzle revisited: Toward an integration of empirical and normative publicness. *Journal of Public Administration Research and Theory* (in press).

Bozeman, B., and S. Pandey. 2004. Public management decision making: Effects of decision content. *Public Administration Review,* 64(5), 553–565.

Bozeman, B., and H.G. Rainey. 1998. Organizational rules and the "bureaucratic personality." *American Journal of Political Science,* 42(1), 163–189.

Bozeman, B., H. Rainey, D. Newton, J. Bull, and G. McGinnis. 2008. Administrative Procedures and Red Tape in the University of Georgia System Office: Assessing Information Technology Administration and Activities. Report submitted to the Office of Information and Instructional Technology, University System of Georgia.

Bozeman, B., P. Reed, and P. Scott. 1992. Red tape and task delays in public and private organizations. *Administration and Society,* 24(3), 290–322.

Bozeman, B., and J. Rogers. 2002. A churn model of scientific knowledge value. *Research Policy,* 31(5), 769–794.

Bozeman, B., and P. Scott. 1996. Bureaucratic red tape and formalization: Untangling conceptual knots. *American Review of Public Administration,* 26(1), 1–17.

Bozeman, B., G.A. Brewer, and R.M. Walker. 2008. An empirical test of Bozeman's external control model of red tape. Paper presented at the International Research Symposium on Public Management, Brisbane, Australia March 25–28.

Bretschneider, S. 1990. Management information systems in public and private organizations: An empirical test. *Public Administration Review,* 50(4), 536–545.

Bretschneider, S.I., and B. Bozeman. 1995. Understanding red tape and bureaucratic delays. In *The Enduring Challenges in Public Management: Surviving and Excelling in a Changing World,* ed. A. Halachmi and G. Bouckaert, 204–215. San Francisco: Jossey-Bass.

Brewer, G.A. 2005. In the eye of the storm: Frontline supervisors and federal agency performance. *Journal of Public Administration Research and Theory*, 15, 505–527.

———. 2006. All measures of performance are subjective: More evidence on U.S. federal agencies. In *Public Service Performance*, ed. G.A. Boyne, K.J. Meier, L.J. O'Toole Jr., and R.M. Walker. Cambridge, UK: Cambridge University Press.

Brewer, G.A., R.L. Facer II, L.J. O'Toole Jr., and J.W. Douglas. 1998. The state of doctoral education in public administration: Developments in the field's research preparation. *Journal of Public Affairs Education*, 4(2), 123–135.

Brewer, G., A., Alisa K. Hicklin, and Richard M. Walker. 2006. Multi-level Modelling Stakeholder Red Tape, Environmental Constraints, Management and Public Service Performance. Determinants of Performance in Public Organizations II, University of Hong Kong, December 7–10.

Brewer, G.A., and S.C. Selden. 2000. Why elephants gallop: Assessing and predicting organizational performance in federal agencies. *Journal of Public Administration and Research*, 10(4), 685–712.

Brewer, G.A., and R.M. Walker. 2005. What you see depends on where you sit: Managerial perceptions of red tape in English local. Paper presented at the 8th Public Management Research Conference, School of Policy, Planning, and Development, University of Southern California–Los Angeles, September 29–October 1, 2005.

———. 2010a. An empirical analysis of the impact of red tape on governmental performance: An empirical evaluation. *Journal of Public Administration Research and Theory*, 20(1), 233–257.

———. 2010b. Explaining variations in perceptions of red tape: A professionalism-marketization model. *Public Administration*, 88, 2.

Brick, Michael. 2003. City's smoking ban grows teeth with fines beginning at midnight. *New York Times*, April 30. www.nytimes.com/2003/04/30/nyregion/city-s-smoking-ban-grows-teeth-with-fines-beginning-at-midnight.html.

Briscoe, F. 2007. From iron cage to iron shield? How bureaucracy enables temporary flexibility for professional service workers. *Organization Science*, 18(2), 297–314.

Brown, M.M., and J.L. Brudney. 1998. A "smarter, better, faster, and cheaper" government: Contracting and geographic information systems. *Public Productivity and Management Review,* 22(3), 470–489.

Brown, T.L., and M. Potoski. 2003. Contract-management capacity in municipal and county governments. *Public Administration Review*, 63(2), 153–164.

———. 2006. Contracting for management: Assessing management capacity under alternative service delivery arrangements. *Journal of Policy Analysis and Management*, 25(2), 323–346.

Buchanan, B. 1975. Red tape and the service ethic: Some unexpected differences between public and private managers. *Administration and Society*, 6(4), 423–444.

Buckley, P., and M. Chapman. 1997. The perception and measurement of transaction costs. *Cambridge Journal of Economics*, 21, 127–145.

Burnier, D. 2005. Making it meaning full: Postmodern public administration and symbolic interactionism. *Administrative Theory and Praxis*, 27(3), 498–516.

Carmines, E.G., and R.A. Zeller. 1994. *Reliability and Validity Assessment*. Thousand Oaks, CA: Sage.

Chanlat, J.-F. 2003. Le managérialisme et l'éthique du bien commun: La gestion de la motivation au travail dans les services publics [Managerialism and the common interest: Work motivation management in the public service]. In Duvillier, T., J.-L. 25.

Chen, G., and D.W. Williams. 2007. How political support influences red tape through developmental culture. *Policy Studies Journal*, 35(3), 419–436.

Chinowsky, P., G.A. Kingsley, B.L. Ponomariov, and A. Dunn. 2003. Strategies to strengthen consultant management in the Georgia Department of Transportation. Unpublished paper.

Chun, Y., and H.G. Rainey. 2005. Goal ambiguity and organizational performance in U.S. federal agencies. *Journal of Public Administration Research and Theory*, 15(4), 529–557.

Cleary, R.E. 2000. The public administration doctoral dissertation reexamined: An evaluation of the dissertations of 1998. *Public Administration Review*, 60(5), 446–455.

Clegg, S. 1981. Organization and control. *Administrative Science Quarterly*, 26(4), 545–562.

Coursey, D., and B. Bozeman. 1990. Decision making in public and private organizations: A test of alternative concepts of "Publicness." *Public Administration Review*, 50(4), 525–535.

Coursey, D.H., and S.K. Pandey. 2007a. Content domain, measurement, and validity of the red tape concept: A second-order confirmatory factor analysis. *American Review of Public Administration*, 37, 342.

———. 2007b. Public service motivation measurement: Testing an abridged version of Perry's proposed scale. *Administration and Society*, 39, 547–568.

Coursey, D., J.L. Perry, J.L. Brudney, and L. Littlepage. 2008. Psychometric verification of Perry's public service motivation instrument: Results for volunteer exemplars. *Review of Public Personnel Administration*, 28(1), 79–90.

Cowen, R. 1994. Snipping the red tape that keeps private enterprise Earthbound. *Washington Post*, September 14, 1994, A4.

Cozzetto, D.A. 1994. Quantitative research in public administration: A need to address some serious methodological problems. *Administration and Society*, 26(3), 337–343.

Cronbach, L. 1971. Test validation. In *Educational Measurement*, 2nd ed., ed. R. Thorndike, 443–507. Washington, DC: American Council on Education.

Crow, M., and B. Bozeman. 1987. A new typology for R & D laboratories: Implications for policy analysts. *Journal of Policy Analysis and Management*, 6(3), 328–341.

———. 1998. *Limited By Design: R&D Laboratories in the U.S. National Innovation System*. New York: Columbia University Press.

Crozier, M. 1964. *The Bureaucratic Phenomenon*. Chicago: University of Chicago Press.

Cummings, R.G., D.S. Brookshire, and W.E. Shulze. 1986. *Valuing Environmental Goods: An Assessment of the Contingent Valuation Method*. Savage, MD: Rowman & Littlefield.

Cyert, R., and J.G. March. 1963. *A Behavioral Theory of the Firm*. Englewood Cliffs, NJ: Prentice-Hall.

Daneke, G.A. 1990. A science of public administration? *Public Administration Review*, 50(3), 383–392.

185

Davis, C.R. 1996. The administrative rational model and public organization theory. *Administration and Society*, 28(1), 39–60.

DeHart-Davis, L. 2000. Environmental permit application costs: The role of red tape, subcontracting, experience and communications. Unpublished doctoral dissertation. Atlanta, GA: Georgia Institute of Technology.

―――. 2007. The unbureaucratic personality. *Public Administration Review*, 67(5), 892–903.

―――. 2009. Green tape: A theory of effective organizational rules. *Journal of Public Administration Research and Theory*, 19(2), 361–384.

―――. 2010. Public Sector Workplace Survey. Department of Public Administration, University of Kansas.

DeHart-Davis, L., and B. Bozeman. 2001. Regulatory compliance and air quality permitting: Why do firms "overcomply"? *Journal of Public Administration Research and Theory*, 11(4), 471–508.

DeHart-Davis, L., and S.K. Pandey. 2005. Red tape and public employees: Does perceived rule dysfunction alienate managers? *Journal of Public Administration Research and Theory*, 15(1), 133–148.

Delamont, S., and P. Atkinson. 2001. Doctoring uncertainty: Mastering craft knowledge. *Social Studies of Science*, 31(1), 87–107.

DeNisi, A.S. 2000. Performance appraisal and control systems: A multilevel approach. In *Multilevel Theory, Research, and Methods in Organizations*, ed. K. Klein and S. Kozlowski, 121–156. San Francisco: Jossey-Bass.

de Zwart, F. 2002. Administrative practice and rational inquiry in postmodern public administration theory. *Administration and Society*, 34(5), 482–498.

DiMaggio, P.J., and W.W. Powell. 1983. The iron cage revisited: Institutional isomorphism and collective rationality. *American Sociological Review*, 48, 147.

Dobbin, F., and T.J. Dowd. 2000. The market that antitrust built: Public policy, private coercion, and railroad acquisition, 1825 to 1922. *American Sociological Review*, 65(5), 631–657.

Dobbin, F., and J.R. Sutton. 1988. The strength of a weak state: The rights revolution and the rise of human resources management divisions. *American Journal of Sociology*, 104, 441–476.

Dodge, J., S.M. Ospina, and E.G. Foldy. 2005. Integrating rigor and relevance in public administration scholarship: The contribution of narrative inquiry. *Public Administration Review*, 65(3), 286–300.

Donahue, J. 1989. *The Privatization Decision: Public Ends, Private Means*. New York: Basic Books.

Donahue, A.K., and S.C. Selden. 2000. Measuring government management capacity: A comparative analysis of city human resources management systems. *Journal of Public Administration Research and Theory*, 10(2), 381–411.

Downs, A. 1967. *Inside Bureaucracy*. Boston: Little, Brown.

Dubin, R. 1951. *Human Relations in Administration: The Sociology of Organization, with Readings and Cases*. New York: Prentice-Hall.

Dubnick, M. 2005. Accountability and the promise of performance: In search of the mechanisms. *Public Performance and Management Review*, 28(3), 376–417.

Dryzek, J.S., and S.T. Leonard. 1988. History and discipline in political science. *American Political Science Review*, 82(4), 1245–1260.

Edwards, R. 1984. Work incentives and worker responses in bureaucratic enterprises: An empirical study. *Research in Social Stratification and Mobility*, 3, 3–26.

Europa. 2009. European Commission, Enterprise and Industry, Better Regulation. VP Verheugen and Dr. Stoiber award the German Confederation of Skilled Crafts (ZDH) for the best idea for red tape reduction. Brussels, May 13. http://europa. eu/rapid/pressReleasesAction.do?reference=IP/09/754&format=HTML&aged=0 &language=EN&guiLanguage=en.

Evans, K.G., and D. Lowery. 2006. Prescriptive thinking: Normative claims as scholarship. *Administration and Society*, 38(2), 147–165.

Feeney, M.K. 2008. Public wars and private armies: Militaries, mercenaries, and public values. Paper presented at the Public Values and Public Interest Research Workshop. Copenhagen, Denmark, May 28–30.

Feeney, M.K., and P.C. Boardman. 2010. Organizational confidence: An empirical assessment of highly positive public managers. *Journal of Public Administration Research and Theory*. First published online: July 29, 2010.

Feeney, M.K., and B. Bozeman. 2009. Stakeholder red tape: Comparing perceptions of public managers and their private consultants. *Public Administration Review*, 69(4), 710–726.

Feeney, M.K, and L. DeHart-Davis. In press. Bureaucracy and public employee behavior: A case of local government. *Review of Public Personnel Administration*.

Feeney, M.K., and G. Kingsley. 2008. Patronage: Have we come full circle? *Public Integrity*, 10(2), 165–176.

Feeney, M.K., and H.G. Rainey. 2010. Personnel flexibility in public and nonprofit organizations. *Journal of Public Administration Research and Theory*.

Fernandez, S., H.G. Rainey, and C.E. Lowman. 2006. Privatization and its implications for human resources management. In *Public Personnel Management: Current Concerns, Future Challenges*, 4th ed., ed. N.M. Riccucci, 204–224. New York: Pearson Education.

Figlioa, D.N., and L.W. Kenny. 2007. Individual teacher incentives and student performance. *Journal of Public Economics*, 91(5–6), 901–914.

Forbes, M., and L.E. Lynn Jr. 2005. How does public management affect government performance? Findings from international research. *Journal of Public Administration Research and Theory*, 15(4), 559–584.

Foss, N.J. 1996. Knowledge-based approaches to the theory of the firm: Some critical comments. *Organization Science*, 7(5), 470–476.

Foster, J.L. 1990. Bureaucratic rigidity revisited. *Social Science Quarterly*, 71, 223–238.

Foster, J.L., and J.H. Jones. 1978. Rule orientation and bureaucratic reform. *American Journal of Political Science*, 22, 348–363.

Frant, H. 1993. Rules and governance in the public service: The case of civil service. *American Journal of Political Science*, 37(4), 990–1007.

Furlong, S. 1997. Interest group influence on rule-making. *Administration and Society*, 29(3), 325–347.

Garnett, J., J. Marlowe, and S.K. Pandey. 2008. Penetrating the performance predicament: Communication as mediator or moderator of organizational culture's impact on public organizational performance. *Public Administration Review*, 68(2), 266–281.

Gershon, S.P. 2004. *Releasing Resources to the Front-Line: Independent Review of Public Sector Efficiency*. London: HM Treasury.

Gilbert, D. 2005. *Stumbling on Happiness*. New York: Random House.

Gill, J., and K.J. Meier. 2000. Public administration research and practice: A methodological manifesto. *Journal of Public Administration Research and Theory*, 10(1), 157–199.

Girosi, F., and G. King. 2008. *Demographic Forecasting*. Princeton, NJ: Princeton University Press.

Glennan, S. 2002. Rethinking mechanistic explanation. *Philosophy of Science*, 69(3), 342–353.

Golembiewski, R. 1977. *Public Administration as a Developing Discipline*. Vols. 1 and 2. New York: Marcel Dekker.

Goodsell, C. 1981. Looking once again at human service bureaucracy. *Journal of Politics*, 43, 763–768.

———. 1985. The Grace Commission: Seeking efficiency for the whole people? *Public Administration Review*, 44(2), 196–204.

———. 1994. *The Case for Bureaucracy: A Public Administration Polemic*, 3rd ed. Chatham, NJ: Chatham House.

Gore, A. 1993. *From Red Tape to Results: Creating a Government That Works Better and Costs Less: Reengineering Through Information Technology*. Washington, DC: U.S. Government Printing Office.

Gouldner, A.W. 1950. The Problem of Succession in Bureaucracy. In *Studies in Leadership,* ed. A. Gouldner, 644–659. New York: Harper.

Grant, R.M. 1996. Toward a knowledge-based theory of the firm. *Strategic Management Journal*, 17(Winter), 109–122.

Grossi, G., and R. Mussari. 2008. Effects of outsourcing on performance measurement and reporting: The experience of Italian local governments. *Public Budgeting and Finance*, 28(1), 22–38.

Gruber, J. 1987. *Controlling Bureaucracies: Dilemmas in Democratic Governance*. Berkeley, CA: University of California Press.

Guriev, S. 1999. A theory of informative red tape with an application to top-level corruption. New Economic School.

———. 2004. Red tape and corruption. *Journal of Development Economics*, 73(2), 489–504.

Hall, J.L. 2007. Implications of success and persistence for public sector performance. *Public Organization Review*, 7(3), 281–297.

Hall, R.H. 1968. Professionalism and bureaucratization. *American Sociological Review*, 33(1), 92–104.

———. 1991. *Organizations: Structures, Processes, & Outcomes*, 5th ed. Englewood Cliffs, NJ: Prentice-Hall.

Hall, R.H., N. Johnson, and J. Haas. 1967. Organizational size, complexity, and formalization. *American Sociological Review*, 32(6), 903–912.

Hall, T.E., and L.J. O'Toole. 2000. Structures for policy implementation: An analysis of national legislation, 1965–1966 and 1993–1994. *Administration and Society*, 31(6), 667–686.

Hanson, N.R. 1971. *Observation and Explanation*. New York: Harper and Row.

Hanushek, E.A., and S.G. Rivkin. 2004. How to improve the supply of high-quality teachers. In *Brookings Papers on Education Policy: 2004*, ed. D. Ravitch, 7–25. Washington, DC: Brookings Institution.

Hays, S.W., and J.E. Sowa. 2006. A broader look at the "accountability" movement: Some grim realities in state civil service systems. *Review of Public Personnel Administration*, 26(2), 102–117.

Heckman, J., C. Heinrich, and J. Smith. 1997. Assessing the performance of performance standards in public bureaucracies. *American Economic Review*, 87(2), 389–395.

Heinrich, C.J., and L.E. Lynn Jr., eds. 2000. *Governance and Performance: New Perspectives*. Washington, DC: Georgetown University Press.

Helmer, O., and N. Rescher. 1959. On the epistemology of the inexact sciences. *Management Science*, 6, 1, 25–52.

Hondeghem, A., and W. Vandenabeele. 2005. Valeurs et motivation dans l'administration publique: Perspective comparative. *Revue française d'administration publique*, 115, 463–480.

Hood, C. 1991. A public management for all seasons. *Public Administration*, 69(1), 3–19.

Hou, Y. 2006. The comparative study of budgeting and Chinese budgeting in a comparative perspective. *Journal of Public Budgeting, Accounting and Financial Management*, 18(4), 421–429.

Houston, D.J., and S.M. Delevan. 1990. Public administration research: An assessment of journal publications. *Public Administration Review*, 50(6), 674–681.

———. 1991. The state of public personnel research. *Review of Public Personnel Administration*, 11(2), 97–111.

———. 1994. A comparative assessment of public administration journal publications. *Administration and Society*, 26(2), 252–271.

Hummel, R.P. 1982. *The Bureaucratic Experience*, 2nd ed. New York: St. Martin's Press.

———. 1991. Stories managers tell: Why they are as valid as science. *Public Administration Review*, 51(1), 31–41.

———. 2007. What do theorists do? *Administrative Theory and Praxis*, 29(2), 292–296.

Isett, K.R., and K.G. Provan. 2005. The evolution of dyadic interorganizational relationships in a network of publicly funded nonprofit agencies. *Journal of Public Administration Research and Theory*, 15(1), 149–165.

Islam, G., and M.J. Zyphur. 2009. Rituals in organizations: A review and expansion of current theory. *Group and Organization Management*, 34(1), 114–139.

Ivancevich, J.M., and J.H. Donnelly. 1975. Relations of organizational structure to job satisfaction, anxiety-stress, and performance. *Administrative Science Quarterly*, 20, 272–280.

Jensen, J.L., and R. Rogers. 2001. Cumulating the intellectual gold of case study research. *Public Administration Review*, 61(2), 235–246.

Johnston, J.M., and B.S. Romzek. 1999. Contracting and accountability in state Medicaid reform: Rhetoric, theories, and reality. *Public Administration Review*, 59(5), 383.

Joregensen, T.B. 1999. The public sector in an in-between time: Searching for new public values. *Public Administration*, 77(3), 565–584.

Jos, P.H. 1993. Empirical corruption research: Beside the (moral) point? *Journal of Public Administration Research and Theory*, 3(3), 359–375.

Kaufman, D., and S.J. Wei. 1999. Does "Grease Money" Speed Up the Wheels of Commerce? Washington, DC: World Bank.

Kaufman, H. 1977. *Red Tape: Its Origins, Uses, and Abuses*. Washington, DC: Brookings Institution.

———. 1986. *Time, Chance and Organization: Natural Selection in a Perilous Environment*. Chatham, NJ: Chathman House.

Kellough, J.E. 1998. Reliability, validity, and the MV index: Toward the clarification of some fundamental issues. *Public Administration Review*, 58(2), 167–173.

Kellough, J.E., and L.G. Nigro. 2002. Pay for performance in Georgia state government: Employee perspectives on Georgia gain after 5 years. *Review of Public Personnel Administration*, 22(2), 146–166.

Kennedy, M.M. 1983. Working knowledge. *Knowledge*, 5(2), 193–211.

Kerwin, C. 1994. *Rulemaking: How Government Agencies Write Law and Make Policy*. Washington, DC: CQ Press.

Kerwin, C., and S. Furlong. 1992. Time and rule-making: An empirical test of theory. *Journal of Public Administration Research and Theory*, 2(2), 113–138.

Kettl, D.F., and J.J. Diulio. 1995. *Inside the Reinvention Machine: Appraising Governmental Reform*. Washington, DC: Brookings Institution.

Kieser, A., and H. Kubicek. 1992. *Organisation*, 3rd ed. Berlin: de Gruyter.

Kim, S. 2009. Revising Perry's measurement scale of public service motivation. *American Review of Public Administration*, 39(2), 149–163.

King, G., C.J.L. Murray, J.A. Salomon, and A. Tandon. 2004. Enhancing the validity of cross-cultural comparability of measurement in survey research. *American Political Science Review*, 98(1), 191–207.

Kingsley, G.A., and B. Bozeman. 1992. "Red tape" in public and private organizations: The impact of task, structure and external environment. Syracuse University.

Kingsley, G.A., and P.N. Reed. 1991. Decision process models and organizational context: Level and sector make a difference. *Public Productivity and Management Review*, 14(4), 397–413.

Kirlin, J. 1996. What government must do well: Creating value for society. *Journal of Public Administration Research and Theory*, 6(1), 161–185.

Knorr-Cetina, K. 1999. *Epistemic Cultures: How the Sciences Make Knowledge*. Cambridge, MA: Harvard University Press.

Kraemer, K.L, and J.L. Perry. 1989. Institutional requirements for academic research in public administration. *Public Administration Review*, 49(1), 9–16.

Kreiner, G., E. Hollensbe, and M. Sheep. 2006. Boundary dynamics at the interface of individual and organizational identities. *Human Relations*, 59(10), 1351–1342.

Kriess, K. 1993. The sick building syndrome in office buildings: A breath of fresh air. *New England Journal of Medicine*, 328(12), 877–878.

Kunreuther, H., and M. Pauly. 2006. Rules rather than discretion: Lessons from hurricane Katrina. *Journal of Risk and Uncertainty*, 33(1–2), 101–116.

Lakatos, I. 1970. Falsification and the methodology of scientific research programmes. In *Criticism and the Growth of Knowledge*, ed. I. Lakatos and A. Musgrave, 91–197. Cambridge, UK: Cambridge University Press.

Lan, Z., and H.G. Rainey. 1992. Goals, rules, and effectiveness in public, private, and hybrid organizations: More evidence on frequent assertions about differences. *Journal of Public Administration Research and Theory*, 2(1), 5–28.

Landau, M. 1969. Redundancy, rationality, and the problem of duplication and overlap. *Public Administration Review*, 29(2), 346–358.

———. 1991. On multiorganizational systems in public administration. *Journal of Public Administration Research and Theory*, 1(1), 5–18.

Landau, M., and R. Stout. 1979. To manage is not to control: Or the folly of type II errors. *Public Administration Review*, 39(2), 148–156.

LaPorte, T., and P. Consolini. 1991. Working in practice but not in theory: Theoretical challenges of high-reliability organizations. *Journal of Public Administration Research and Theory*, 1(1), 19–47.

LaPorte, T., and C. Thomas. 1990. Regulatory compliance and the ethos of quality enhancement: Surprises in nuclear power plant operations. Paper presented at the American Political Science Association, San Francisco.

Laudan, L. 1977. *Progress and Its Problems*. Berkeley: University of California Press.

Layder, D. 1998. *Sociological Practice: Linking Theory and Social Research*. Thousand Oaks, CA: Sage.

Leahey, E. 2008. Overseeing research practice: The case of data editing. *Science, Technology and Human Values*, 33(5), 605–630.

Leahey, E., B. Entwisle, and P. Einaudi. 2003. Diversity in everyday research practice: The case of data editing. *Sociological Methods and Research*, 32(1), 64–89.

Leazes. 1997. Public accountability: Is it a private responsibility? *Administration and Society*, 29(4), 395–411.

Lee, M. 2006. Empirical experiments in public reporting: Reconstructing the results of survey research, 1941–1942. *Public Administration Review*, 66(2), 252–262.

Leveson, N., N. Dulack, K. Marais, and J. Carroll. 2009. Moving beyond normal accidents and high reliability organizations: A systems approach to safety in complex systems. *Organization Studies*, 30(2–3), 227–249.

Levitt, B., and J.G. March. 1988. Organizational learning. *Annual Review of Sociology*, 14, 319–340.

Lieberson, S., and J. O'Connor. 1972. Leadership and organizational performance: A study of large corporations. *American Sociological Review*, 37(1), 117–130.

Light, P. 1999. *The True Size of Government*. Washington, DC: Brookings Institution.

Lindblom, C.E. 1959. The science of muddling through. *Public Administration Review*, 19(1), 79–99.

Lindblom, C.E., and D.K. Cohen. 1979. *Usable Knowledge: Social Science and Social Problem Solving*. New Haven, CT: Yale University Press.

Lippman, W. 1955. *Essays in the Public Philosophy*. Boston: Little, Brown.

Lord, R.G., and K.J. Maher. 1993. *Leadership and Information Processing: Linking Perceptions and Performance*. London: Routledge.

Loveless, S. 1985. Sector Status, Structure and Performance: A Comparison of Public and Private Research Units. Unpublished doctoral dissertation, Syracuse University, Syracuse, NY.

Lowery, D., and K.G. Evans. 2004. The iron cage of methodology: The vicious circle of means limiting ends limiting means. *Administration and Society*, 36(3), 306–327.

Luton, L.S. 2007. Deconstructing public administration empiricism. *Administration and Society*, 39(4), 527–544.

———. 2008. Beyond empiricists versus postmodernists. *Administration and Society*, 40(2), 211–219.

Lynch, M. 1994. *Scientific Practice and Ordinary Action*. Cambridge, UK: Cambridge University Press.

Lynn, L.E., C.J. Heinrich, and C.J. Hill. 2008. The empiricist goose has not been cooked! *Administration and Society*, 40(1), 104–109.

MacRoberts, M., and B. MacRoberts. 1989. Problems of citation analysis: A critical review. *Journal of the American Society for Information Science*, 40(5), 342–349.

Magat, W.A., A.J. Krupnick, and W.J. Harrington. 1986. *Rules in the Making: A*

Statistical Analysis of Regulatory Agency Behavior. Washington, DC: Resources for the Future.

Malkin, E. 2009. For redress of grievances, Mexicans turn to bureaucracy contest. *New York Times*, January 9. www.nytimes.com/2009/01/09/world/americas/09iht-09mexico.19210715.html.

Manning, P. 1977. Rules in organizational context: Narcotics law enforcement in two settings. *Sociological Quarterly*, 18(1), 44–61.

March, J.G., M. Schulz, and X. Zhou. 2000. *The Dynamics of Rules.* Palo Alto, CA: Stanford University Press.

March, J.G., and J.P. Olsen. 1983. Organizing political life: What administrative reorganization tells us about government. *American Political Science Review*, 77(2), 281–296.

March, J.G., and H. Simon. 1958. *Organizations.* New York: Wiley.

Mauro, P. 1995. Corruption and growth. *Quarterly Journal of Economics*, 110(3), 681–712.

Maynard-Moody, S., and M. Musheno. 2000. State agent or citizen agent: Two narratives of discretion. *Journal of Public Administration Research and Theory*, 10(2), 329–358.

McCurdy, H.E., and R.E. Cleary. 1984. Why can't we resolve the research issue in public administration? *Public Administration Review*, 44(1), 49–55.

McGarrity, T. 1991. The internal structure of EPA rulemaking. *Law and Contemporary Problems*, 54, 57–65.

Meier, K.J. 2005. Public administration and the myth of positivism: The Antichrist's view. *Administrative Theory and Praxis*, 27(4), 650–668.

Meier, K.J., and J.L. Brudney. 1993. *Applied Statistics for Public Administration*, 3rd ed. Belmont, CA: Wadsworth.

Meier, K.J., and L.J. O'Toole. 2002. Public management and organizational performance: The effect of managerial quality. *Journal of Policy Analysis and Management*, 21(4), 629–643.

———. 2007. Deconstructing Larry Luton: Or what time is the next train to Reality Junction? *Administration and Society*, 39(6), 786–796.

Merton, R. 1940. Bureaucratic structure and personality. *Social Forces*, 18(3), 560–568.

Meyer, M. 1979a. *Change in Public Bureaucracies.* London: Cambridge University Press.

———. 1979b. Debureaucratization? *Social Science Quarterly*, 60(1), 25–33.

Meyer, J.W., W.R. Scott, D. Strang, and A. Creighton. 1985. Bureaucratization without centralization: Changes in the organizational system of American public education, 1940–1980. In *Institutional Patterns and Organizations*, ed. L.G. Zucker. Boston: Pitman.

Meyer, M.W., and C.M. Brown. 1977. The process of bureaucratization. *American Journal of Sociology*, 83, 364–385.

Milward, H.B. 1996. Symposium on the hollow state: Capacity, control, and performance in interorganizational settings. *Journal of Public Administration Research and Theory*, 6(2), 193–195.

Miner, A.S. 1987. Idiosyncratic jobs in formalized organizations. *Administrative Science Quarterly*, 32, 327–351.

———. 1991. Organizational evolution and the social ecology of jobs. *American Sociological Review*, 56(6), 772–785.

Mintzberg, H. 1996. Managing government, governing management. *Harvard Business Review*, 74(3), 75–83.

Mladenka, K. 1981. Citizen demands and urban services: The distribution of bureaucratic response in Chicago and Houston. *American Journal of Political Science*, 25, 693–714.

Moloney, S. 1996. 1996. The lady in red tape. *Policy Review*, 79(2), 147–154.

Moon, M.J. 1999. The pursuit of managerial entrepreneurship: Does organization matter? *Public Administration Review*, 59(1), 31–43.

Moon, M.J., and S.I. Bretschneider. 2002. Does the perception of red tape constrain IT innovativeness in organizations? Unexpected results from a simultaneous equation model and implications. *Journal of Public Administration Research and Theory*, 12(2), 273–291.

Moriarty, E. 2005. Gov. Perdue approves anti-smoking legislation. *Atlanta Business Chronicle*, May 9. www.bizjournals.com/atlanta/stories/2005/05/09/daily10.html.

Moynihan, D.P. 2006. What do we talk about when we talk about performance: Dialogue theory and performance budgeting. *Journal of Public Administration Research and Theory*, 16(2), 151–168.

———. 2008. *The Dynamics of Performance Management: Constructing Information and Reform*. Washington, DC: Georgetown University Press.

Moynihan, D.P., and S.K. Pandey. 2007a. Comparing job satisfaction, job involvement, and organizational commitment. *Administration and Society*, 39(7), 803–832.

———. 2007b. The role of organizations in fostering public service motivation. *Public Administration Review*, 67(1), 40–53.

Naff, K.C., and J. Crum. 1999. Working for America: Does public service motivation make a difference? *Review of Public Personnel Administration*, 19(4), 5–16.

Nelson, R.R., and S.G. Winter. 1982. *An Evolutionary Theory of Economic Change*. Cambridge, MA: Belknap.

Roethlisberger, F.J., and W.J. Dickson. 1939. *Management and the Worker*. Cambridge, MA: Harvard University Press.

Occupational Safety and Health Administration (OSHA). 1995. *Reinventing Worker Safety and Health*. Washington, DC: U.S. Government Printing Office.

O'Connor, R.E., R.J. Bord, and A. Fisher. 1999. Risk perceptions, general environmental beliefs, and willingness to address climate change. *Risk Analysis*, 19(3), 461–471.

Office of Public Service Reform. 2002. Reforming our public services: Principles into practice. London: Prime Minister's Office of Public Service Reform.

Osborne, D., and T. Gaebler. 1993. *Reinventing Government: How the Entrepreneurial Spirit Is Transforming the Public Sector*. New York: Plume/Penguin.

O'Toole, L.J., and K.J. Meier. 2004. Parkinson's law and the new public management? Contracting determinants and service-quality consequences in public education. *Public Administration Review*, 64(3), 342–352.

Pandey, S.K. 1995. Managerial perceptions of red tape. PhD diss., Syracuse University.

———. 2003. *National Administrative Studies Project (NASP-II): A National Survey of Managers in State Health and Human Service Agencies*. Camden, NJ: Rutgers University.

Pandey, S., and S. Bretschneider. 1997. The impact of red tape's administrative delay on public organizations' interest in new information technologies. *Journal of Public Administration Research and Theory*, 7(1), 113–130.

Pandey, S.K., D.H. Coursey, and D.P. Moynihan. 2004. Management capacity and organizational performance: Can organizational culture trump bureaucratic red tape? Paper prepared for presentation at the annual meeting of Academy of Management, New Orleans, Illinois, August 6–10.

———. 2007. Organizational effectiveness and bureaucratic red tape: A multimethod study. *Public Performance and Management Review*, 30(3), 398–425.

Pandey, S.K., and J.L. Garnett. 2006. Exploring public sector communication performance: Testing a model and drawing implications. *Public Administration Review*, 66(1), 37–51.

Pandey, S.K., and G.A. Kingsley. 2000. Examining red tape in public and private organizations: Alternative explanations from a social psychological model. *Journal of Public Administration Research and Theory*, 10(4), 779–799.

Pandey, S.K., and J. Marlowe. 2009. Taking stock of survey-based measures of bureaucratic red tape: Mere perceptions or more than meets the eye? Paper presented at the 10th Public Management Research Conference.

Pandey, S.K., and D.P. Moynihan. 2006. Bureaucratic red tape and organizational performance: Testing the moderating role of culture and political support. In *Public Service Performance*, ed. G.A. Boyne, K.J. Meier, L.J. O'Toole, and R.M. Walker. Cambridge, UK: Cambridge University Press.

Pandey, S.K., and H.G. Rainey. 2006. Public managers' perceptions of organizational goal ambiguity: Analyzing alternative models. *International Public Management Journal*, 9(2), 85–112.

Pandey, S.K., and P.G. Scott. 2002. Red tape: A review and assessment of concepts and measures. *Journal of Public Administration Research and Theory*, 12(4), 553–580.

Pandey, S.K., and E.W. Welch. 2005. Beyond stereotypes: A multistage model of managerial perceptions of red tape. *Administration and Society*, 37(5), 542–575.

Pandey, S.K., and B.E. Wright. 2006. Connecting the dots in public management: Political environment, organizational goal, and the public manager's role in ambiguity. *Journal of Public Administration Research and Theory*, 16(4), 511–532.

Parsons, D.O. 1991. Self-screening in targeted public transfer programs. *Journal of Political Economy*, 99(4), 859–876.

Pentland, B.T., and M.S. Feldman. 2005. Organizational routines as a unit of analysis. *Industrial and Corporate Change*, 14(5), 793–815.

Perrow, C. 1972. *Complex Organizations*. Glenview, IL: Scott, Foresman.

Perry, J.L. 1996. Measuring public service motivation: An assessment of construct reliability and validity. *Journal of Public Administration Research and Theory*, 6(1), 5–24.

Perry, J.L., and A. Hondeghem. 2008. Directions for future theory and research. In *Motivation in Public Management: The Call of Public Service*, ed. J.L. Perry and A. Hondeghem, 294–314. Oxford, UK: Oxford University Press.

Perry, J.L., and K.L. Kraemer. 1986. Research methodology in the *Public Administration Review*, 1975–1984. *Public Administration Review*, 46(3), 215–226.

Pfeffer, J., and G. Salancik. 1977. Organizational context and the characteristics and tenure of hospital administrators. *Academy of Management Journal*, 20(1), 74–88.

Pitts, D., and S. Fernandez. 2007. How effective is public management research? An analysis of scope and methodology. Paper presented at the 9th Public Management Research Conference. Tucson, Arizona, October 25–27.

Podgursky, M.J., and M.G. Springer. 2007. Teacher performance pay: A review. *Journal of Policy Analysis and Management*, 26(4), 909–950.

Podsakoff, P., S.B. MacKenzie, J.-Y. Lee, and N.P. Podsakoff. 2003. Common method biases in behavioral research: A critical review of the literature and recommended remedies. *Journal of Applied Psychology*, 88(5), 879–903.

Pollitt, C., and G. Bouckaert. 2000. *Public Management Reform: A Comparative Analysis.* New York: Oxford University Press.

Ponomariov, B., and C.P. Boardman. In press. Organizational pathology compared to what? The impacts of job characteristics and career trajectory on perceptions of organizational red tape. *Public Administration Review.*

Ponomariov, B., and G. Kingsley. 2006. Experiential learning and the evolution of outsourcing at a state transportation agency. Academy of Management Best Conference Papers, 2006 PNP, F1–F6.

Pratchett, L., and M. Wingfield. 1996. Petty bureaucracy and woolly-minded liberalism? The changing ethos of local government officers. *Public Administration Review,* 74(4), 639–656.

Provan, K.G. 1993. Embeddedness, interdependence, and opportunism in organizational supplier-buyer networks. *Journal of Management,* 19(4), 841–856.

Provan, K.G., K.R. Isett, and H.B. Milward. 2004. Cooperation and compromise: A network response to conflicting institutional pressures in community mental health. *Nonprofit and Voluntary Sector Quarterly,* 33(3), 489–514.

Pugh, D.S., D.J. Hickson, C.R. Hinings, and C. Turner. 1969. The context of organization structures. *Administrative Science Quarterly,* 14(1), 91–114.

Raadschelders, J.C.N. 1999. A coherent framework for the study of public administration. *Journal of Public Administration Research and Theory,* 9(2), 281–303.

Raadschelders, J.C.N., P. Wagenaar, M.R. Rutgers, and P. Overeem. 2000. Against a study of the history of public administration: A manifesto. *Administrative Theory and Praxis,* 22(4), 772–791.

Radin, B.A. 2006. *Challenging the performance movement: Accountability, complexity and democratic values.* Washington, DC: Georgetown University Press.

Rai, G.S. 1983. Reducing bureaucratic inflexibility. *Social Service Review,* 57(1), 44–58.

Rainey, H.G. 1983. Public agencies and private firms: Incentive structures, goals and individual roles. *Administration and Society,* 15(2), 207–242.

———. 2009. *Understanding and Managing Public Organizations, Fourth Edition.* San Francisco: Jossey-Bass.

Rainey, H.G., S.K. Pandey, and B. Bozeman. 1995. Research note: Public and private managers' perceptions of red tape. *Public Administration Review,* 55(6), 567–574.

Rainey, H.G., and P. Steinbauer. 1999. Galloping elephants: Developing elements of a theory of effective government organizations. *Journal of Public Administration Research and Theory,* 9, 1–32.

Ranson, S., B. Hinings, and R. Greenwood. 1980. The structuring of organizational structures, *Administrative Science Quarterly,* 25(1), 1–17.

Reason, J. 1990. *Human Error.* New York: Cambridge University Press.

Reynaud, B. 2005. The void at the heart of rules: Routines in the context of rule-following. The case of the Paris Metro Workshop. *Industrial and Corporate Change,* 14(5), 847–871.

Richardson, Elliot. 1996. *Reflections of A Radical Moderate.* New York: Pantheon.

Rivkin, J.W., and N. Siggelkow. 2003. Balancing search and stability: Interdependencies among elements of organizational design. *Management Science,* 49(3), 290–311.

Roethlisberger, F.J., and W.J. Dickson. 1939. *Management and the Worker.* Cambridge, MA: Harvard University Press.

Rosenfeld, R.A. 1984. An expansion and application of Kaufman's model of red tape:

The case of community development block grants. *Western Political Quarterly*, 37, 603–620.

Roulet, C., F. Flourentzou, F. Foradini, F. Bluyssen, P. Cox, and C. Aizlewood. 2006. Multicriteria analysis of health, comfort and energy efficiency in buildings. *Building Research and Information*, 34(5), 475–482.

Savas, E.S. 1982. *Privatizing the Public Sector. Privatizing the Public Sector.* Chatham, New Jersey: Chatham House.

Schroeder, L. O'Leary, R. Jones, and D. Poocharoen. 2004. Routes to scholarly success in public administration: Is there a right path? *Public Administration Review*, 64(1), 92–105.

Schulz, M. 1998a. Limits to bureaucratic growth: The density dependence of organizational rule births. *Administrative Science Quarterly*, 43(4), 845–876.

———. 1998b. A model of organizational rule obsolescence. *Journal of Computational and Mathematical Organization Theory*, 4(3), 241–266.

———. 2003. Impermanent institutionalization: The duration dependence of organizational rule changes. *Industrial and Corporate Change*, 12(5), 1077–1098.

Schulz, M., and N. Beck. 2000. Iron laws of bureaucracy: Comparing incremental and radical change of organizational rules in the U.S. and in Germany. University of Washington, Department of Management and Organization. Unpublished paper.

———. 2002. Organizational rules and rule histories: A review of current research on rule-based models of organizational learning. Unpublished manuscript.

Schwab, D.P. 1980. Construct validity in organizational behavior. *Research in Organizational Behavior*, 2, 3–43.

Sclar, E.D. 2000. *You Don't Always Get What You Pay For: The Economics of Privatization.* Ithaca, NY: Cornell University Press.

Scott, P.G. 1997. Assessing determinants of bureaucratic discretion: An experiment in street-level decision making. *Journal of Public Administration Research and Theory*, 7(1), 35–58.

Scott, P.G., and S.K. Pandey. 2000. The influence of red tape on bureaucratic behavior: An experimental simulation. *Journal of Policy Analysis and Management*, 19(4), 615–633.

———. 2005. Red tape and public service motivation: Findings from a national survey of managers in state health and human services agencies. *Review of Public Personnel Administration*, 25(2), 155–180.

Scott, W. Richard. 1987. *Organizations: Rational, Natural, and Open Systems*, 2nd ed. Englewood Cliffs, NJ: Prentice-Hall.

Seidman, H. 1970. *Politics, Position and Power: The Dynamics of Federal Organization.* New York: Oxford University Press.

Simon, H. 1957. *Administrative Behavior*, 2nd ed. New York: Macmillan.

Snizek, W., and J. Bullard. 1983. Perception of bureaucracy and changing job satisfaction: A longitudinal analysis. *Organizational Behavior and Human Performance*, 32, 275–287.

Sorenson, J.E., and T.L. Sorenson. 1974. The conflict of professionals in bureaucratic organizations. *Administrative Science Quarterly*, 19(1), 98–106.

Spicer, M.W. 2005. Public administration enquiry and social science in the postmodern condition: Some implications of value pluralism. *Administrative Theory and Praxis*, 27(4), 669–688.

Springer, M.G., and M.A. Winters. 2009. The NYC teacher pay-for-performance program: Early evidence from a randomized trial. *Civic Report*, 56 (April).

Stallings, R.A., and J.M. Ferris. 1988. Public administration research: Work in *PAR*, 1940–1984. *Public Administration Review*, 48(1), 580–587.

Stevenson, W. 1986. Change in the structure of bureaucracy: A longitudinal analysis. *Sociological Perspectives*, 29, 307–336.

Straussman, J., and M. Zhang. 2001. Chinese administrative reforms in international perspectives. *International Journal of Public Sector Management*, 14(5), 411–422.

Streib, G., and C. Roch. 2005. Strengthening public administration research: Identifying boundaries and horizons. *International Journal of Public Administration*, 28(1–2), 37–55.

Sutton, J.R., and F.R. Dobbin. 1996. The two faces of governance: Responses to legal uncertainty in U.S. firms, 1955 to 1985. *American Sociological Review*, 61(5), 794–811.

Sutton, J.R., F.R. Dobbin, J.W. Meyer, and R.W. Scott. 1994. The legalization of the workplace. *American Journal of Sociology*, 99, 944–971.

Teece, D., and G. Pisano. 1994. The dynamic capabilities of firms: An introduction. *Industrial and Corporate Change*, 3, 537–556.

Thompson, V. 1961. *Modern Organization*. New York: Alfred Knopf.

Thompson, F. 1975. *At That Point in Time: The Inside Story of the Senate Watergate Committee*. New York: Quadrangle Books.

Ting, M.M. 2003. A strategic theory of bureaucratic redundancy. *American Journal of Political Science*, 47(2), 274–292.

Tolbert, P., and L.G. Zucker. 1983. Institutional sources of change in the formal structure of organizations: The diffusion of civil service reform, 1880–1935. *Administrative Science Quarterly*, 28, 22–39.

Tsui, A.S. 2006. Contextualization in Chinese management research. *Management and Organization Review*, 2(1), 1–13.

Turaga, R.M.R., and B. Bozeman. 2005. Red tape and public managers' decision making. *American Review of Public Administration*, 35(4), 363–379.

U.S. Government Accountability Office. 2001. Managing for Results: Using GPRA to Assist Oversight and Decisionmaking. Testimony Before the Subcommittee on Government Efficiency, Financial Management and Intergovernmental Relations, Committee on Government Reform, House of Representatives. Statement of J. Christopher Mihm, Director, Strategic Issues, June 19, 2001. GAO-01-872T.

———. 2005. Matter of: Food and Drug Administration—Use of Appropriations for "No Red Tape" Buttons and Mementoes. November 6, 1995. B-257488. http://redbook.gao.gov/11/fl0050298.php.

Vandenabeele, W., S. Scheepers, and A. Hondeghem. 2006. Public service motivation in an international comparative perspective: The UK and Germany. *Public Policy and Administration*, 21(1), 13–31.

Vickers, J., and G. Yarrow 1991. Economic perspectives on privatization. *Journal of Economic Perspectives*, 5(2), 111–132.

Waldo, D. 1948. *The Administrative State*. New York: Ronald Press.

Walker, R.M., and G.A. Brewer. 2008. An organizational echelon analysis of the determinants of red tape in public organizations. *Public Administration Review*, 68(6), 1112–1127.

———. 2009a. Can management strategy minimize the impact of red tape on organizational performance? *Administration and Society*, 41(4), 423–448.

———. 2009b. Can public managers reduce red tape? The role of internal management in overcoming external constraints. *Policy and Politics*, 37(2), 255–272.

Walters, J. 2002. Life after civil service reform: The Texas, Georgia, and Florida experiences. Human Capital Series. IBM Endowment for the Business of Government.

Wamsley, F.L., and J.F. Wolf. 1996. *Refounding Public Administration*. Thousand Oaks, CA: Sage.

Warwick, D. 1975. *A Theory of Public Bureaucracy*. Cambridge, MA: Harvard University Press.

Watson, J.D. 1968. *The Double Helix: A Personal Account of the Discovery of the Structure of DNA*. New York: Atheneum.

Waugh, W.L. 2006. The political costs of failure in the Katrina and Rita Disasters. *Annals of the American Academy of Political and Social Science*, 604, 10–25.

Welch, E.W., and S.K. Pandey. 2007. E-government and bureaucracy: Toward a better understanding of intranet implementation and its effect on red tape. *Journal of Public Administration Research and Theory*, 17, 379–404.

Welch, E.W., and W. Wong. 1998. Public administration in a global context: Bridging the gaps of theory and practice between Western and non-Western nations. *Public Administration Review*, 58(1), 40–49.

West, W.F. 2004. Formal Procedures, Informal Processes, Accountability, and Responsiveness in Bureaucratic Policy Making: An Institutional Analysis. *Public Administration Review*, 64(1), 66–80.

———. 2005. Administrative rulemaking: An old and emerging literature. *Public Administration Review*, 65(6), 655–668.

White, J.D. 1986a. On the growth of knowledge in public administration. *Public Administration Review*, 46(1), 15–24.

———. 1986b. Dissertations and publications in public administration. *Public Administration Review*, 46(3), 227–234.

Williamson, O.E. 1981. The economics of organization: The transaction cost approach. *American Journal of Sociology*, 87(3), 548–578.

———. 1985. *The Economic Institutions of Capitalism*. New York: Free Press.

———. 1999. Public and Private Bureaucracies: A Transaction Cost Economics Perspective. *Journal of Law Economics and Organization*, 15(4), 306–342.

Wittmer, D., and D. Coursey. 1996. Ethical work climates: Comparing top managers in public and private organizations. *Journal of Public Administration Research and Theory*, 6(4), 559–572.

Woodhouse, D. 1997. *In Pursuit of Good Administration—Ministers, Civil Servants and Judges*. Oxford, UK: Clarendon Press.

Wright, B., L. Manigault, and T. Black. 2004. Quantitative research measurement in public administration: An assessment of journal publications. *Administration and Society*, 35(6), 747–764.

Yang, K., and S.K. Pandey. 2009. How do perceived political environment and administrative reform affect employee commitment? *Journal of Public Administration Research and Theory*, 19(2), 335–360.

York, R., and H. Henley. 1986. Perceptions of bureaucracy. *Administration in Social Work*, 10(1), 3–13.

Zhou, X. 1993. The dynamics of organizational rules. *American Journal of Sociology*, 98(5), 1134–1166.

Zmud, R.W. 1982. Diffusion of modern software practices: Influence of centralization and formalization. *Management Science*, 28(12), 1421–1143.

Index

199

About the Authors

Barry Bozeman is Regent's Professor and Ander Crenshaw Professor of Public Policy at the University of Georgia. Previously he held appointments at Georgia Tech and at Syracuse University's Maxwell School. His research focuses on public management, organization theory, and science and technology policy. Bozeman's most recent book is *Public Value and Public Interest* (2007). His PhD in political science was granted by Ohio State University.

Mary K. Feeney is Assistant Professor in the Department of Public Administration at the University of Illinois at Chicago. Her research focuses on public management, sector distinctions, mentoring, and science and technology policy. The University of Georgia granted her PhD in public administration and policy. She holds a master's in public policy from Rutgers University, New Brunswick, New Jersey, and a bachelor's in political science from the University of Wyoming.